The English Countryside between the Wars

Regeneration or Decline?

The English Countryside between the Wars

Regeneration or Decline?

Edited by
Paul Brassley
Jeremy Burchardt
Lynne Thompson

THE BOYDELL PRESS

First published 2006
The Boydell Press, Woodbridge

ISBN 1 84383 264 X

The Boydell Press is an imprint of Boydell & Brewer Ltd
PO Box 9, Woodbridge, Suffolk IP12 3DF, UK
and of Boydell & Brewer Inc.
668 Mt Hope Avenue, Rochester, NY 14620, USA
website: www.boydellandbrewer.com

A CIP catalogue record of this publication is available
from the British Library

This publication is printed on acid-free paper

Typeset in Adobe Caslon Pro
by David Roberts, Pershore
Printed in Great Britain by
MPG Books Ltd, Cornwall

❦ Contents

List of illustrations

§ Contributors

Caitlin Adams

Dr Caitlin Adams teaches sociology and cultural studies at Witan International College, Reading. Her research interests include interwar rural history, gender and drama. She is currently working on a book about the Arts League of Service Travelling Theatre.

Christopher Bailey

Christopher Bailey is Dean of Arts and Society at Leeds Metropolitan University. He has published in rural industries, cultural policy and the impact of digital technology on the discipline of art history. He was the founder editor of the *Journal of Design History* (OUP), serving as its Editorial Secretary 1987–2000.

Paul Brassley

Dr Paul Brassley is a senior lecturer rural history and policy in the School of Geography at the University of Plymouth, having previously undertaken research at Oxford University in the early modern agricultural history of north-east England. He has published on agricultural science and technological development in the nineteenth and twentieth centuries, and his research is now mainly concerned with rural England in the twentieth century. He is currently chair of the British Agricultural History Society and treasurer of the Interwar Rural History Research Group.

Roy Brigden

Dr Roy Brigden is Keeper of the Museum of English Rural Life at the University of Reading. He has published works on the history of farming techniques and has research interests centring on the links between agriculture and landscape in the twentieth century.

Jeremy Burchardt

Dr Jeremy Burchardt is a lecturer in history in the Department of History at the University of Reading. He is currently chair of the Interwar Rural History Research Group. His research focuses on the social and cultural history of the countryside in the nineteenth and twentieth centuries, especially leisure and rural social relations and attitudes to the countryside. He is the author of *Paradise Lost: Rural Idyll and Social Change* (I. B. Tauris, 2002) and *The Allotment Movement in England, 1793–1873* (Boydell & Brewer, 2002).

CLARE GRIFFITHS

Dr Clare Griffiths is lecturer in Modern British History in the Department of History at the University of Sheffield. She is the author of *Labour and the Countryside: The Politics of Rural Britain between the Wars* (OUP, for publication in 2007). Her research has focused on early twentieth-century political culture, on agricultural and rural policy, and on attitudes towards commemoration and the history of the countryside. She is currently working on a study of landscape art during the Second World War.

ALUN HOWKINS

Alun Howkins is a Professor of Social History at the University of Sussex. He left school at the age of 15 and worked in a variety of manual and white-collar jobs before going to Ruskin College, an Oxford trade-union college for adult students, in 1968. He read History at Oxford and completed his PhD at Essex. He has written on a wide range of subjects from the paintings of Turner to the politics of the Communist Party in the 1930s. However, his central commitment has always been and remains the history of the rural areas and the rural poor. His most recent book is *The Death of Rural England: A Social History of the Countryside since 1900* (Routledge, 2003).

DAVID JEREMIAH

David Jeremiah is a design historian and Research Professor at the University of Plymouth. His special interests are concerned with the 19th and 20th centuries, and he has published *Architecture and Design for the Family in Britain, 1900–1970* (MUP, 2000). He is currently completing *Visual Representation of British Motoring* (MUP, 2007).

NICK MANSFIELD

Dr Nick Mansfield has been Director of the People's History Museum since 1989, and is an Honorary Research Fellow at the Universities of Manchester and Salford. He is the author of *English Farmworkers and Local Patriotism, 1900–1930* (Ashgate, 2000) and is currently researching class and regional identity in the British army with reference to the county regiment.

MARK RAWLINSON

Dr Mark Rawlinson is senior lecturer in the Department of English at the University of Leicester. He is the author of *British Writing of the Second World War* (Clarendon Press, 2000) and is finishing a sequel on the Second World War in fiction after 1945. He has written widely on twentieth-century poetry and prose with a special interest in the English novel from 1920–1950. He is currently editing the Norton Critical Edition of Anthony Burgess's *A Clockwork Orange*, writing a monograph on Pat Barker and researching a book on the cultural significance of camouflage.

MARION SHAW

Marion Shaw is Emeritus Professor of English at Loughborough University. Her research has focused on Victorian literature, particularly Tennyson. She has also worked on the literature of the interwar period and published *The Clear Stream*, a biography of Winifred Holtby (Virago, 1999). She has recently completed a variorum edition of Elizabeth Gaskell's *Sylvia's Lovers* (Pickering & Chatto, 2006) and is currently working on a study of general practitioners from 1815 to 1911 in relation to their literary representations and their writing about themselves.

JOHN SHEAIL

Dr John Sheail is an environmental historian and Research Fellow of the Centre for Ecology and Hydrology (Natural Environment Research Council) at Monks Wood, Huntingdon, of which he was deputy head before his retirement. His most recent book is *An Environmental History of Twentieth-Century Britain* (Palgrave, 2002).

LYNNE THOMPSON

Lynne Thompson is an Honorary Fellow of the School of Education and Lifelong Learning at the University of Exeter. During her career as a lecturer in continuing and adult education she published work on modern and historical aspects of adult education in England and Wales, with particular emphasis on women's groups and the early WI movement. She is currently researching on agricultural education in the interwar period and the history of Young Farmers' Clubs in the UK, and was until recently secretary of the Interwar Rural History Research Group.

MICK WALLIS

Mick Wallis is Professor of Performance and Culture and Director of Research in the School of Performance and Cultural Industries at the University of Leeds. His publications include work on the historical pageant in England, and he is co-author with Simon Shepherd of *Drama/Theatre/Performance* (Routledge, 2004).

❧ Introduction

Paul Brassley, Jeremy Burchardt, and Lynne Thompson

S INCE the Second World War the conventional view has seen a period
of continuity in the history of rural England from the 1870s to the 1930s,
only briefly interrupted by the First World War. It was a continuity of decline
that culminated in the interwar years, which thus form a sad contrast to the
expansionary decades after 1940.[1] Despite the proliferation of undergraduate
and graduate courses on twentieth-century history and cultural studies, this
view has remained unchallenged, since for a long time little work was done on
the interwar countryside. The various contributions in this book have emerged
from a growing sense that much of the existing historiography on interwar
rural England is narrow and one-sided, and so fails to reflect the complexity
of the period. Much of the emphasis has been on agriculture and its problems; much of the analysis has been almost entirely economic; and its effect
has been to produce an image of gloom. What follows, in this introductory
chapter, aims to show why this view has persisted, and so to explain why the
authors believe that a new look at the period and the subject to challenge such
opinions is worth while.

From the perspective of Europe as a whole, the interwar years, in the
words of one historian who lived through them as a working journalist, were
a period of 'unhappy ferment' with 'much bitter discontent and disturbance'.[2]
A younger historian, writing thirty years later, refers to the period as a 'crisis
of capitalism'.[3] The focus is upon revolution, strikes, unemployment, an 'economic abyss', wars, rumours of wars, and preparations for wars, not only in
Europe, but also in North America and the Far East.[4] At first sight, rural
society and culture make little impact on this story except as a refuge for
the worried: '... as the political outlook in Europe darkened ... [the] public
love affair with an idealized countryside intensified ...', and the Tudorbethan
semis of suburban England were echoed in suburban public housing schemes
with private gardens, or pseudo villages, from Scandinavia to Central Europe.

---

[1] See, for example, R. Perren, *Agriculture in Depression, 1870–1940* (Cambridge,
1995).

[2] E. Wiskemann, *Europe of the Dictators, 1919–1945* (1966), p. 9.

[3] M. Mazower, *Dark Continent: Europe's Twentieth Century* (1998), p. 106.

[4] E. Hobsbawm, *Age of Extremes: The Short Twentieth Century, 1914–1991* (1995),
p. 85; P. Brendon, *The Dark Valley: A Panorama of the 1930s* (2001).

More seriously, in the 1930s Fascist regimes glorified land, blood and soil as they strove for self-sufficiency in case of war.[5] Vinen argues that the effect of the First World War was to exacerbate the differences between the urban working classes and the countryside over most of Europe. If the results were most dramatic in the great wave of collectivisation in the Soviet Union, there were also political impacts in other countries. Peasant parties were formed in Croatia, Poland and Bulgaria, radical and Marxist parties in France had peasant support, land reform was an issue in Hungary, Czechoslovakia, Italy and Spain, and a ruralist rhetoric produced much support for the Nazi Party in the Protestant countryside of Germany, for example.[6] As in the towns, the emphasis is upon struggle, strife and the problematics of change.

Many of the generation that grew up in the Britain of the 1940s and 50s would have heard similar stories when their parents spoke of the pre-war years: unemployment and hunger marches in the old industrial areas, and 'dog and stick' farming in rural areas, all flavoured with a whiff of appeasement, became part of the image of the wasted years or the 'low, dishonest decade'.[7] How-ever, over the last thirty years a generation of British historians has set about modifying, if not exploding, the myth. Indeed, A. J. P. Taylor, *English History, 1914–1945*, published in 1965, argued that unemployment and appeasement needed to be balanced against motor cars and cinemas: 'Public affairs were harsh and intense; private lives increasingly agreeable … The two sides of life did not join up.'[8] In the following decade Stevenson and Cook first produced their influential revisionist study, highlighting the reasons to be cheerful in the 1930s and their political effects, and at the same time Glynn and Oxborrow published their economic and social history of the period.[9] Each of them set out to analyse the paradox of economic growth and rising living standards at a time when depression was afflicting both home and international markets. Both books concluded that it was a matter of economic restructuring. Depres-sion was geographically concentrated in the old industrial areas, while the growth industries – cars, chemicals and electricals in particular – were located

---

5 Mazower, *Dark Continent*, p. 95.

6 R. Vinen, *A History in Fragments: Europe in the Twentieth Century* (2000), pp. 165–70.

7 W. H. Auden, 'September 1 1939': 'I sit in one of the dives / On Fifty-second Street / Uncertain and afraid / As the clever hopes expire / Of a low dishonest decade.' We are grateful to Tony Gould for identifying the source of the phrase for us.

8 A. J. P. Taylor, *English History, 1914–1945* (Oxford, 1965), p. 317.

9 J. Stevenson and C. Cook, *The Slump: Society and Politics during the Depression* (1977); S. Glynn and J. Oxborrow, *Interwar Britain: A Social and Economic History* (1976).

elsewhere. Most people benefited from the process, but a substantial and geographically concentrated minority paid the price.

Although subsequent work may have modified the details of this revisionist position, it has not been substantially changed.[10] However, since Britain was an urban industrial country, many of the general histories of the period have little to say about the countryside, even though about 20 per cent of the population (roughly 9 million out of 45 million in 1931) lived in rural areas.[11] Glynn and Oxborrow have about three pages on agriculture, but nothing on other aspects of rural life; Stevenson and Cook mention motoring, cycling and rambling in the countryside as forms of entertainment, but say nothing about rural areas in their discussion of nutrition and health; Clarke has one or two pages and Robbins about half a dozen.[12] Stevenson's social history of the period mentions agriculture several times, and discusses the countryside in the context of land use planning and leisure, but none of his chapters is specifically devoted to rural life.[13] Dewey's page count on rural issues is almost into double figures, but he clearly feels that they need not be a major feature of an economic and social history of interwar Britain.[14] Of these general works, perhaps only Michael Thompson's major social history can be said to give any real weight to the countryside in this period.[15] In accounts of the United States, it might be noted, agriculture merits greater attention, perhaps because its depressed state stood out from other industries, or because of the Jeffersonian myth of the the independent small farmer as the bedrock of American democracy.[16] Given this neglect of the rural in the general run of revisionist histories of the period, it is hardly surprising that they have produced no great re-examination of rural issues. They have certainly done little to contradict the view of one of the first historians of the period, who painted a picture of

[10] See the opening survey in the second edition of Stevenson and Cook's book, published as *Britain in the Depression: Society and Politics, 1929–39* (1994). Andrew Thorpe also concludes that there were 'solid grounds for being optimistic about the 1930s'. See A. Thorpe, *Britain in the 1930s: The Deceptive Decade* (Oxford, 1992), p. 126.

[11] P. Dewey, *War and Progress: Britain, 1919–1945* (1997), p. 159.

[12] Glynn and Oxborrow, *Interwar Britain*, pp. 100–3; Stevenson and Cook, *Britain in the Depression*, pp. 32–4 and chapter 3; P. Clarke, *Hope and Glory: Britain, 1900–1990* (1996); K. Robbins, *The Eclipse of a Great Power: Modern Britain, 1870–1975* (1983), pp. 146–7, 223–4, 227–8.

[13] J. Stevenson, *British Society, 1914–45* (1984).

[14] P. Dewey, *War and Progress: Britain, 1914–1945* (1997), pp. 94–6, 159–61, 189, 196–7.

[15] W. A. Armstrong, 'The countryside', *The Cambridge Social History of Britain, 1750–1950*, vol. 1: *Regions and Communities*, ed. F. M. L. Thompson (1990), pp. 87–154.

[16] See e.g. Brendon, *The Dark Valley*, and J. L. Bronstein, *Land Reform and Working-Class Experience in Britain and the United States, 1800–1862* (Stanford, 1999).

depressed agriculture and substandard rural housing, in which 'The old order changed little' despite state subsidies and the popularity of rural writers.[17]

It was these rural writers who first established the image of rural England between the wars. George Sturt, A. G. Street, Adrian Bell, Henry Williamson, W. H. Hudson, H. J. Massingham, H. V. Morton, Constance Holme and Mary Webb, to identify only some of the better known, all published novels and memoirs on rural themes. The genre was recognisable enough for Stella Gibbons to parody it in 1932 in *Cold Comfort Farm*. The publishing firm of Batsford produced numerous non-fiction works, often copiously illustrated, introducing the countryside to the traveller.[18] Most of these were elegiac in tone: 'I have been informed by a friendly critic, who has watched with interest my amateurish struggles in attempting this book, that this portion of it lacks charm as compared with the earlier pages. I am afraid that this is only too true. Success and money-making, although they are often sordid, can be charming, but failure and loss never can be'.[19] So wrote A. G. Street as he began to describe the way he made his farm management system react to the decreasing corn prices of the 1920s. Many of the other writers listed above set their work in earlier times when it was easier to charm the reader. They idealised the countryside, much as the British pavilion at the Paris International Exposition of 1937, with its emphasis on recreation and its 'cardboard cut-out of Neville Chamberlain fishing in long rubber boots' presented a countryside of consumption.[20] Not that the countryside of production was entirely neglected, although Malcolm Muggeridge described the Ministry of Agriculture as 'the grave of political expectations'.[21] There were surveys of rural industries – see the chapter by Brassley below – and especially of the problems of agriculture, and it is these that appear to have most influenced rural historians.[22]

With some recent exceptions, the great bulk of specialist historical writing on this period has been concerned with agriculture. Most, indeed, has been solely concerned with British agriculture, with only Tracy attempting to set

---

[17] C. L. Mowat, *Britain between the Wars, 1918–1940* (1955), pp. 250–8, 436–41.

[18] See C. Brace, '"A pleasure ground for noisy herds?" Incompatible encounters with the Cotswolds and England, 1900–1950', *Rural History* 11/1 (2000): 75–94.

[19] A. G. Street, *Farmer's Glory* (new edn, 1959; first published 1932), p. 218.

[20] Brendon, *The Dark Valley*, p. 493. But see also R. Graves and A. Hodge, *The Long Weekend: A Social History of Great Britain, 1918–1939* (1940), p. 271.

[21] M. Muggeridge, *The Thirties: 1930–1940 in Great Britain* (1940), p. 180.

[22] C. S. Orwin, 'Commodity prices and farming policy', *Journal of the Royal Agricultural Society of England* 83 (1922); J. R. Currie and W. H. Long, *An Agricultural Survey in South Devon* (Newton Abbott, 1929); J. P. Maxton (ed.), *Regional Types of British Agriculture* (1936); Viscount Astor and B. Seebohm Rowntree, *British Agriculture: The Principles of Future Policy* (1939).

it in a European context.[23] Several authors have seen the interwar period as merely part of a longer phase of *laissez-faire* agricultural policy and low prices lasting from about 1870 to the Second World War, in which the high prices of the First World War appear as just a minor disturbance.[24] Joan Thirsk also sees the interwar years as part of this longer period, but argues that it makes more sense to see the decline of cereal and meat production as part of a process of adjustment to changing demands and market forces, balanced by an increase in dairying, horticulture, intensive livestock and industrial crops.[25] Two-thirds of Edith Whetham's volume in the *Agrarian History of England and Wales* series deals with the interwar period, but, unlike some of the other volumes in the series, which cover the wider social history of the countryside, it confines itself exclusively to the history of agriculture.[26] Her work has been considerably updated, for Wales, by Moore-Colyer.[27] In recent years Martin and Wilt have discussed the latter years of the period, but again, their concerns were exclusively agricultural.[28] Among the general surveys it is only the most recent, by Alun Howkins, that finds space for a wider rural history outside the farm gate.[29] He provides a valuable reminder of the significance of urban expansion and the growth of rural tourism and recreation. Even so, much of his discussion of this period is devoted to agriculture and the people connected with it, and it is perhaps fair to say that he provides more of an initial sketch of what a social history of interwar England might look like than a final definitive account.

There are, of course, several studies of particular aspects of the interwar countryside. Penning-Rowsell, Fenton Cooper, Griffiths and Tichelar have examined agricultural policy, Blaxter and Robertson agricultural science, and

[23] M. Tracy, *Agriculture in Western Europe*, 2nd edn (1982).

[24] J. Brown, *Agriculture in England: A Survey of Farming, 1870–1947* (Manchester, 1987); Perren, *Agriculture in Depression*; P. Brassley, 'Output and technical change in twentieth-century British agriculture', *Agricultural History Review* 48/1 (2000): 60–84.

[25] J. Thirsk, *Alternative Agriculture: A History from the Black Death to the Present Day* (Oxford, 1997), pp. 147–222.

[26] E. H. Whetham, *The Agrarian History of England and Wales*, vol. 8: *1914–1939* (Cambridge, 1978).

[27] R. J. Moore-Colyer, 'Farming in depression: Wales between the wars, 1919–39', *Agricultural History Review* 46/2 (1998): 177–96.

[28] J. Martin, *The Development of Modern Agriculture: British Farming since 1931* (2000); A. F. Wilt, *Food for War: Agriculture and Rearmament in Britain before the Second World War* (Oxford, 2001).

[29] A. Howkins, *The Death of Rural England: A Social History of the Countryside since 1900* (2003), pp. 95–111.

Conford the organic movement.[30] Burchardt, following Wiener, Howkins, Miller and Mandler, has written about the increasingly strong relationship between the countryside and national identity.[31] From a different standpoint, Matless has explored the relationship between landscape and culture.[32] Sheail and Bowers have brought environmental history perspectives to the period.[33] Carol Twinch has charted the long and bitter struggle over tithes in this period.[34] Howkins has explored the experience of the farm worker.[35] But much of the available material on the wider picture of rural life appears scattered through the periodical literature, especially that published in *Rural History*.[36] The implicit revisionism of the writers identified here has not been drawn together or focused to produce any new paradigm.

It is the growing strength and impact of this recent work, together with the perception that the economic and social forces that produced urban regeneration might have had some rural equivalents, which led to the establishment of

[30] K. Blaxter and N. Robertson, *From Dearth to Plenty* (Cambridge, 1995); P. Conford, 'A forum for organic husbandry: the *New English Weekly* and agricultural policy, 1939–49', *Agricultural History Review* 46/2 (1998): 197–210; P. Conford, *The Origins of the Organic Movement* (Edinburgh, 2001); A. F. Cooper, *British Agricultural Policy, 1912–36: A Study in Conservative Politics* (Manchester, 1989); E. Penning-Rowsell, 'Who 'betrayed' whom? Power and politics in the 1920/1 agricultural crisis', *Agricultural History Review* 45/2 (1997): 176–94; C. Griffiths, 'Red Tape Farm? The Labour Party and the farmers, 1918–1939', in *Agriculture and Politics in England, 1815–1939*, ed. J. R. Wordie (2000), pp. 199–241; M. Tichelar, 'The Labour Party and land reform in the inter-war period', *Rural History* 13/1 (2002): 85–102.

[31] J. Burchardt, *Paradise Lost: Rural Idyll and Social Change since 1800* (2002); M. J. Wiener, *English Culture and the Decline of the Industrial Spirit* (Cambridge, 1981); A. Howkins, 'The discovery of rural England', in *Englishness: Politics and Culture, 1880–1920*, ed. R. Colls and P. Dodd (1986); S. Miller, 'Urban dreams and rural reality: land and landscape in English culture, 1920–45', *Rural History* 6/1 (1995): 89–102; P. Mandler, 'Against Englishness: English culture and the limits to rural nostalgia, 1850–1940', *Transactions of the Historical Society* 6th ser. 7 (1997): 155–75.

[32] D. Matless, *Landscape and Englishness* (1998).

[33] J. Bowers, 'Inter-war land drainage policy in England and Wales', *Agricultural History Review* 46/1 (1998): 64–80; J. Sheail, 'Elements of sustainable agriculture: the UK experience, 1840–1940', *Agricultural History Review* 43/2 (1995): 178–92.

[34] C. Twinch, *Tithe War, 1918–1939: The Countryside in Revolt* (Norwich, 2001).

[35] A. Howkins, *Poor Labouring Men: Rural Radicalism in Norfolk, 1872–1923* (1990).

[36] J. R. Gold and M. M. Gold, 'To be free and independent: crofting, popular protest and Lord Leverhulme's Hebridean development projects, 1917–25', *Rural History* 7/2 (1996): 191–206; R. J. Moore-Colyer, 'From Great Wen to Toad Hall: aspects of the urban-rural divide in inter-war Britain', *Rural History* 10/1 (1999): 105–24; R. J. Moore-Colyer, 'A voice clamouring in the wilderness: H. J. Massingham (1888–1952) and rural England', *Rural History* 13/2 (2002): 199–224; M. Morgan, 'Jam making, Cuthbert Rabbit and cakes: redefining domestic labour in the Women's Institute, 1915–60', *Rural History* 7/2 (1996): 207–20.

the Interwar Rural History Research Group (IRHRG). This in turn produced the impetus to bring together a wide range of speakers at a conference held at Dartington in Devon in January 2002. From its beginning the IRHRG had involved not only socio-economic and political historians but also environmental, cultural, educational, architectural and art historians, and this was reflected in the papers offered at the conference. This multiplicity of perspectives in itself added to the perception that we were seeing interwar England in a new light. As a group of rural historians, we were dissatisfied with the way in which the countryside has been eliminated from our national history, or at best seen as nothing more than the location of the agricultural industry, and we now contend that the evidence for decline and regeneration in interwar England should be evaluated. Hence the impetus to bring the conference papers together in this book. It is restricted to England rather than covering the entire United Kingdom, and for this reason, if no other, we cannot claim that it forms a complete history; rather we see it more as a challenge to produce further work.

In organising the conference we made a deliberate attempt to attract historians from a wide range of specialisms. In addition to the social and economic historians who have often dominated rural history, the authors of the following chapters also include political, art, literary, drama, educational and environmental historians. The order and arrangement of their contributions is perhaps bound to be somewhat arbitrary. On the other hand, we feel that it does not do too much violence to their individuality to group them under four conventional headings: society, culture, politics and economics.

Under the heading of society, the chapter by Alun Howkins begins the book with a general survey of its main theme: was the story of interwar rural England one of decline or regeneration, or, as he calls it, death and rebirth? Howkins demonstrates that although there were clearly intimations of mortality in established industries and occupations such as agriculture and some rural crafts, there were at the same time signs of a new rural population gaining in numbers and vitality. The other three chapters in this section are more specialised. Burchardt examines the leisure aspirations of rural people as revealed by the widespread building of village halls in the period after the First World War, while Caitlin Adams and Lynne Thompson consider education in and for rural life from two different perspectives. It is clear from these four chapters that, in writing about rural change, any division between rural society and rural culture is bound to be arbitrary and artificial. The chapters in the following section also discuss changes in rural society; it is the perspectives of their authors that are cultural. Marion Shaw and Mark Rawlinson review the period through the works of two writers at opposite ends of the political spectrum: Winifred Holtby and Henry Williamson. Mick Wallis looks at the way that drama was used in attempts to deliver adult education and regenerate village life. David Jeremiah's chapter on Dartington Hall brings an art historian's perspective to one of the best-known experiments in integrating social, cultural and economic change in this period, and a design historian, Christopher Bailey, explains how the products of rural crafts and industries could be used both as metaphors of a lost English past and as sources of regeneration. The first of the chapters on politics, by John Sheail, uses a wide definition of the term that includes the activities of officials, experts, advisers and planners as well as ministers and MPs, concentrating especially on the 1920s and concluding that there was not one but several overlapping strands in the rural politics of the decade. Clare Griffiths concentrates on the way in which agricultural and food policy was seen and developed from a left-wing perspective, while Nicholas Mansfield, in contrast, explains why the right wing remained dominant among the rural working class in the Welsh Marches. The final three papers deal with rural life from a mainly economic perspective. Brassley's chapter on agriculture attempts to explain why farmers felt that they had had a hard time in the interwar years. Brigden's chapter on the Leckford estate in Hampshire examines one of the more radical experiments by a landowner to deal with those economic problems, and Brassley's second chapter uses both economic and literary evidence to analyse the construction of socio-economic change, in this case as it applies to rural crafts and trades. Finally the editors have combined to produce a conclusion that brings together the evidence of the various chapters to answer the question posed at the beginning: is the interwar period one of decline or regeneration in rural England?

We cannot claim that the chapters contained in this book cover all of the possible approaches and areas of study that might be relevant to our principal question. On the other hand, many of the topics that we have not covered have been dealt with elsewhere, often comprehensively. We have said little about Conservative agricultural policy, but it has already been the subject of a detailed study by Fenton Cooper.[37] His conclusions do not seem to differ seriously from ours. Except in John Sheail's paper we say little about the legislative framework from its beginnings in the First World War Ministry of Reconstruction to what might be seen as its climax in the Scott Report of 1942. In this case it is not so easy to point to an obvious substitute. Fortunately, in the cases of preservationism, or the rise of urban leisure and rambling, there are again recent and comprehensive studies.[38] Similarly, in the case of preparations for war and their impact on the regeneration of agriculture, there is also

---

[37] Cooper, *British Agricultural Policy.*

[38] Matless, *Landscape and Englishness*; M. Shoard, *This Land is Your Land: The Struggle for Britain's Countryside* (1997); M. Shoard, *A Right to Roam* (1999).

a relevant recent study.[39] Although there is no comprehensive treatment of the range of alternative or idealist communities or approaches to rural life in this period, there are several works that deal with individual examples, such as the organic movement, the Land Settlement Association, Rolf Gardiner's 'English Mistery', and informal groups such as the women's smallholding community at Lingfield.[40] Perhaps the most glaring omission is any discussion of the impact of the changing pattern of rural landownership. Surprisingly, Edith Whetham paid little attention to it, and although Madeleine Beard has some interesting impressionistic material, it is mostly concerned with large landowners and their activities.[41]

What follows, therefore, is not so much a comprehensive study of interwar rural England, but an attempt to make a revisionist case. As we have pointed out above, this has already been done in the general histories of the period, and in the economic histories, but not so far in the histories of rural England in this period. We believe that there is now sufficient evidence to make a revisionist argument that this should not just be seen as a period of rural decline, and we present this evidence in the following chapters.

[39] Wilt, *Food for War*.

[40] Conford, *Origins of the Organic Movement*; P. Dearlove, 'Fen Drayton, Cambridgeshire: an estate of the Land Settlement Association', in *The English Rural Landscape*, ed. J. Thirsk (Oxford, 2000), pp. 323–35; P. Wright, *The Village that Died for England: The Strange Story of Tyneham* (1995); A. Meredith, 'From ideals to reality: the women's smallholding colony at Lingfield, 1920–39', *Agricultural History Review* 54/1 (2006): 105–21.

[41] Whetham, *The Agrarian History of England and Wales*, vol. 8; M. Beard, *English Landed Society in the Twentieth Century* (1989), chapter 4.

I Death and rebirth? English rural society, 1920–1940

Alun Howkins

IN the last twenty years the social and economic history of interwar Britain has been the subject of substantial revision. Most notably, following on from the work brought together in Stevenson and Cook's *The Slump*, the 1920s and especially the 1930s have taken on a new face.[1] Gone are the grim years of mass unemployment and political extremism, which dominated earlier historiography and the political memories of the generation of 1945. In their place we have a more complex picture in which unemployment was a phenomenon of a few years, notably 1929–35, and a small number of industries, most obviously the Victorian 'staples': iron and steel, heavy engineering, textiles, ship-building and coal. Reflecting this, the text most studied by many undergraduate students as a 'contemporary' account is now more likely to be J. B. Priestley's *English Journey*, with its portrait of three Englands in different stages of economic success and failure, than George Orwell's *The Road to Wigan Pier*, with its universally black picture.

Until much more recently this 'revisionist' view had touched little on the rural areas: Stevenson and Cook, for example, make virtually no reference to agriculture. Here the dominant image of the interwar period remained one of desperate and unrelieved gloom. The story is familiar enough. During the Great War farmers had served their county well, saving the nation's food supply from the threat of the U-boat campaign. Their justified reward was the Agriculture Act of 1920, which guaranteed minimum prices for cereal crops, and promised long-term price stability. By an act of unparalleled treachery perpetrated by the urban world and a sycophantic government frightened of the power of the urban demand for cheap food, this act was repealed in 1921, plunging farming into desperate crisis. Following on from this the English market was flooded with cheap (and inferior) foreign imports. Worse still, many farmers who had bought their farms with crippling loans in the period between 1918 and 1921 now found repayments increasingly difficult.[2]

---

[1] J. Stevenson and C. Cook, *The Slump: Society and Politics during the Depression* (1977).

[2] This is of course a parody in some respects – but it does accord with what many country people, and especially farmers, believed to have happened. For more serious accounts from different viewpoints see A. Howkins, *The Death of Rural*

There is, it has to be said, some strength in this view. Clearly some sectors, especially the arable ones, were doing very poorly indeed. Throughout the interwar period many cereal-producers, especially in East Anglia, and particularly those who had bought their own farms in the early 1920s, suffered very badly. Alec Douet's study of Norfolk charts the descent of the breadbasket of England into despair. In 1932 Lord Hastings summed it up in the House of Lords. 'What has happened', he said, 'is a catastrophe. There is the gravest risk of the whole of the corn producing area becoming derelict and impoverished.' By the end of that year Douet suggests farmers owed over £3.5 million to Barclays Bank in Norwich.³ Nor was Norfolk alone. The heavy clays of Essex, Suffolk and the Lincolnshire Wolds were at least as badly hit. Throughout these areas of the eastern counties farm buildings were derelict, fields untended and farms unlet, giving to both the farming community and to the general public a profound sense of the end of English agriculture

This image, which found its place in, among other things, Cecil Day Lewis's long poem 'The Magnetic Mountain' of 1933, has had a lasting effect on how the farming community views the interwar years.⁴ This account was well established by the mid-1920s. In 1927 S. L. Bensusan followed in the footsteps of Sir Henry Rider Haggard and produced his *Latter-Day Rural England*. Although the book as a whole presents a diverse picture of the fortunes of agriculture, its preface feeds into a growing sense of agriculture in crisis:

> … farmers who had been forced to buy their holdings in the years imme-
> diately following the War and had been sorry for themselves ever since;
> tenant farmers who realize that the old landmarks have been removed by
> the march of events, and that their landlords are now, and must remain,
> powerless to help them; small-holders struggling desperately and often
> successfully for the right to live; agricultural labourers doing their best
> … to meet the farmer's needs.⁵

More powerful, and with a much wider impact, was A. G. Street's *Farmer's Glory* of 1932.⁶ Here, in the thinly disguised autobiography of a working farmer, the whole sorry tale of post-war agriculture was exposed. Along

England: A Social History of the Countryside since 1900 (2003), and R. Perren, *Agriculture in Depression, 1870–1940* (Cambidge, 1995).

3 A. Douet, 'Norfolk Agriculture, 1914–1972' (unpublished PhD thesis, University of East Anglia, 1989), p. 132.

4 C. Day Lewis, *The Magnetic Mountain* (1933): '… passing derelict mills and barns roof rent / Where despair has burnt itself out – hearts at a standstill'.

5 S. L. Bensusan, *Latter-Day Rural England, 1927* (1928), pp. 9–10.

6 A. G. Street, *Farmer's Glory* (1932).

with Adrian Bell's farming trilogy, *Corduroy*, *Silver Ley* and *The Cherry Tree*, published between 1930 and 1935, the personal and emotional tone of Street's work obscured his often rather hard-nosed analysis to produce a popular and generalised sense of agricultural decay.[7]

Nor was it only within popular writing that the idea of the decay of agriculture seemed almost all-pervasive. As late as 1939 Lord Addison, who had been Minister of Agriculture in the Labour Government of 1929–31, wrote

> Millions of acres of land have passed out of active cultivation and … the process is continuing; … an increasing extent of good land is reverting to tufts of inferior grass, to brambles and weeds, and often to the reedy growth that betrays water logging; … multitudes of farms are beset with dilapidated buildings and that a great a rapid diminution is taking place in the number of those who find employment upon them.[8]

Less surprisingly, perhaps, this view found support on the political right. Viscount Lymington's *Famine in England* of 1938[9] presents an even more desperate picture, as does Henry Williamson's *The Story of a Norfolk Farm* of 1940.[10] Furthermore the youthful organic movement, as Phillip Conford has shown, added a powerful critical voice to the argument.[11]

Most assiduously of all, the idea of agricultural collapse was pushed by the farmers organisations and the farming press. Crucial here was *Farmers Weekly*, which first appeared in 1934. Designed for farmers and their families, it also spoke to the countryside as a whole. It covered a broad range of country life issues and presented an increasingly unified voice on agricultural politics. The account of the 'great betrayal' of English farming was a central theme of *Farmers Weekly* from the very first. For example, in August 1934, two months after its first issue, it carried a leader looking back to August 1914 which, under the headline 'Does Britain so Easily Forget?', outlined the ill treatment of Britain's farmers since they 'saved' the nation in the Great War.[12] This theme was revisited constantly for the rest of the 1930s and, indeed, into the Second World War.

However, as with the account of the interwar urban areas, that of the rural has undergone revision in the last decade. Most notably in the work of Richard Perren, John Martin and, most recently, Alan Wilt, the picture of agriculture's

---

7   A. Bell, *Corduroy* (1930), *Silver Ley* (1932), *Cherry Tree* (1935).

8   Lord Addison, *A Policy for British Agriculture* (Left Book Club, 1939), p. 14.

9   Viscount Lymington, *Famine in England* (1938).

10   H. Williamson, *The Story of a Norfolk Farm* (1940).

11   P. Conford, *The Origins of the Organic Movement* (Edinburgh, 2001).

12   *Farmer's Weekly*, 5 Aug 1934.

interwar fortunes has become much more nuanced.[13] As with the urban areas the periods of most intense depression are seen to be much shorter, from 1922 to 1925, and from 1929 to 1932. At a macro level E. J. T. Collins argued in a paper presented to the 2001 Economic History Society Conference (as yet unpublished) that through the interwar period as a whole, and especially in the 1930s, farm productivity was much higher than has hitherto been thought. Crucially the effects of the depression, it is argued, were much more regionally specific that it was once argued. The work of David Taylor has shown that in the dairying districts the interwar years were a period of some success, and that where farmers, especially in areas of mixed farming, switched to milk production, a decent living could still be made.[14] Other sectors also had some successes. Joan Thirsk has argued persuasively for a dynamic sector centred on small-scale 'alternative husbandry', a view which is strongly supported by the history of, for example, the Preston and District Farmers Trading Society (now Amalgamated Farmers).[15] Founded in 1911 by a handful of Lancashire chicken farmers, by 1931 it had helped the Preston area produce a third of England's eggs, and in November 1937 it achieved an annual turnover of £1 million.[16]

Nor was farming as helpless as the traditional account suggests. David Cannadine has argued that the power of the aristocracy in the countryside declined in the interwar period as they withdrew from county government:

> By the 1930s, the county councils were no longer the old rural oligarchy under a new name, but a professional hierarchy and structured bureaucracy which might – or might not – be sheltering behind a façade of patrician authority ... The aristocracy's part in the government of the countryside was increasingly moving towards that non-contentious and essentially ornamental role that that during the same period they were perfecting and practising in the towns and the empire.[17]

They were replaced, albeit gradually, by farmers. Lee's study of Cheshire shows

[13] Perren, *Agriculture in Depression*; J. Martin, *The Development of Modern Agriculture: British Farming since 1931* (2000); A. F. Wilt, *Food for War: Agriculture and Rearmament in Britain before the Second World War* (Oxford, 2001).

[14] D. Taylor 'Growth and structural change in the British dairy industry, c.1860–1930', *Agricultural History Review* 35/1 (1987).

[15] J. Thirsk, *Alternative Agriculture: A History from the Black Death to the Present Day* (Oxford, 1997)

[16] See Howkins, *The Death of Rural England*, pp. 72–3. The papers of the Preston Farmers Co-op are held at the Museum of English Rural Life, University of Reading (henceforth MERL).

[17] D. Cannadine, *The Decline and Fall of the British Aristocracy* (1990), p. 167

the local NFU emerging as an 'independent party' on the County Council in the 1920s, a pattern which appears to have been repeated elsewhere.[18] By the end of the interwar period much of county government in England at least was in the hands of farmers.

This growth in local power was parallelled by the growth of the NFU. Founded in 1908, its membership grew from 10,000 in 1910 to 60,000 by 1918, reaching more than 125,000 by the 1930s and thus representing over half of British farmers. Dominated from the first by farmers rather than landowners, the formal involvement of the NFU in government policy between 1917 and 1921 gave it the ear of government – an ear into which it whispered ever more frequently in the 1930s. In 1939 Sir Reginald Dorman Smith, the president of the NFU from 1936 to 1938, became Minister of Agriculture. During the 1930s an increasingly confident NFU had a greater and greater effect on government policy on agriculture.[19] As Wilt writes: 'This was basically for two reasons: to keep the demands of the increasingly powerful Union in bounds, and to gain the support of the farmers as the government attempted to deal with the Depression and preparations for war.'[20] By the mid-1930s the NFU was more and more serving as the National Government (if not the Tory Party) in the fields. In return government gave the NFU an increasingly privileged position in shaping agricultural policy. This was most obvious in the 'protective' legislation imposed in the early 1930s. In November 1931 tariffs were imposed on soft fruit and potatoes and this was extended in early 1932 to include wheat via the Wheat Act. This essentially returned to the old principles of the Corn Production Act with deficiency payments to guarantee a minimum price. However, unlike the old Agriculture Act the money was raised by a tax on milled flour, both home produced and imported, and was in fact, as Brown says 'a disguised tariff'.[21] The effects were remarkably swift. In 1933 and 1934 there was a large increase in the area sown to wheat, and in 1934 the long established sugar beet subsidy was renewed further helping the arable farmer.[22]

---

[18] J. M. Lee, *Social Leaders and Public Persons: A Study of County Government in Cheshire since 1888* (Oxford, 1963), p. 89.

[19] See G. Cox, P. Lowe and M. Winter, 'The origins and early development of the National Farmers' Union', *Agricultural History Review* 39/1 (1991), and A. Flynn, P. Lowe and M. Winter, 'The political power of farmers: an English perspective', *Rural History* 7/1 (1996).

[20] Wilt, *Food For War*, p. 134.

[21] J. Brown, *Agriculture in England: A Survey of Farming, 1870–1947* (Manchester, 1987), p. 113.

[22] For this complex process see Martin, *The Development of Modern Agriculture*, and Wilt, *Food for War*.

However, the countryside is not only about agriculture; its history is also about the problems and changes within rural society as a whole. Again the picture drawn from contemporary accounts is a grim one. In this the old social order was destroyed by the carnage of the Great War. As Bensusan says, 'the old landmarks have been removed', with the old and trusted gentry and aristocracy driven out by upstarts and 'urban syndicates' like the one which buys up farms in Bell's *Corduroy*.[23] Alongside the vanished aristocracy go the old and 'real' countrymen (nearly always men), particularly those associated with the 'dying' rural crafts. As with agriculture these were seen as the victims of change and unfair competition over which they had no control. Finally rural depopulation drew not only these craftsmen and women out of the villages but removed their markets.

Again there is some truth in this. George Sturt's account of the decay and death of the village craftsman and women may be tinged with nostalgia, but cannot simply be dismissed out of hand.[24] Even a cursory glance through the country directories over the period 1900–1950 shows a huge reduction in numbers of blacksmiths, wheelwrights, basket-makers and hurdle-makers. It was in the interwar period that the rural potteries of Surrey and Sussex finally vanished. For example, the East Grinstead Pottery closed in 1937; Meeds and Leaney's potteries at Burgess Hill closed in the late 1930s or very early 1940s; while Norman's bigger works had closed in 1930. Only the Dicker and Boship potteries continued any substantial level of production after the Second World War, and they vanished in the 1960s.[25]

To many contemporaries this decline in craftsmanship and in the village was worse than the decay of agriculture itself. In the 1900s the English village had begun to be seen as an ideal community by sections of the artistic and intellectual elite. To Ebenezer Howard and, perhaps more importantly, Raymond Unwin, the architect who worked with him at Letchworth, the English village was the perfect expression of community and the finest form of human social organisation. Rural depopulation and the lure of what some at least saw as the unnatural world of the towns was destroying a 'natural' and organic system.[26] To Lymington the decay of farming lead to the collapse not only of the countryside and the village but the whole race.

Thus without hesitation one can say that from Land's End to John O'Groats the soil in general is degenerating. Its best servants among the

---

[23] Bensusan, *Latter-Day Rural England*, p. 9.

[24] G. Sturt [as G. Bourne], *Change in the Village* (1984).

[25] J. M. Baines, *Sussex Pottery* (Brighton, 1980).

[26] For a good account of Letchworth see S. Meacham, *Regaining Paradise: English-ness and the Early Garden City Movement* (1999).

labourers are disappearing and the ancient skill is being lost. The disappearance of the arable sheep has meant the disappearance of the hurdle-maker, who lost his market for barrel hoops at the same time. This has meant the ruin of the old oak and coppice system of woodland. ... Rates go up to put out-of-door gypsies in new council houses, which they ruin and where they languish. The faceless and unfit are better treated than any healthy labourer could ever hope to be ...[27]

This is an extreme view, but organisations as impeccably worthy as the Rural Industries Bureau and books which had an enormous impact, like Clough Williams Ellis's *Britain and the Beast* of 1937, contained all or at least most of these ideas.

The picture of the 'decline' of rural England was apparently supported by the Census. In 1921 there were just over 1.4 million men and women in England and Wales working in agriculture. They were already a declining group and had been since the 1850s, when agricultural employment was at its height. The interwar years were to see the numbers decline still further, falling by about 100,000 by 1931, and possibly a similar figure up to 1941. By using the statistics provided by the annual agricultural returns, we can get a clear sense of relative decline in agricultural labourers over the twenty-year period. Between 1921 and 1930 – that is, up to the onset of the 'worst' years – the number of male and female farm workers declined by about 10 per cent. Between 1930 and 1939 numbers fell by a further 18 per cent. Looking more closely still, we see that numbers employed dropped rapidly from 1919–23, when they picked up, remaining fairly constant until 1932, when they fell again, and continued to drop very rapidly until 1939.

These are crude figures and they conceal a good deal of regional variation. Particularly they conceal the fact that the interwar period shows marked change in the ratio of farmers to farm workers, with the latter group declining much faster than the former, especially after 1932. However, to see the rural areas of England and Wales simply in these terms is to ignore a massive problem. The numbers employed in agriculture was certainly declining throughout the interwar period, but the population of rural areas was not. In 1891 there were 8,107,021 people living in the rural areas, and this fell in 1901 to 7,469,488. However, in 1911 the rural population increased by about 500,000, and it remained much the same in 1921; but, as the Census report notes, using the same boundaries to define rural in 1921 as 1911, the rural population had in fact increased by about 4.3 per cent. This growth was to continue throughout the interwar years, and what the 1951 Census says could be applied to the whole of that period:

[27] Lymington, *Famine in England*, p. 125.

In the twenty years since 1931 the Southern and Eastern Regions still had the largest percentage increases and Wales and the Northern Region the smallest … The large migration gain by rural areas does not, of course, indicate any return of population to farming but merely a movement of population away from their workplaces in the towns to more residential areas in the surrounding countryside. The almost uniformly outward migration from the conurbations is another indication of this change.[28]

This growth in population in the 'rural' areas was, of course, the other sign of rural crisis in the 1930s, the urban beast or octopus of Williams Ellis's two interwar attacks on the growth of the urban areas.[29] It was observed first in the south and east. As property prices in Inner London grew (outside the slum areas at least) both businesses and their workers moved out. In 1921 the census had noted that 'increases above the average are recorded for all the Home Counties with an exception in the case of Kent'.[30] By 1940 the Barlow Report saw this trend as a major change. 'The continued drift of the industrial population to London and the Home Counties constitutes a social, economic, and strategical problem, which demands immediate attention.'[31]

Those who moved out came in search of rural or at least semi-rural England. As Thomas Sharp wrote in 1932:

People have lived too long in dreary streets. They have seen too few trees and too little grass in their sordid towns. They were tired the squalid paved back yards. They wanted gardens of their own, back and front, with a space between their house and the next.[32]

They also, though, as Best and Rogers argue, wanted modern houses near to shops, schools and transport; hence it was the hamlet, the small town and the village which were the epitome of rural life.[33] Where they came, they built in country style. As Barret and Phillips write in *Suburban Style*

---

[28] *Census 1951, England and Wales: General Report*, p. 82.

[29] C. Williams-Ellis, *England and the Octopus* (1928); C. Williams-Ellis (ed.), *Britain and the Beast* (1937).

[30] *Census of England and Wales 1921*, p. 21.

[31] Royal Commission on the Distribution of the Industrial Population, *Report*, Cmd 6153 (1940), p. 152.

[32] T. Sharp, *Town and Countryside: Some Aspects of Urban and Rural Development* (1932), pp. 6–7.

[33] R. H. Best and A. W. Rogers, *The Urban Countryside: The Land-use Structure of Small Towns and Villages in England and Wales* (1973), p. 24.

It was this rejection (in the inter war-period) of the uncompromising images of the neo-Georgian and the Modernist style favoured by the architectural establishment that provoked the most acute criticism ... The haphazard combination of architectural details – mock beams, lattice windows, weatherboarding, pebble dash and fancy brickwork – created, in Osbert Lancaster's words an 'infernal amalgam' of the 'least attractive materials and building devices known in the past' a view shared by the architectural profession and social commentators alike.[34]

'By-pass variegated' was a middle-class invention, or rather reinvention of the rural. 'Moderne' houses, like those built by Laings between the wars, were far out numbered by 'traditional' or 'cottage' styles. The visual evidence of this remains with us today in every city, town and even many villages, in the form of the 'mock-Tudor' house.

Behind these cultural ideas of an essentially 'English' countryside was a new economic reality. The economic growth of the 1920s but especially the 1930s was, as we have already indicated, essentially regional and occupational, in which the 'traditional' skilled manual and male industries of the nineteenth declined while the new, and especially the commercial and largely south-eastern, prospered. The impact of this was swift. Even in 1921 white-collar workers were the third largest occupational group in country districts after those working in agriculture and domestic servants. If we take together commercial, public and professional occupations in that year we find these groups employed 483,656 men and women in the rural areas – only 100,000 less than were employed as farm workers. These figures are even more striking if we look at the Home Counties. In 1921 the largest number of white-collar workers lived in Surrey, with about 21.5 per cent of the population in these occupations. Middlesex follows this with 21 per cent; Essex has 16 per cent. This meant that there were more white-collar workers in Surrey and Middlesex than in London. Nor was regional spread solely a southern phenomenon. Cheshire, perhaps Manchester's equivalent of Surrey, had 13.2 per cent of its population in white-collar occupations, although no other area in the north comes anywhere near this figure. The other point that needs to be made about this figure is the large number of women involved: women made up 172,721 or 36 per cent of the white-collar work-force, even in country districts.

Quite how startling this change was, even at the beginning of the interwar period, can be shown by a simple comparison. For much of the nineteenth century the third largest group of workers in the rural areas (after agricultural

---

34 H. Barrett and J. Phillips, *Suburban Style: The British Home, 1840–1960* (1988), p. 125.

workers and domestic servants) was coal miners, 297,968 of them in 1921 (all the figures are for men and women workers). In fact there were over half as many coal miners living in rural areas as there were farm workers. If we add other quarrying employment, there were 336,485 employed in these trades – a group over a third of the size of those in agriculture. The next largest group, and one which was also growing in importance, were transport and communication workers (177,521). Already by 1921 the majority of these were working in road transport, although railways constituted an important, and homogeneous, group. Close behind transport workers came metal workers (168,798). This presents an interesting group with both 'traditional' and modernising elements. For instance, there were 28,860 smiths and skilled forge workers – a firmly traditional group. However, they had already been overtaken in the fast lane by the future, with 59,637 men and women who worked in branches of the motor trade and mechanical engineering. The only other group employing more than 100,000 people in rural districts was the building trades (135,218).[35]

In the southern areas of England many of these new 'rural' workers were commuters, travelling daily from the rural areas to London by railway. The Southern Railways assiduously promoted Kent, Sussex and above all Surrey with posters illustrating slogans like 'Live in Surrey Free From Worry' and 'Live in Kent and Be Content'. In the early 1930s it published a guide, *Country Homes at London's Door*, arguing that as a result of electrification there were great areas in easy reach of London which were 'actually in and surrounded by the real and beautiful country', where 'London's daily workers can spend their leisure, and sleep, in pure air and in a beautiful country which before was more or less inaccessible'. The guide gave details of housing, lighting, soils, and schools and even gave advice of how to borrow money to buy or build a house.[36] The growth of the railways was followed by, and sometime went hand in hand with, suburban development. The population of Epsom and Ewell increased from 22,953 in 1921 to 35,228 in 1931 and 62,960 in mid-1939; Leatherhead expanded from 11,233 in 1921 to 21,170 in mid-1938; and Caterham and Warlingham from 17,108 to 27,100 in the same period.[37] At Stoneleigh, also in Surrey, the development was even more remarkable. It barely existed in 1930, when two farms were sold to developers, who contributed half the cost of a new station which was opened in July 1932. By 1935 313,647 people were travelling from Stoneleigh each year – the vast majority to London.[38]

35 *Census of England and Wales 1921*.

36 C. A. Lockwood, 'The changing use of land in the Weald region of Kent, Surrey and Sussex, 1919–1939' (unpublished PhD thesis, University of Sussex, 1991), p. 32.

37 A. A. Jackson, *The Railway in Surrey* (Southend-on-Sea, 1999), p. 109.

38 Jackson, *The Railway in Surrey*, p. 118.

Not all these new countrymen and women were the same. At one extreme there were hated *nouveaux riches* of John Betjeman's poem 'Slough.'[39]

> It's not their fault they do not know
> The birdsong from the radio,
> It's not their fault they often go
> To Maidenhead
> And talk of sports and makes of cars
> In various bogus Tudor bars
> And daren't look up and see the stars
> But belch instead.

These were perhaps the typical inhabitants of Stoneleigh, with its typically unpretentious 'semis', its grand new roadhouse/pub by the station and, by 1938, the 1,462-seat Rembrandt Cinema, or perhaps Oxted, which expanded vigorously in the 1920s and 1930s. Here 'Tudorbethan shopping parades' sprang up in Station Approach, along with another cinema, the 'new Kinema', also in Tudorbethan style.[40]

Elsewhere in suburban England, and even in Surrey's crowded land, lived wealthier, and one assumes from other of Betjeman's suburban poems, more acceptable commuters. St George's Hill near Weybridge, the site of the Diggers' doomed and heroic experiment of common ownership of 1649, became from the late 1920s one of Surrey's most exclusive estates. Here in contrast to the humble 'semi' of the clerk, grand houses built by the developer Walter G. Tarrant stood in grounds of never less than an acre and enjoyed two eighteen-hole golf-courses and private tennis and croquet clubs.[41] Grander still were the houses making up what Jackson calls 'high quality residential scatter'.[42] In the area around Leith Hill in Surrey, F. E. Green wrote in 1914, 'I can point out to you the residences of people who have amassed wealth out of ships, law, tea, pottery, ink, banking and "contracting" …'[43]

Nor was this solely a southern phenomenon, although it was at its most obvious in the south and east of England. In the English Midlands the demand for cars, bicycles, household and electrical goods saw all these sectors increase in size. As in the south and east this led to a largely middle-class move out of the cities of the Industrial Revolution to the countryside around. Around Birmingham and Wolverhampton suburban development of a kind familiar in

---

39 J. Betjeman, *Collected Poems*, enlarged edn (1977), p. 23.

40 Jackson, *The Railway in Surrey*, p. 139.

41 Jackson, *The Railway in Surrey*, p. 133.

42 Jackson, *The Railway in Surrey*, pp. 148–52.

43 F. E. Green, *The Surrey Hills* (1915).

the south and east spread into the rural districts. By the mid-1930s the decline of the rural population in both rural Staffordshire and rural Warwickshire had been reversed, while, for example, the population of Stoke-on-Trent declined as the areas around 'began to attract young couples who worked in Stafford or the Black country and travelled daily to work by bus, train or car'.[44] In the former industrial village of Neston in the Wirral the 1930s were remembered as a time of similar change, with 'the building trade … one of the few steady occupations':

> The whole area in the 1930s was slowly but surely changing, if not already changed, into the irreversible dormitory town for the city gent … while the rank and file of the populace had to follow suit. The city was where the new work was, and new staff were needed, from manager to office boy, from manageress to typist … To town they went on trains and crowded buses everyday.[45]

Even in the northeast, one of the areas worst hit by the depression, the Council for the Preservation of Rural England could still bemoan the development of the Jesmond area of Newcastle. 'There is a pathos in the rush to build dwellings in green surroundings, which, through lack of early planning, blots out those green surroundings.'[46]

What these new countrymen and women had in common, though, was that they were *in* the country but not, at least in the traditional sense, *of* the country. The men of these families, and a substantial part of the unmarried women, travelled daily to an urban place of work, returning for evenings and weekends. The women and children of the new suburbs and suburbanised villages and towns stayed at home. This has led many historians to see these places, particularly for women, as 'a cultural desert', providing a 'life of extreme monotony':

> … these estates embodied a way of life which was atomised and individualised, that lacked social cohesion except of a passive, flock-of-sheep, variety, and which generated no networks of associations or communities to stand between individuals, or families, and the state.[47]

[44] M. B. Rowlands, *The West Midlands from AD 1000* (1987), pp. 335ff.

[45] G. W. Place (ed.), *Neston, 1840–1940* (Chester, 1996), p. 244. The memories of David Scott.

[46] Museum of English Rural Life, Reading CPRE File 37/1 Batch 4, Northumberland and Newcastle Society.

[47] F. M. L. Thompson, 'Town and City', in *The Cambridge Social History of England, 1750–1950*, vol. 1: *Regions and Communities*, ed. F. M. L. Thompson (Cambridge, 1990), p. 84.

Yet this seems more to do with what Andy Medhurst has called 'the sheer vitriol which cultural practitioners and commentators have felt compelled to pour over the suburbs' than with historical reality.[48] What few memoirs there seem to be of suburbia talk about endless clubs and societies, from the ubiquitous amateur opera society through to rambling and cycling clubs – indeed, as Medhurst writes, clubs and societies were in some ways the defining feature of suburbia.[49] It was not only the elite of St George's Hill that had tennis, golf and even croquet clubs. No new suburb was complete without a 'Tudor Bar' or two, and even the Left Book Club, as George Orwell reminds us, found a cosy niche in the world of 'Dunroamin'.[50] Nor were the women and children quite so trapped at home as is often suggested. Between 1927 and 1935 the number of ordinary tickets sold at Epsom Downs increased from 329,778 to 859,794 as the suburb grew, and the wives and children of the largely male commuters went 'up to town' for the day.[51]

The growth of white-collar employment, commuting and the 'suburb' in all its forms changed that face of rural England. In 1931 Surrey had only 6 per cent of it population employed on the land despite a very high number in horticulture. Against that, 32 per cent of the working population were employed in white-collar occupations – an increase of 11 per cent in a decade. Even more obviously agricultural counties showed similar change. West Sussex continued to find work in agriculture for 16 per cent of its population, but still had 26 per cent in white-collar work. Moving away from London, 21 per cent of the working population in Devon worked in agriculture, but only 18 per cent in white-collar jobs, while Norfolk, hardly surprisingly, is the most rural of the arable counties, with 36 per cent in agriculture as against a mere 15 per cent in white-collar occupations. In these 'truly' rural counties the older crafts and trades also survived. It can only be an impression but it seems that the village social and economic infrastructure remained central here until at least the 1950s, and, as a result, traditional trades and crafts, as well as local shops, pubs and other village services remain much more important employers of labour.

So where does this leave death and rebirth? Trying to draw together an overview brings a number of basic points to mind, which in turn perhaps help towards a general reworking of the history of the interwar countryside.

First chronology. In terms of agricultural history it seem possible to make a crude division, especially in the arable areas, although not only here, around

48 A. Medhurst, 'Negotiating the Gnome Zone', in *Visions of Suburbia*, ed. R. Silverstone (1997), pp. 240–1.

49 Medhurst, 'Negotiating the Gnome Zone', p. 257.

50 G. Orwell, *Coming up for Air* (Penguin, 1980, original edition 1938), pp. 146–56.

51 Jackson, *The Railway in Surrey*, p. 120.

about 1932. Before that date farming was certainly in decline; after that date it shows signs of recovery. That chronology could equally be applied to rural society as a whole. The period after 1931 seems to mark, as the 1951 census argued, the real take-off into urban development in the countryside. If we look again at the proportion of the work-force employed in agriculture but move to the immediate post-war period this becomes clear. In Surrey, symbolically at least the most suburban county in England, the agricultural proportion of the population had nearly halved to 3.7 per cent; in Norfolk, a truly 'rural' county, by 1951 it had fallen to 17 per cent. This kind of drop, and a parallel rise in white-collar occupations was repeated all over rural England, even though the farm work-force had gone up dramatically during the Second World War. Interestingly, in some counties the decline then slowed between 1951 and 1971, before beginning again.[52]

Second, and related to the same chronology, the late 1920s and early 1930s mark a shift in political attitudes. In agriculture this is clear in government policy after 1931, but it spreads beyond that. Cooper has shown that the Conservative Party after the late 1920s was committed to large modern farms which were to be brought into being by state intervention.[53] Even the Liberal Party abandoned its long-held belief in smallholdings and back-to-the-land in favour of a big-farms policy, while Labour, if it had a policy at all, followed similar lines. This was supported by a growing body of 'trade' and scientific opinion which supported the large mechanised and scientific farm, be it in the arable or pastoral sector.[54]

This is replicated in the 'social' history. The Town and Country Planning Act of 1932, though widely criticised at the time and since for its weakness, does mark a step forward to planned intervention in the rural areas. Similarly, the growing demand for access to the countryside, marked spectacularly by the mass trespasses in the Peak District in the early 1930s, and less dramatically by the Access to Mountains Bill of 1939 and the foundation of the Standing Committee on National Parks in 1936, brought government into previously untouched aspects of rural life.

Third – and perhaps most difficult although most seductive to the historian of the current generation – is the image of all this, and the relation between the shadow and the substance. The idea of a depressed and broken interwar

---

52 Much of this material is discussed in more detail in Howkins, *The Death of Rural England.*

53 A. F. Cooper, *British Agricultural Policy 1912–1936: A Study in Conservative Politics* (Manchester, 1989).

54 Many of these discussion were conveniently summarised in the different editions of Viscount Astor and B. Seebohm Rowntree, *British Agriculture: The Principles of Future Policy,* which appeared as a Penguin Book in 1939.

countryside remains a fundamental part of farming's current self-image, but it was much more central at the time. The careful cultivation of the idea of a rural England betrayed, ruined and depopulated passed from the farming community into government policy ably assisted *en route* by a generation of writers and critics. This not only enabled agriculture to get state aid denied to, say, mining or shipbuilding, but to convince political and public opinion that state aid was essential to farming's future. In 1942 Mass Observation sent out a directive asking what people though the future of agriculture would be. Nearly all the replies, which were overwhelmingly urban, began from a sense that agriculture had been badly treated before the war. For example, a panellist wrote from urban Lancashire, 'Agriculture must never be allowed to fall into the condition into which it had descended prior to the war in this country.' There was, as a result of this feeling, a widespread belief that wartime controls and subsidies should continue after the war – to a remarkable degree fore-shadowing the policies of all post-war governments.[55] We may as historians 'prove' that interwar agriculture was not as badly off as used to be argued, but we should not lose sight of the dominating power of 'myth'.

And that brings us to another image which might be a bit more difficult to blow away. There is no doubt that the agricultural population declined in the interwar period, and alongside that decline was a real fall in the number of country workers, especially craftspeople, of all kinds. This has always been put alongside the problems of agriculture as indicating the 'end' of an old rural England. It may well be that that is so. However, that ignores the rebirth of rural England. By 1931 those who worked in agriculture were a minority of the rural population. Only in a very small number of counties were they even the largest single occupational group. They had been replaced by new country men and women, 'the resident trippers' as George Sturt called them – the commuter, the weekender, and the suburbanite and the holiday-maker were the people of new rural England.

That is clearly a very simplistic view. Until the 1950s, if not later, agriculture clearly provided a massive amount of indirect employment in rural areas which is hidden by simply counting those who worked the land. The very landscape of every rural county is still largely shaped by agriculture – even in the south east. Yet it raises huge problems for the historian. Perhaps somewhere around 1930 rural history, in the way we have hitherto understood it – as cows and ploughs, as landlord, farmer and labourer, or as cottage and castle – comes to an end. Or, at least (to paraphrase Churchill), comes to the beginning of the end.

---

[55] For this survey and attitudes during the war see A. Howkins, 'A country at war: Mass-Observation and rural England, 1939–45', *Rural History* 9/1 (1998).

It is easy to dismiss the new countrymen and women of the 1930s. Reactionaries like Betjeman and Waugh made a career out of it, and the Countryside Alliance wishes to deny even their existence as country people at all. Yet they, just as much as the revival of agriculture after 1931–2, are a central part of revising the history of the interwar countryside. What this means is that we as historians need to reshape the way in which we view the recent past of the rural areas. Certainly continuities are central; certainly my assertions of change in one or two years make little sense in some ways; yet we do have to confront change as well.

2 'A new rural civilization': village halls, community and citizenship in the 1920s

Jeremy Burchardt

THE traditional account of rural leisure in the interwar period takes its cue from the identification of these years as an era of agricultural depression. It is argued that the seemingly remorseless downwards trend of farm product prices in the 1920s and early 1930s undermined what little confidence had returned to the sector in the wake of the First World War, and that low wages, the failure of agricultural trade unionism and declining population struck particularly hard at agricultural workers. I have taken issue with this view elsewhere, arguing that, on the contrary, the interwar years witnessed a remarkable expansion in the quantity and, in many ways, the quality of rural leisure opportunities. An impressive array of new leisure organisations were established during and immediately after the First World War, and, despite some decline in the numbers participating after 1929, rural leisure in 1939 was more varied and extensive than it had been in 1914.[1] In this chapter I would like to consider what was perhaps the single most important component of the revitalisation of rural leisure: the provision of village halls.

The first and in some ways most important question about village halls is when they originated. Were they a new creation of the years during and after the First World War? The answer to this depends in large part on what we define as a village hall. Certainly there were important precursors to village halls in the years before the First World War. A variety of buildings had been used as indoor meeting places for villagers in the nineteenth century. In terms of the number of leisure hours spent there, the pub was the most important of these. Many pubs had not only one or more bars, but also private function rooms. These were often the venue for meetings of village friendly societies, which had a significant subsidiary leisure function. Other important venues for public leisure events in nineteenth-century villages included church and chapel rooms, school rooms and reading rooms. All of these, however, were normally much smaller than a village hall and could rarely seat more than thirty or so adults in comfort: a fraction of the population of all but the least

---

[1] J. Burchardt, 'Deference and democracy: village social organisations as rural institutions', in *Rural Institutions in the North Sea Area, 1850–1950*, ed. J. Bielemann, L. van der Molle and E. von Thoen (forthcoming).

populated villages. Each of them also suffered from a less obvious but equally serious disadvantage: they were only in practice available to defined subgroups of the village population. The pub was probably the venue, of those mentioned, which was least restrictive from this point of view, but even the pub was in effect a closed territory to most 'respectable' women (and, of course, to tee-totallers). Church and chapel rooms were under the control of the religious denomination in question, and were thus inhospitable not only to members of other denominations but also to a wide and indeterminate variety of causes, organisations and activities which were regarded with disfavour by the own-ers of the room. School rooms suffered from the same problem, particularly before non-denominational schools became common in the countryside. They were also inconvenient because of the child-sized furniture. Reading rooms were in many respects the most direct precursor of village halls, because they too were primarily intended to accommodate gatherings of a cross-section of the population meeting together for the purpose of amusement or entertain-ment. However, reading rooms were not only much smaller than most village halls, but were often under the direct control of the incumbent clergyman or the major local landowner, and were accordingly often governed by strict regulations. Furthermore, they usually excluded women. So although village halls may not have been the first indoor public meeting places available to vil-lagers, they were the first large indoor meeting places under public rather than sectional control.

A more pertinent objection to the claim that village halls were an innova-tion of the years after the First World War is, not that village halls had precur-sors, but that some of them were built before 1914. This is clearly the case, and these early village halls are a subject deserving more detailed investigation than has yet been made. Some of the most lavish and spectacular halls were in fact built before the war, including Nettlebed in Oxfordshire (1913) and Kemsing in Kent (1910). But the vast majority were built after 1914.[2] System-atic data is not yet available, but research into the halls of Oxfordshire identi-fied three known to have been built before 1914, one between 1914 and 1918, and nineteen between 1919 and 1939. The three halls pre-dating the war were Chalgrove (1906), Checkendon (1913) and Nettlebed (also 1913). In Berkshire the pattern was similar, with four halls with confirmed opening dates prior to 1914, five prior to 1918 and twenty-six prior to 1940.[3] It seems that village halls manifest the same pattern apparent in so many other aspects of British and,

[2] L. Weaver, *Village Clubs and Halls* (1920), pp. 62–83. Weaver also provides repro-ductions of the ground plans of twenty-six other village halls and institutes in England and Wales built before the outbreak of the war.

[3] J. Burchardt, 'Reconstructing the rural community: village halls and the National Council of Social Service, 1919 to 1939', *Rural History* 10/2 (1999): 193–216.

indeed, European society: early signs of developments which were to become major features after 1918 were already apparent in the years immediately before the war. The problem here is in many respects one of emphasis: some will be more impressed by the fact that a few halls did pre-date the war, others by the fact that far more were established after the war, and that the rate of hall provision accelerated impressively after 1918 (between two and threefold, to judge by the Oxfordshire figures). There may also have been a change in the character of hall-building after the war: several of the pre-war halls, including both Nettlebed and Kemsing, were impressive buildings financed in their entirety by wealthy individuals (typically local landowners), whereas post-1918 village halls were typically financed at least in part by a wider cross-section of the local community, reflecting more democratic origins. It seems possible that pre-war halls were, as a result, larger and more expensive than post-war halls.[4]

The dramatic acceleration in the rate of village hall provision after 1918 had two main causes: popular pressure on the one hand, and proactive sponsorship by the voluntary sector on the other. The first of these has been described in revealing detail by Keith Grieves in his article on hall provision in Sussex after 1918, and also by myself in a previous article, so I will provide only a brief summary here.[5] Virtually all contemporary accounts of rural society in 1918–20 mention the discontent of the mass of the rural population with existing leisure provision in the countryside. As Sir Henry Rew said in his address to the 1920 NCSS conference in Oxford,

> the demand [for better rural leisure facilities] is universal. The organisers of the Village Clubs' Association have only been actively at work for a very few months, but in all parts of the country they have visited – from Lancashire to Sussex, from Norfolk to Devonshire, from Hertfordshire to North Wales, from every county and district, the demand is the same. The Women's Institutes … testify to the same urgent need. All recent enquirers into the rural problem are insistent on the subject.

---

4 Lawrence Weaver cites costs for seven pre-war village halls, the average of which is £1,378. The average cost of twenty-eight post-war halls financed in part by the NCSS Village Halls Loan Fund was £624. These figures take no account of inflation, so probably understate the difference. However, it is not clear whether the cost of furnishings was always included in the raw data on which these calculations are based. See Weaver, *Village Clubs and Halls*, pp. 14, 18, 23, 40, 43, 45, 74; National Council of Social Service, *Cooperation in Social Service: Being the Annual Report of the National Council of Social Service for the Years 1928–9* (1929), p. 35.

5 K. Grieves, 'Common meeting places and the brightening of rural life: local debates on village halls in Sussex after the First World War', *Rural History* 10/2 (1999): 171–92; Burchardt, 'Reconstructing the rural community', pp. 193–216.

As Rew's remarks emphasise, this demand for improved rural leisure applied to women, whose exclusion from public leisure spaces before the war had been on a larger scale, at least as much as to men. Women as well as men had had their lives disrupted by the war and had often experienced new leisure possibilities through war work or through contact with women from urban backgrounds. This kind of experience and contact was, of course, not new in 1914; indeed, the interfusion and interdependence of town and country is as old as are the two categories, but the war accelerated the rate of mixing, bringing the two into more frequent, abrupt and prolonged contact.

The second force stimulating village hall provision was the policies of a close-linked network of individuals and voluntary organisations with an interest in rural social life. Amongst these were the rural community councils, the National Council of Social Service, the Village Clubs Association, the YMCA, the Red Triangle Federation and the WI. Behind these organisations stood the Carnegie UK Trust and the Development Commission, which offered financial backing for many of their initiatives, including the building of village halls. The remainder of this chapter is primarily concerned with the aims of these organisations, especially with the two which were principally responsible for developing the administrative infrastructure to support village halls, the rural community councils (RCCs) and the National Council of Social Service (NCSS).

Both the RCCs and the NCSS were new organisations created in the wake of the First World War. I have examined their origins elsewhere, and will only briefly summarise them here.[6] The NCSS, established in 1919, was in some respects a successor to the late nineteenth-century Charity Organization Society (COS), in that it aimed to co-ordinate voluntary social action and to make it more efficient. Where the NCSS departed from the model of the COS, other than in its greater ideological flexibility, was in its relationship to government. Many of the leading figures within the NCSS, including its long-standing chairman W. G. S. Adams, were or had been public servants, and saw the purpose of the organisation as being in large part to mediate between government and society, channelling information and finance from government to the voluntary sector and responding to social need in a more fluid and less conflictual form than was possible for government.[7] The RCCs derived from a small group of voluntary sector organisers based in Oxford. The key figure here was Grace Hadow, the vice-president of the WI and later Principal of the Society of Oxford Home Students (now St Anne's College).

---

6 Burchardt, 'Reconstructing the rural community', pp. 193–216.

7 H. Deneke, *Grace Hadow* (1946), p. 101. See also R. J. Morris, 'Clubs, societies and associations', in *The Cambridge Social History of Britain, 1750–1950*, vol. 3: *Social Agencies and Institutions*, ed. F. M. L. Thompson (1990), p. 440.

Hadow had close links to Adams, who, as Gladstone Professor of Political Theory and Institutions, was himself an Oxford man, and it was at his behest that she took on the leadership of Barnett House, a centre for social research and organisation established in Oxford shortly before the First World War.[8] Hadow, whose background and interests were rural, developed Barnett House into a clearing house for voluntary organisations active in the Oxford area. From the meetings of the leaders of these organisations emerged what was subsequently formalised as the Oxfordshire Rural Community Council.[9] This was a model in which the NCSS, guided by Adams, took a keen interest, and a number of conferences were held in Oxford under its aegis. One of the first results of this was that the NCSS established a rural department; subsequently it was decided to seek to generalise the Oxford model to other counties. This was done with the help of a grant from the Carnegie UK Trustees, and by 1939 the RCCs had become integral to organised social life in rural England.[10] The NCSS and the RCCs jointly administered a scheme under which village halls could be financed by loans from the Carnegie Trust and by grants from the Development Commission.

Both the NCSS and the RCCs regarded the building of village halls as of central importance. This was not merely because of the strength of popular demand for them, nor because of the lack of suitable alternatives, but because halls were seen as an essential step towards a much more ambitious goal: the creation of a 'new rural civilization'. This vision of a new rural civilisation had several components. At its core lay the concept of community, construed as a distinctively rural quality. The village, it was believed by Adams, Hadow and their followers, held the potential for the creation of true community in a way not possible in urban areas. As the sixteenth annual report of the NCSS explained, the rural work of the NCSS was 'in a very real sense the apex of that work. For it is in the country village more than anywhere else that the meaning of "community" and the fact of common interest can be most easily realised.' A village was a face-to-face society in which everyone could know each other and in which individuals stood in a clearly defined relationship to each other, as opposed to the amorphous, shifting and uncertain relationships assumed to characterise urban social interaction. Furthermore, because people who lived in the countryside were thought to be closer to nature, a capacity to 'assess the quality of things that is easily blunted by the artificial environment of streets'

---

[8] M. Brasnett, *Voluntary Social Action: A History of the National Council of Social Service, 1919–1969* (1969), p. 33.

[9] Brasnett, *Voluntary Social Action*, p. 32.

[10] National Council of Social Service, *Third Annual Report of the National Council of Social Service for the Year 1922* (1923), p. 5.

was attributed to them.[11] However, if this rich potential for community was to be achieved in practice, it was essential that villagers had opportunities for meeting. It was from this point of view that a village hall was the 'key to good progress'.[12] Even the process of planning and building a hall would, the NCSS believed, have community-forming properties. The collective effort required to raise the share of the funding which the NCSS required, even where it provided a grant or loan, would, it was thought, bring villagers together: they would find their common identity in shared work. It was, of course, essential that this work should be provided on a voluntary basis, for what the NCSS and the RCCs were seeking to nourish was a delicate tissue of feelings. No crude cash payments or inducements could substitute for this spontaneous growth.

The spirit of community which the NCSS and RCCs were so keen to foster was an end in itself, but it was also a means to another, more practical end with which it was closely intertwined. This was the development of an active, informed, reflective citizenship among rural voters, many of whom, including, of course, all female voters, had been enfranchised for the first time in 1918. Community was the proper foundation for citizenship because the sense of common purpose, social unity, individual restraint and responsible action to which it gave rise were also the necessary qualifications for the responsible democratic citizen. The NCSS believed that the small size of villages meant that they offered a training in self-government: 'the village has a special value as a school of democracy and whatever tends to draw out the capacity for self-government in village life is enhancing this value.' Meeting together in the village hall and, perhaps still more, taking a share in the running of the hall would provide the ideal education in citizenship for new rural electors.

A further aspect of the 'new rural civilization' that the NCSS and the RCCs hoped to bring to life through the village halls policy was the maintenance of the rural as a distinctive and separate sphere from the urban world. The special qualities of rural life from which it was hoped community and citizenship could be constructed were perceived as 'easily corrupted by town influences that are permeating the countryside'.[13] A sense that the countryside was under threat was pervasive amongst the cultural establishment in the late nineteenth and early twentieth centuries. Partly this was because of the collapse of agricultural prices from the 1870s onwards and the social disruption that came

---

[11] National Council of Social Service, *Constructive Citizenship: The Annual Report of the NCSS (Inc.) for the Year 1930–31* (1931), p. 9.

[12] National Council of Social Service, *Voluntary Service: Being the Twelfth Annual Report of the NCSS for the Year 1931–2* (1932), p. 15.

[13] NCSS, *Voluntary Service*, p. 9.

with this, notably the economic difficulties of landowners and the mass out-migration of agricultural labourers. But still more powerful was a conviction that urbanism as a way of life was the coming universal condition. Writers like Hardy, Sturt and Lawrence charted the intrusion both of urban influences into the countryside not only in their more obvious physical forms, such as suburbanisation or mechanisation, but in the increasing marginalisation or even extinction of rural culture. The First World War served to crystallise such fears. Just as the organicist thinkers of the 1940s denounced Nazism as a manifestation of the brutal domination of the machine and the 'urban mind', so there was also a sense that the extreme destructiveness of the First World War was linked to its unprecedentedly mechanised and industrial character.[14] From this point of view it was a short step to diagnosing urbanism, as leading to a reversion to barbarism. What was needed, evidently, was a restoration of the proper 'balance' of rural and urban elements. In this way, hope for the future of human civilisation depended on the maintenance of the rural as a distinct and separate sphere, defended so far as possible against insidious urban influences. For this reason, the NCSS and the RCCs sought to buttress distinctive rural traditions wherever they could find them. A notable feature of their village halls policy was using control of the purse strings to insist on (often more expensive) 'traditional' local building materials and styles. Villages applying for funding from the NCSS had to demonstrate that their plans had been approved by a panel of architects appointed by the Royal Institute of British Architects, an organisation with close links to the NCSS and (later) the Council for the Preservation of Rural England, and one committed to respecting what were perceived as authentic regional building traditions. The NCSS emphasised that village halls should be beautiful as well as serviceable, citing their role in persuading the Carnegie Trustees to provide financial assistance for the wall paintings at Woodgreen village hall (Hampshire).[15] Characteristic of the close involvement of the NCSS in the planning of individual halls and of its determination to ensure that halls were in keeping with their rural setting was the hall at Taynton in Oxfordshire, built 1938. The NCSS made the grant which permitted the hall to be built conditional on the roof being constructed from cedar shingles rather than asbestos.[16]

Why did the NCSS and the RCCs seek to foster community, voluntary

---

[14] P. Conford, *The Origins of the Organic Movement* (Edinburgh, 2001); P. Fussell, *The Great War and Modern Memory* (1975).

[15] NCSS, *Voluntary Service*, p. 32.

[16] Copy letter from the secretary of the Taynton village hall to T. F. Thompson, Town Planning Surveyor, Witney and District Joint Town Planning Committee of Oxfordshire County Council and Witney Urban and Witney Rural District Councils, dated 26 May 1938.

service, citizenship and rural distinctiveness in the countryside? We need to look not just at the justifications and explanations given by these organisations, but at the social provenance and connections of the leading figures within them. What is striking about the leaders of the NCSS and the RCCs is that they were almost all public servants. Many of them, including both Adams and Hadow, had experienced government service during the First World War, and it is clear that this had a considerable effect on them.[17] Interestingly, few of those who were most active in the NCSS or the RCCs had fought in the trenches. Perhaps for this reason, they exhibit a kind of idealism that was an extension of the untarnished conviction that the war was a noble struggle of democracy against autocracy and militarism. The same kind of 'social service' that Adams and Hadow willingly offered to the voluntary organisations they worked for, they hoped and expected would be tendered by villagers participating in the organisation of events at village halls.

A second common feature of the social provenance of many of those within the RCCs and the NCSS was an academic background. Again, this is well illustrated by Adams and Hadow, although many others who were less prominent in the movement also shared it. Professor Peers of the University of Nottingham, the chairman of the joint East Midlands RCC, is another example. Once again, the non-commercial, public service aspect is apparent. It may even be no exaggeration to suggest that for some within the movement, especially those based in Oxford, the university provided a model of how a democratic village community could operate. Just as universities reached decisions – at least in theory – by calm, well-informed deliberation, mediated through a network of voluntary committees, so villages could become true communities through coming together in their halls.

What this points to is that the ideals of the village hall movement – and here I am referring solely to that component of it which was 'from above' – corresponded in large part to the characteristic values of a social stratum which was increasingly influential within British society in the interwar years – the professional middle class. In this I am following Harold Perkin. Perkin argues that professionals tended to favour a meritocratic, and therefore democratic, model of society. Like the NCSS and the RCCs, they were keen to sweep away the vestiges of aristocratic oligarchy. They justified their social role in terms of service to the community, which axiomatically shared common interests transcending those of individuals. These common interests it was the purview of professionals to interpret and serve.[18]

---

[17] W. G. S. Adams obituary, *The Times*, 1 Feb 1966, p. 12e; Grace Hadow obituary, *The Times*, 22 Jan 1940, p. 9c; 'Grace Hadow', *Dictionary of National Biography* (1931–40), p. 386.

[18] H. J. Perkin, *The Rise of Professional Society: England since 1880* (1989).

If we interpret the ideology of rural community manifest in the advocacy and sponsorship of village halls by the voluntary organisations as characteristic of professional values, the question arises of whether this ideology was an alien one to rural society, and if so, how viable it could be. Pedley makes the interesting observation that the RCCs had sometimes been 'the means whereby independent and retired people express their benevolence towards the villages' and suggests that the unwillingness of several northern counties to form rural community councils may be attributable to a suspicion of this.[19] However, the history of village halls appears to demonstrate that they did meet real needs, since they remained well used in most villages throughout the interwar period and have survived almost everywhere (and in fact increased their numbers) into the twenty-first century. But the fact that they have survived and prospered does not necessarily indicate that they met the aspirations of the organisations that originally promoted and in part funded them. On the contrary, in one important respect village halls actually militated against the hopes of the NCSS and the RCCs. It seems quite clear that halls facilitated the influx into rural society of urban cultural forms – cinema, jazz, modern dance, keep-fit classes, to cite the most obvious examples. So far from preserving the separateness of the 'rural way of life', village halls probably hastened its decline.[20]

In other respects, village halls did more to meet the aspirations of the NCSS and the RCCs. They do seem to have furthered democratisation and perhaps even political participation by villagers, at least if the evidence of village hall committee minutes is anything to go by. Hall committees, partly at the insistence of the NCSS, were established on a democratic basis, and although it took time, by the 1930s the traditional elite of landowners and clergymen was often being shouldered aside by 'ordinary' villagers. Still clearer is the success of village halls in brightening rural life and extending the range of leisure activities that took place in the interwar countryside.[21] Village halls also clearly helped to perpetuate the tradition of voluntaryism in the countryside, so contributing to the marked success of the more privileged elements within rural society in blurring the lines of class conflict. In all these respects, village

---

[19] W. H. Pedley, *Labour on the Land: A Study of the Developments between the two Great Wars* (1942), p. 162.

[20] Films were often shown in village halls. Evidence from the *Oxford Times* shows that films were shown in at least six Oxfordshire halls in January 1919, for example. See also Weaver, *Village Clubs and Halls*, p. 82: 'The provision of picture palaces in all English villages would be a doubtful advantage, if they showed the baser sort of 'cowboy' and other sensational films. Given some restraint in the choice of subject, however, moving pictures make winter evenings more changeful.'

[21] Burchardt, 'Reconstructing the rural community', pp. 193–216.

halls ministered to the real needs or interests of important sections of rural society, and it is to this rather than to the intentions of the NCSS and the RCCs that their success should be attributed. It may not be unfair to suggest that village halls did create a new civilisation in the countryside – or at least enrich rural social life and community integration very considerably – but not a distinctively rural civilisation. With regard to leisure opportunities in the countryside, then, a strong case can be made for regeneration rather than decline after the First World War. Regeneration, however, came at least in part from outside traditional agricultural society and, if it enhanced rural life, also served to erode what made it distinctive.

3 Rural education and reform between the wars[*]

Caitlin Adams

As Colin Ward points out, the village school has an iconic significance within English culture. Childhood, but especially country childhood, is typically recalled in nostalgic terms, and contact with the natural environment is a mark of special favour.[1] Within literary and visual representations of the countryside, the village school, like the parish church and the village green, is often an emblem of community and cohesiveness. This is a compelling and enduring image, but one that masks religious and other divisions. Historically the village school was not intended for all local children, but only those whose parents could not afford to send them elsewhere.

Rural reformers in this period were profoundly anxious about geographical mobility, suburban development and a perceived loss of community. Observers across the political spectrum believed that the old landlords, or 'squirearchy', were abdicating their responsibilities. Reformers feared continuing depopulation as country people were lured to the towns, and as agriculture continued to decline in economic importance. Some social reformers looked to state education to counteract negative external influences and to keep young people on the land. Meaningful change was difficult, however, because of the existing state system – inadequate and compromised by a competing private system for the privileged – and the difficulty of finding resources to support small, isolated populations.

Educational policy is inherently political in nature, because it forms social actors in accordance with the wishes (explicit or otherwise) of administrators, parents and the wider mainstream society. What makes a good citizen or subject? What behaviours and values should a child learn in order to grow into a capable and useful adult within a capitalist economy? Education, when it is mass education, is a tricky balancing act: literacy has a notorious habit of failing to produce citizens obedient to their elders and betters.[2]

[*] This article is based on the second chapter of C. Adams, 'The Idea of the Village in Interwar England' (unpublished PhD thesis, University of Michigan, 2001), pp. 72–104. Thanks are owed to Anna Davin, Catherine Dille, and my dissertation committee for their comments, and to all the conference contributors.

[1] C. Ward, *The Child in the Country* (1988), p. 18.

[2] See J. Rose, *The Intellectual Life of the British Working Classes* (2001).

What follows is a discussion of interwar educational reform in rural areas, beginning with the problematic legacy of the Victorian period and then considering how observers defined the rural school as a special problem. I will look at how education was supposed to fit country boys and girls for rural life, and the range of adult education provision supported by new organisations such as the women's institutes and rural community councils (RCCs). The one great innovation of the period was the village college, an attempt to solve the problems of rural education by concentrating resources in small population centres and integrating vocational and academic training. By any standards an enduring success, the colleges brought together different rural groups in a common social enterprise. But these colleges and other efforts at rural educational reform did not entirely bypass existing social hierarchies or reject traditional assumptions about the special characteristics and needs of country people.

THE VICTORIAN LEGACY: VILLAGE SCHOOLS BEFORE 1918

Mass education (that is, omitting elite private schools) developed in the nineteenth century essentially as a religious enterprise funded by competing Anglican and nonconformist organisations in association with the state. Through most of the nineteenth century there were also many 'dame schools', whose educational efficiency is still debated. These schools often served as sweatshops for learning localised trades such as lace-making.[3] From the 1830s the religious societies for schools received public money for providing educational services, but it was not until 1870 that legislation was finally passed that established state responsibility for funding and overseeing schools.[4] Historians generally see this development within a larger Victorian creation of the concept of childhood as a special, distinct period of life. Thus mass education proceeded in tandem with the official attempts to abolish child labour.[5]

After the 1870 Act and subsequent legislation, all children were expected to attend school until the age of eleven (later rising to thirteen, fourteen and then ultimately to sixteen). The state inspected schools and contributed to the costs of schooling, though tuition fees were not entirely abolished until

---

3 For a positive view, see P. Gardner, 'Schools', in *The Lost Elementary Schools of Victorian England: The People's Education* (1984), pp. 147–87. However, Rose has reservations: *The Intellectual Life of the British Working Classes*, pp. 151–6.

4 The relevant Act was never meant as a first step in creating a secular state system, and the Church of England retained a considerable amount of control. P. Chadwick, *Shifting Alliances: Church and State in English Education* (1997), p. 10.

5 C. Steedman, *Childhood, Culture and Class in Britain: Margaret McMillan, 1860–1931* (1990), pp. 62–8.

1918. Where the old voluntary schools failed to meet the needs of local children – through mismanagement or lack of adequate funding – administration moved to elected school boards. In rural England relatively few school boards were created in this period, as ratepayers seem to have resisted the necessary expenditure, or feared the waning of Anglican influence.

The existence of a school board did not guarantee that it would meet its statutory obligations to provide enough school places for children or ensure their attendance.[6] Teachers had to be in sympathy with the religious and political views of the managers, and they were not protected from arbitrary dismissal. They were also very badly paid, and their salaries depended for some years on success as determined by examination results. Sanitary inspection, the building of new schools and other necessary developments occurred gradually and unevenly; where the managers were obstructive, it was extremely difficult to force them to improve school conditions. In 1902 the school boards were abolished and replaced by local education authorities, or LEAs, which assumed control on a more systematic basis but were overseen by the central Board of Education. Nonconformists protested strongly at being forced to support Anglican schools, resulting in local 'rate strikes' in England and Wales. In Willingham, Cambridgeshire, for instance, 400 people demonstrated in 1905. Some of those who refused to pay the new education rate went to prison or had their goods sold at public auction.[7]

All of the standard difficulties of limited resources and poor and malnourished children are magnified in isolated country settings. In the late Victorian era classes were large and materials inadequate, with underpaid teachers rarely able to supplement them effectively. Mandatory attendance placed the schools at odds with impoverished parents who needed their children's wages. In addition, many schools were poorly built and by modern standards dirty, smelly and uncomfortable, despite the regulations of the Board of Education. In fact it was commonplace into the 1940s to make the excuse that country children were accustomed to poor living conditions and 'unpleasant smells'.[8]

---

[6] P. Horn, *Education in Rural England, 1800–1914* (Dublin, 1978), pp. 135–6. T. W. Bamford shows that some school boards in the East Riding remained deliberately inactive for years at a time, necessitating intervention from London: T. W. Bamford, *The Evolution of Rural Education: Three Studies of the East Riding of Yorkshire*, Research Monographs 1 (Hull, 1965), pp. 24–42.

[7] These had ended by 1911 in Wales. Horn, *Education in Rural England*, p. 266. In Willingham the auctioneer was in sympathy with the resisters, and photographs of the event survive. Cottenham Village College Local History Group, *Charity School to Village College: Cottenham, Rampton, Willingham* (Loughborough, 1968), pp. 52–5.

[8] H. M. Burton, *The Education of the Countryman* (1944), pp. 28–9.

As schoolteachers also appeared to represent an extension of the authority of the Anglican Church in many areas, it is easy to see why some parents were indifferent or even hostile to compulsory schooling.

This brief outline of the system in place before the First World War helps to explain the terrible conditions still found in country schools in the 1920s. As so often in the field of education, a small number of reformers correctly identified the worst problems of schooling decades before the emergence of the political will needed for action. In 1918 an education bill was introduced that raised the school-leaving age to fourteen and took a first step toward expanding secondary schooling to all students who showed academic ability. Briefly it seemed there would be a new approach, but instead government expenditure was cut across the board and any dream of a golden age ended quickly.

VILLAGE SCHOOLS BETWEEN THE WARS: TEACHING AND ADMINISTRATION

If the 1918 act did not change education as many reformers and teachers had hoped, certain progressive assumptions – many of them derived from the Labour Party's policy statements – did in fact enter public discussion and gradually became part of mainstream educational theory. The most important of these ideas were that the school-leaving age should be raised again to the mid-teens, and that all children with ability deserved a chance to attend a secondary school. In addition, teachers gradually won better salaries and conditions with the adoption of nationwide scales of pay. Progressive theories about curriculum and the psychological and physical needs of the child affected teaching enough so that learning by rote slowly fell out of favour and was replaced in many areas by hands-on work and lessons that moved across traditional disciplinary boundaries.

Surveys of rural education in the interwar period show, however, that for a number of reasons country schools nearly always lagged behind town schools. Religious or political views were sometimes a bar to hiring the best graduates of the training colleges; about two-thirds of the village schools were 'non-provided' (that is, founded by one of the two religious foundations) and therefore mostly Anglican in origin.[9] Even the structure of the pay scale and system of recruitment discouraged innovation.

It was a striking feature of rural schools that they used a far higher percentage of 'uncertificated' and 'supplementary' teachers than town schools. 'Certificated' teachers had attended a teacher-training college and passed examinations, whereas 'uncertificated' teachers had (in theory, at least) attended

9 Burton, *The Education of the Countryman*, p. 59.

teacher-training colleges for a short period without graduating. 'Supplementary' teachers had no educational qualifications whatsoever: they were required only to be eighteen years old and vaccinated against smallpox. In 1936/7 some 87 per cent of the 'supplementary' teachers in England were in areas run by county LEAs.[10] 'Supplementary' and 'uncertificated' teachers were nearly all women, and they could be paid much less than trained teachers of either sex. Although there was reported progress in staffing village schools with trained teachers by the later 1930s, the 'certificated' teachers were just over 65 per cent of the total rural teaching force in 1937.[11] 'Supplementary' teachers were supposed to be closely supervised, but often had complete oversight over the infants' class.

The special place of women teachers in rural areas deserves attention. Women were, of course, always paid less than men wherever they taught. In 1932 the National Union of Women Teachers reported that county schools that paid the lowest salaries had some 10,370 women, against 2,647 men. A contemporary commentator observed that rural education was therefore 'in the main a woman teacher's problem'.[12] Some urban LEAs had a 'marriage bar'; thus trained women who chose to marry sometimes taught in rural schools by default rather than by choice. In the late 1930s most rural LEAs apparently preferred to hire men to run schools that had more than about ninety pupils; in Oxfordshire in the early 1920s the cut-off point for a school to be run by a headmistress was sixty students.[13]

Qualified teachers sometimes avoided working in rural areas because of social pressures as well as extra work. Marjorie Wise reported that one teacher found 'the prejudices of religious sect and class distinction were so bitter' that she avoided involvement in any local organisations.[14] But it was more common to have the opposite problem: the teacher might have responsibility for many local clubs, or be the main source of writing services and general legal advice. If there were continuing education activities in the village, the teacher had to serve as a local liaison or, in many cases, the instructor. Hence a committed country headmaster or headmistress could be on duty many more hours than the average city teacher.[15]

---

[10] Burton, *The Education of the Countryman*, p. 31.

[11] Burton, *The Education of the Countryman*, p. 31.

[12] E. E. Crosby, *A Survey of the Problem of Education in Rural Areas* (1932), paper read at the Conference of Educational Associations in London, 5 January 1932.

[13] Burton, *The Education of the Countryman*, p. 32, and A. W. Ashby and P. Byles, *Rural Education* (Oxford, 1923), p. 62.

[14] M. Wise, *English Village Schools* (1931), p. 43.

[15] Burton, *The Education of the Countryman*, pp. 42–3.

Aside from the difficulties already mentioned, village schools had a very high proportion of poor children, and the farming context presented special problems. Harvests required child labour, which disrupted the school schedule, and parents were anxious for their children to go into domestic service for a regular wage. Thus many pupils did not stay until the legal minimum leaving age. Some teachers complained that their students were exhausted and under-nourished, raised in badly overcrowded homes. In Oxfordshire in 1920 A. W. Ashby and Phoebe Byles found cases of a family of seven in a one-bedroom cottage, and of ten in a cottage with one bedroom and a landing.[16]

Another frequent complaint among educationists was that rural conditions produced children who were 'backward' mentally as well as physically because of social isolation, poverty and the monotony of farm work.[17] It is one of the inconsistencies of rural stereotyping that these characteristics could be given a positive gloss: producing children who were reliable, self-contained and morally sound. Indeed, some writers on rural matters thought that country people had a different and possibly better form of intelligence than townspeople. H. M. Burton wrote that working the land inspired 'a certain patient, watchful stolidity', but also initiative and mental agility. He insisted that rural children had a different process of reasoning than town children, rather than less overall mental capacity:

A proportion of them appear to hold on to what they have been taught more firmly, even if it took them a little longer to learn it. Their power of concentration, once they have settled down to a job, would surprise the town teacher: and the job does not have to be one which they like. They are, on the whole, more patient and more reliable than the town children.[18]

Religious differences and class divisions did not disappear in the twentieth century. Many teachers probably continued to depend directly on local benefactors for coal and other supplies, and there would have been pressures from 'notables' who subsidised so many village activities. Students at one Kent school found that in cold weather, '[s]eats near to the fire were reserved for the offspring of the farmers and the squire's agent.'[19] In the Victorian period a

[16] Ashby and Byles, *Rural Education*, pp. 104–5.

[17] Ashby and Byles, for example, claimed that a school of ninety-five students had 'one lot of twelve and another of ten [who] are cousins, and hardly any of them have any real stamina either physical or mental': Ashby and Byles, *Rural Education*, p. 108.

[18] Burton, *The Education of the Countryman*, p. 56.

[19] Horn, *Education*, p. 121, quoting an unnamed student in *Countryman* 18/4 (Winter 1976/7), p. 163.

few school managers had worked actively against the ideal of mass education, hoping that the rural work-force would remain docile. By the interwar period it was no longer so acceptable for the well-off automatically to denigrate mass schooling, but there was a residual prejudice against 'over-educating' those destined to be labourers: one reformer felt that '[a]s a class the farmers regard education much in the same way as they regard "blight" or "rust".'[20]

In theory, at least, the vicar no longer reigned supreme in the interwar period as he had done in many schools in the past.[21] However, in practice school managers could still refuse to authorise funds for repairs or alterations if they wanted to keep the rates down, or if they took a dislike to a teacher; Marjorie Wise found instances of school managers who were ignorant and indifferent.[22] Such matters pale into insignificance when placed against the conflict at Burston, Norfolk, where a vicar brought about the dismissal of teachers who were nonconformists, supporters of the Labour Party and closely tied to the local agricultural labourers' union. Sixty-six of the pupils went on strike, with their parents supporting the fired teachers; eventually a 'strike school' was built by public subscription. Although it was a uniquely bitter twenty-five-year conflict, this episode illuminates the extent to which Victorian relationships of patronage and control still endured into the 'modern' era.[23]

CONTINUING AND ADULT EDUCATION

Both governmental bodies and social reformers were greatly interested in what is now called 'life-long learning'. Secondary and grammar schools had a narrow academic curriculum and were designed to produce teachers, university students, or members of the 'black-coated' occupations (such as clerks). This began to change, especially after the publication in 1926 of a report of the Board of Education Consultative Committee called *The Education of the Adolescent* (the Hadow Report), which argued for a well-organised system of

---

[20] Quoted anonymously in Ashby and Byles, *Rural Education*, p. 163.

[21] Horn notes a case in Boston Spa, Yorkshire in 1876, in which a teacher was sacked by the vicar for refusing to punish a student who failed to curtsey to the vicar's wife: Horn, *Education in Rural England*, p. 121, citing J. Lawson, *Primary Education in East Yorkshire, 1560–1902* (York, 1959), p. 24.

[22] Wise, *English Village Schools*, p. 147.

[23] A. Howkins, *Poor Labouring Men: Rural Radicalism in Norfolk, 1872–1923* (1985), pp. 115–16; B. Edwards, *The Burston School Strike* (1974); and T. Jeffs, *Henry Morris: Village Colleges, Community Education and the Ideal Order* (Nottingham, 1998), p. 39. The school is now a listed building with a museum of the strike. The Burston Strike School (3 July 2001), website: http://www.burstonschoolstrike.org [15 Aug 2005].

secondary schooling. In essence the report suggested that there should be two main streams in secondary education: one that would continue the academic tradition, and another that would feed the needs of industry, commerce and agriculture by providing vocational training. Pupils would be assigned to one stream or the other based on an examination taken at the age of eleven.[24] Those students who were not academically inclined, or who did not win a scholarship for secondary education, left school at their fourteenth birthday. Consequently it was almost impossible for children from poor rural backgrounds to attend a secondary school. For example, in 1920 the total number of pupils in elementary education in Oxfordshire was 18,600, with about 2,000 children leaving school each year. The number of public scholarships available to students at fourteen to attend secondary schools was just thirty.[25]

Because of this, there was a partial (but inadequate) system of continued education in evening classes funded by the LEAs. The classes were usually run by the overworked teachers of the elementary school, and this limited the range of subjects that were offered. Demand for practical instruction in cooking, gardening and woodwork was high, but in many villages it went unmet. The Board of Education provided grants only for six or more lectures and a class of at least ten students. If a teacher was unenthusiastic or the population too sparse, there was no continuing education for young people at all.

Adult education in England to this point was largely a product of working-class co-operation and self-improvement, allied at times with university extension efforts.[26] The Workers' Educational Association, founded in 1903, met some of the demand for adult learning. Each local branch set up courses using WEA tutors and public lectures or conferences on various topics – often concerning international relations, economics or local history. Affiliated trade unions would refund in whole or in part the tuition fees of their members. There was a strong emphasis on university-level work (tutorial classes), and in some places students achieved undergraduate standard. However, it was only possible to send tutors for this purpose where demand was high, because grants depended on the rate of participation. It was therefore easier to form WEA branches and to find students willing to commit to the equivalent of a long-term degree course within a dense urban population.

The WEA increasingly joined forces with university extension schemes, but this did not meet the demand for recreational or vocational education.

[24] S. J. Curtis, *History of Education in Great Britain*, 5th edn (1963), p. 351.

[25] Ashby and Byles, *Rural Education*, pp. 210–11.

[26] T. Kelly, *The History of Adult Education in Great Britain*, 3rd edn (Liverpool, 1992); A. Mansbridge, *An Adventure in Working-Class Education: Being the Story of the Workers' Educational Association, 1903–1915* (1920); and Rose, *The Intellectual Life of the British Working Classes*, chapter 8.

The National Federation of Women's Institutes and the Ministry of Agriculture first addressed this gap during the war by creating an extensive network of lectures and short courses in all aspects of domestic science and food production. In addition WI members could learn about the latest animal husbandry techniques and the principles of co-operative selling and distribution.[27] After the war the WI continued this strand of its adult education activities, focusing especially on music, drama, local history and international relations, as well as practical training. Lectures and demonstrations usually took place as part of the regular WI meeting. Many rural community councils (RCCs), of which the county WI federations were members, then followed this lead by working closely with LEAs to provide a variety of subjects. By the end of the 1930s most counties had at least one full-time tutor and several part-time tutors to help with this work.

The classes undertaken by LEAs in conjunction with the rural community councils varied widely in order to meet the demand for both academic and non-academic training. In Oxfordshire, for example, despite cutbacks in the early 1930s, there were twenty-two classes and courses of lectures in 1936, not counting instruction meant specifically for the unemployed. The courses had a heavy emphasis on politics and the situation in Europe, although literature and general interest subjects were also offered. Apparently about 90 per cent of the students were poor and could pay only very low fees.[28] In Gloucestershire the rural community council and WEA worked together to provide twenty-two classes in 1930/1, and presented over 130 talks in villages.[29] In Somerset the county council provided a grant to full-time residential tutors, hired from Bristol University, who gave almost 100 lectures in twenty-two short courses. Single lectures were also provided on drama, fitness and physical training. The Kent Council of Social Service and many other RCCs gave advisory lectures on subjects such as music, drama and local history in the hopes of training local leaders in these areas.[30]

[27] P. Dudgeon (ed.), *Village Voices: A Portrait of Change in England's Green and Pleasant Land, 1915–1990* (1989), p. 57, and M. Andrews, *The Acceptable Face of Feminism: The Women's Institute as a Social Movement* (1997). Lynne Thompson is undertaking extensive research on the WI and agricultural education.

[28] Average attendance came to about nineteen students per class over five years. 'Adult Education in Oxfordshire', 1931/32 to 1935/36 ([1936]). Oxfordshire Public Record Office [OPRO], ORCC Box: 'ORCC Villages, Chilson 1950–63'.

[29] E. Green, 'Members of the Rural Community Council 1: The Workers' Educational Association', *Gloucestershire Countryside* 1/1 (Oct 1931), p. 5, and 'Notes and News', *Gloucestershire Countryside* 1/1 (Oct 1931), p. 15.

[30] 'RCC's and Adult Education', paper for a meeting of the Oxfordshire RCC, 23 Jan 1936. OPRO, ORCC Box: 'Squatters' Camp 1947–51; RCC.'s 1935 …',

There is little surviving evidence from those who took these classes, especially in the absence of any systematic attempt to chart student satisfaction. H. M. Burton later estimated that in 1938 one in every 300 or 400 adults was attending non-vocational courses of some kind in villages. He suggested that demand would soar if only more funds were forthcoming from local authorities and the Board of Education, whose rules added to the difficulty of running classes in rural areas for small numbers of students.[31] Oxfordshire's RCC education committee reported with some chagrin in 1936 that it was trying hard *not* to encourage demand for an extension of subjects, because it could not promise to provide new courses.[32]

It is difficult to know why people attended such courses and what benefit they derived. Some undoubtedly went for social reasons, especially in areas that lacked a village hall and alternative amusements. Others may well have had political interests, or a desire to study non-academic and technical subjects. Formal, advanced farming education at the agricultural institutes was available to relatively few. For contemporary reformers it almost did not matter. To them, the particular conjunction of economic and social interests in the countryside meant that almost any educational activity that involved villagers meeting together – engaging in communal discussion – was valuable. Or, as Henry Morris put it, life-long education in rural communities was meant to 'abolish the duality of education and ordinary life.'[33]

VILLAGE COLLEGES

For rural education reformers between the wars, one central problem was how to create a practical curriculum for country people. What material would fit children for life in the countryside? How could their needs be defined, and then met, to make them intelligent rural citizens? The first topic for debate was technical work, and how this might be adapted and extended to children who, it was assumed, were likely to grow up to work on the land or in domestic service. The second was how academic subjects might be taught so that they were interesting and relevant to rural children. As noted, there were still middle-class people who expressed the view that country children were 'only

pp. 4–6. Local authorities and WIs were also active in counties that did not have community councils but their work there is harder to trace.

31 Burton, *The Education of the Countryman*, p. 171.

32 Oxfordshire Rural Community Council, Conference Report, 30 Nov 1936. OPRO, ORCC Box: 'ORCC Villages, Chilson 1950–63 …'

33 H. Morris, *The Village College: Being a Memorandum on the Provision of Educational and Social Facilities for the Countryside, with Special Reference to Cambridgeshire* (Cambridge, 1924), p. 21.

capable of limited education, and anything further is a waste of time.'[34] The village college movement was one visionary response to the general difficulties of rural education.

Henry Morris (1889–1961) first published his ideas for village colleges in 1924. It then took six years before the first institution was built with a combination of public and private funds. Morris chose the village of Sawston, about ten miles from Cambridge, as the best site for the experiment, not only because of its size (about 1,530 people), but also because it was not a 'purely agricultural' village. There was a local industry in curing pelts for chamois leather for gloves and domestic use, and a thriving paper mill. In addition Sawston already had a successful central school of 227 pupils from the neighbouring villages.[35] This village college, which still exists, brought a meeting hall, local library, adult education rooms and 'magnet' secondary school under one roof. It symbolised a rethinking of the relationship between voluntary and statutory authorities at the local level and a significant investment of public money in the idea of rural adult and continuing education.

Morris was a socialist with extensive connections within the world of progressive educators. G. D. H. Cole and the Webbs were friends, as was J. W. R. Scott, the crusading countryside journalist.[36] Before coming to Cambridgeshire Morris had served an apprenticeship in the reforming county of Kent (though he was never a classroom teacher). Before that, as a student at Oxford, he befriended like-minded educational thinkers and those, such as Professor W. G. S. Adams, who would go on to lead the RCC movement. He kept in touch with new experiments in education, though many of these were being developed overseas or within England's private schools.[37]

Morris claimed that the system of rural education whereby all classes for advanced pupils were held in country towns had two related and equally negative results. First, children who were schooled away from home lost a sense of place and, by implication, a desire to stay where they were born. Second, the curriculum of town-based education was not what was required for forming

34 A professional man quoted anonymously by Ashby and Byles, *Rural Education*, p 130.

35 Morris, *The Village College*, pp. 24–5.

36 Founder of the *Countryman* and author of *The Story of the Women's Institute Movement* (Idbury, 1925) among many other works.

37 These connections are discussed in H. Rée, *Educator Extraordinary: The Life and Achievements of Henry Morris, 1889–1961* (1985; first published 1973). See also H. Rée (ed.), *The Henry Morris Collection* (Cambridge, 1984). For an overview of progressive educational theory in this period, see R. J. W. Selleck, *English Primary Education and the Progressives, 1914–1939* (1972), and W. A. C. Stewart, *The Educational Innovators*, vol. 2: *Progressive Schools, 1881–1967* (1968).

what he termed first-class rural citizens. This meant that the better country students were given a literary and academic education 'under urban conditions divorced from the life and habits of the countryside. Either they are lost to the villages and become town workers, or return to their homes unfitted and untrained for life as countrymen and countrywomen.'[38] Morris did not entirely spell out what the curricular remedy might be for such a problem, but it should not preclude preparation for higher education, nor err on the side of being 'prematurely vocational'.[39] Unlike A. W. Ashby and Phoebe Byles, with whose work (published in 1923) he must have been familiar, Morris does not seem to have allowed for the possibility that many schoolchildren from the countryside would inevitably end up in the towns or engaged in industrial work.[40]

It was common for progressive reformers and reactionary educationists alike to insist that country children receive schooling appropriate to remaining on the land. Morris took this to mean that the education of youth in a rural context was essentially familial and social, not just individual. 'Our modern educational institutions provide only for units of the family, or separate the individual from the family by time and space so that they may educate it apart and under less natural conditions.'[41] What he called 'a localized and indigenous system of education' was crucial, because it would protect these 'natural conditions' of learning for rural boys and girls. This 'indigenous' venture would nevertheless have a 'warden' who was likely to be an outsider: someone with a university education who would take the widest possible interest in the social welfare of the whole community.[42]

Morris envisioned the village college as a social centre, not just a school. In fact almost every part of the building would have a double use. The student dining room would become the village hall out of hours; school workrooms would serve as evening classrooms for adult learners. The social benefit would work in both directions between young and adult people from the surrounding area using the building together. And the vitality of the whole would spring

---

[38] Morris, *The Village College*, p. 1.

[39] Morris, *The Village College*, p 2.

[40] Ashby and Byles, *Rural Education*, pp. 81, 198–9.

[41] Morris, *The Village College*, p. 21. See J. Dewey, 'The school and society', in *The School and the Child and the Curriculum* (1990; first published 1915), pp. 1–160.

[42] Morris, *The Village College*, p. 23. In this Morris was influenced not only by the model of the settlement house movement, but also medieval institutions, particularly universities. Several historians discuss these sources of inspiration, including Jeffs, *Henry Morris*, p. 15. On Danish folk high schools, which Morris felt were unlike the village colleges, see T. Rørdham, *The Danish Folk High Schools*, trans. S. Mammen (Copenhagen, 1965).

from the interaction between voluntary and statutory authorities. There was room not only for the branch of the county library and the district nurse, but also groups such as the Women's Institute and British Legion, which, though they shared the building, would remain completely autonomous.[43]

Morris identified ten large villages that already served as a focus for their respective districts in Cambridgeshire. He believed that only relatively large population centres had any chance of survival in the face of demographic shifts and changes in agricultural techniques. Thus it was here that the county council ought to concentrate its funds and energies.

Morris stressed the fact that the village college would be not only a new institution but also, in its practicality and amalgamation of different interests, a concrete manifestation of communal country values. Like other reformers, he felt this was necessary not only because of the agricultural depression and depopulation of rural areas, but also because England's squirearchy, which had formerly been the custodian of the countryside's values and culture, was dying.

> The village college will be the seat and guardian of humane public traditions in the countryside, the training ground of a rural democracy realising its social and political duties. Without some such institution as the village college a rural community consisting largely of agricultural workers, small proprietors and small farmers will not be equal to the task of maintaining a worthy rural civilisation. The alternative would be a countryside like that in some continental countries, prosperous perhaps, but narrow and materialistic, without native distinction and charm, and with no instinct for even the popular arts.[44]

In other words, rural culture was distinct from urban culture, was in imminent danger of collapse, and only expert outsiders – such as the university-educated warden – could save it.

The Prince of Wales opened Sawston Village College on 30 October 1930. Its existence owed a great deal to the Carnegie UK Trust, which not only made an initial donation toward the adult education part of the building but also stepped in when the Treasury refused to send £2,500 that had been promised by the Development Commission.[45] The Elmhirsts of Dartington Hall made

43 Morris, *The Village College*, pp. 20–1.

44 Morris, *The Village College*, p. 22.

45 W. Robertson, *Welfare in Trust: A History of the Carnegie United Kingdom Trust, 1913–1963* (Dunfermline, 1964), p. 103. The Spelman Foundation, based in the US, was also extremely generous.

a contribution as well, seeing in the village college idea something related to their own attempts to create a radical school and social centre.[46]

The new building housed the Women's Institute and the British Legion, and also the Boy Scouts, the Girl Guides and an infant welfare centre. The central dining hall seated 500 and was used daily by 118 pupils, while the remaining 132 went home for lunch. Girls and boys used different entrances but were then allowed to sit where they chose, so long as girls were on the right side of each long table and boys on the left. (This segregation was reflected in some subject teaching, as was common in the period.) The site covered eight acres, including gardens, demonstration plots and recreation grounds.[47] Some of the land had been donated by the owners of the local paper mill, while funds for the central hall had been raised from local donors. In theory, at least, Sawston appeared to fulfill its creator's vision of a fully co-operative institution.

In reality the governing board of the college was not as representative of different groups and classes as Morris had hoped. Instead of being directly elected, members of the board were appointed by the county council, the rural district council and the parish council. Injunctions were laid upon these bodies to appoint several women and a representative of the university.[48] The results were perhaps predictable. The chairman of the governors, for example, was Commander Eyre-Huddleston, who owned nearby Sawston Hall and had guaranteed the loan for the village hall. (In fact in 1939 villagers had to remind the college management that the 'adult wing' of the building had been paid for by the villagers themselves and by voluntary organisations on their behalf, and therefore it was unfair that they should subsidise educational activities through paying high fees for rent of the hall.)[49]

Morris initially won full support from the owners of the local paper mill, the Spicer family, convincing them that their interests would be met by contributing to the college rather than by building a separate cinema. The Spicers

[46] Despite charging low fees for the kindergarten and primary school at Dartington (to encourage local attendance), the focus was on student recruitment from the professional classes. W. B. Curry, 'The School', in V. Bonham-Carter, *Dartington Hall: The History of an Experiment* (1958), p. 179, p. 181 and *passim*, and M. Young, *The Elmhirsts of Dartington: The Creation of an Utopian Community* (1982), p. 180.

[47] Editor's note, 'Building Jerusalem', *Home and Country*, Dec 1930, pp. 604–5. David Matless describes how Impington Village College, discussed below, served as an example of 'right living' to postwar planners; 'right living' apparently depended partly on the maintenance of rigid gender distinctions: D. Matless, *Landscape and Englishness* (1998), p. 239.

[48] M. Dybeck, *The Village College Way: The Relevance of the Cambridgeshire Village College Philosophy to the Present Community Education Movement* (Coventry, 1981), p. 42.

[49] Dybeck, *The Village College Way*, pp. 31–4.

were very generous with land and money, like other members of the local elite.[50] Once the village college was built, however, Mr and Mrs Spicer felt that their cinema shows should take precedence over other uses, and proposed that other village associations might use the hall one Thursday a month and on Sunday – and only with four weeks' notice. Mrs. Spicer was a member of the governing board of the new college, which also made up the letting committee of the hall; when the board agreed to the cinema schedule there was an outcry at this special treatment, and the county council intervened. Despite efforts to find a compromise, the Spicers then withdrew their support from the college and built their own cinema hall on land next to the college.[51]

The overall success of Sawston helped to spur the Cambridgeshire County Council to continue investing in the college idea. Bottisham Village College opened its doors in the spring of 1937, and Linton Village College in the fall of the same year. The managers' minute books of both these colleges show that, as at Sawston, evening classes were very well attended.[52] At Linton the records showed that the college was serving thirteen population centres.[53] The last interwar village college, which was finally built at Impington (opened in September 1939), was more controversial. The parish council of Cottenham, only a mile and a half from Impington, insisted that Cottenham was already the natural centre of the area, and that Impington was a suburb, not a real village: 'It would be wrong to send the rural children of Cottenham to school in an industrial and semi-urban area.'[54] As a result of these objections, there were no fewer than six different schemes for what eventually became Impington Village College, although Cottenham finally obtained its own institution in 1963.[55]

Impington was astonishingly modern in design and a symbol of the commitment Henry Morris made to aesthetic as well as vocational education.

50 Jeffs (*Henry Morris*, pp. 27–8, 38–40) suggests that village colleges were far more acceptable to employers than some of the other radical educational programmes being mooted at the time – and the strike school at Burston.

51 Dybeck, *The Village College Way*, pp. 36–7.

52 The total enrolment of 245 was considered high in this period. Dybeck, *The Village College Way*, pp. 36–70.

53 Public Record Office, Cambridgeshire [PRO], Linton V. C. Minute Book, May 1937 – Oct 1945, 28 Jan 1938.

54 Letter from the Cottenham school managers, the parish council, the trustees of the British school and the eleemosynary charity trustees to the LEA, 12 February 1937, reproduced in D. J. Farnell, 'Henry Morris: An Architect of Education' (Thesis for the Associateship Diploma in Secondary Education, Cambridge Institute of Education, 1967/8), appendix 1, pp. 128.

55 The whole correspondence is reproduced in Farnell, 'Henry Morris', appendix 1, pp. 123–36.

A pioneer in bringing the fine arts into the classroom, Morris believed that art and design were integral to successful education. To use public resources for beauty was a natural duty. At Impington Henry Morris hired Walter Gropius and Maxwell Fry to design the new building in the international style. A school inspector was baffled by the long windows, as they made the rooms difficult to heat.[56] However, the college was unlike anything that had been seen in school architecture previously, and Nikolaus Pevsner later called it one of the best buildings of its date in England.[57]

After the war the Cambridgeshire colleges were copied elsewhere, first in neighbouring areas and then wherever Morris's disciples thrived. The colleges have changed over time in accordance with educational policy and the changing demographics of the countryside, although still dedicated to serving adult learners and the wider community as well as schoolchildren in the area. At the time of writing, Sawston Village College is about the celebrate its 75th anniversary as a comprehensive secondary school and technology college with over 1,000 students and at least 1,500 community users. Impington Village College, also comprehensive, is a specialist language college offering the International Baccaleaureate and outstanding facilities for students with disabilities.[58]

CONCLUSION

Curriculum, administrative organisation and expenditure are sources of endless debate and controversy. Who should decide the goals of education and govern the institutions that provide it? What is 'adequate' funding for something as difficult to measure and standardise as learning? The special difficulties of providing for a scattered and poor population in rural areas highlighted such questions for reformers in the interwar period. Unfortunately, while individual teachers no doubt did their best, in general the wider educational programme was characterised by lack of resources and innovation. It was really not until Henry Morris made the case for village colleges that there was a large-scale

---

[56] It was impractical in other ways: the corridor on one side of the classrooms was open to the elements and was later enclosed. Dr Roberts, Visitor's Report, Impington V. C. Minute Book, Apr 1939 – Dec 1945, 19 May 1941, PRO.

[57] N. Pevsner (ed.), *Cambridgeshire*, The Buildings of England Series (1970; first published 1954), pp. 412–13.

[58] Sawston Village College (2005), website: http://www.school-portal.co.uk/GroupHomepage.asp?GroupID=25029 [15 Aug 2005]; Sawston Village College Inspection Report (2000), website: http://www.ofsted.gov.uk/reports/110/110902.pdf; Impington Village College (2005), website: http://cgu.e2bn.net/e2bn/leas/c99/schools/cgu/ [15 Aug 2005]; Impington Village College Inspection Report (2002), website: http://www.ofsted.gov.uk/reports/110/110861.pdf [15 Aug 2005].

effort, based on rational planning and focusing on the needs and aspirations of students, fundamentally to alter rural education.

The village college movement was part of an attempt to regenerate the countryside through new democratic and inclusive institutions. As the example of Sawston demonstrated, however, dependence on wealthy patrons limited what could be accomplished. The work of Henry Morris in providing rural children, including many deprived and poor children, with the best available facilities, was exemplary. In describing country people and their needs, these reformers – even Morris – sometimes made assumptions about the differences between rural and urban 'character' and 'culture' that were not entirely divorced from older stereotypes and traditional attitudes. Even left-wing reformers could betray an attachment to elements of traditional, hierarchical community in their insistence on the 'specialness' of country people. Were rural children in the interwar period best served by an education meant to keep them in the occupational categories of their parents? Was this compatible with the reformers' commitment to expanding their economic and geographical options?[59] Such questions are provocative but necessary to understanding the successes and limitations of rural educational reform in this period.

---

59 Ashby and Byles (*Rural Education*, pp. 197–8) warned against narrowly vocational training, or over-dependence on agriculture in the revival of rural fortunes.

4 Agricultural education in the interwar years

Lynne Thompson

THIS chapter considers why and how agricultural education assisted in the regeneration of the countryside between 1918 and 1939. It provides an over-view of state funding and the nature of provision available under the auspices of local government, and that of the voluntary bodies co-operating with them. It describes the promotion of what was commonly known as 'rural bias' in the elementary school curriculum, and concludes with a case-study of interwar Devon, since this county implemented many of the agricultural educational initiatives discussed below. Although little research has been undertaken on these aspects of interwar rural history, I argue that such initiatives assisted in developing and expanding the 'durable framework' of agricultural education already in place.[1] Whilst this expansion cannot compare with that following the 1947 Agriculture Act, when agriculture became an integral part of state policy, the interwar countryside offered examples of educational innovation which were adopted later. At least, lessons were learned in terms of what was effective, and what needed to be improved.

Improvement was a focus of the Ministry of Agriculture and Fisheries' (MAF) *Yellow Book* in 1939, in a section on agricultural education provided outside universities. Confidence was displayed in the potential for the 'fruit-ful' development of the countryside through this medium, but MAF warned that there was much to accomplish before the legacy of 'apathy' and an 'obsta-cle'-ridden past was eradicated.[2] One obstacle may have been the variable quality of county agricultural staffs. Another was that, largely due to financial constraints, the committee structures set up to provide agricultural education

[1] The contribution of agricultural education in improving agricultural efficiency during the interwar period is mentioned in E. H. Whetham, *British Farming, 1939–1949* (1952), p. 163. See also N. M. Comber, *Agricultural Education in Great Britain* (1948); A. Cheeseborough, 'A short history of agricultural education up to 1939', *Journal of Education Administration and History* 1/1 (1968): 181–200. See also D. Parker, '"Just a stepping stone": the growth of vocational education in the elementary school curriculum, 1914–1939', *Journal of Educational Administration and History* 35/1 (2003): 3–21.

[2] P. Brassley, 'Agricultural science and education', in *The Agrarian History of Eng-land and Wales*, vol. 7: *1850–1914*, ed. E. J. T. Collins (2000), p. 649; PRO/MAF 38/58: *Agricultural Statistics*, Mar 1939.

had been slow in developing. Table 1, for example, illustrates the vagaries of local government expenditure on agricultural education in relation to the male agricultural population by 1913. Such uneven patterns of expenditure were to continue throughout the interwar period.

TABLE 1 Local government expenditure on agricultural education, 1913

County	Male agricultural population	Total expenditure	Expenditure per capita
Devon	40,000	£3,800	1s 11d
Essex	40,000	£3,300	1s 8d
East Sussex	18,000	£2,400	2s 8d
Lancashire	40,000	£7,700	3s 10d
Lincoln (Kesteven)	13,500	£134	2d
Norfolk	47,000	£1,710	9d
Suffolk	36,500	£580	4d

Source: PRO/MAF/33/59 File TE942/1922; Devon Record Office, Minutes of Devon County Council, 12/6/13. 'Expenditure per capita' figures computed from preceding data.

AGRICULTURAL EDUCATION AND RURAL REGENERATION

The need for self-sufficiency in home-produced food after the experiences of wartime shortages provided the impetus for agricultural reconstruction, and education relating to this was one area in which the state became actively involved. Moreover, the depressed condition of much of British agriculture after the repeal of the 1921 Corn Production Act made it important to promote educational opportunities for young, unqualified persons in rural areas to prevent further migration to the towns, whilst also assisting in kick-starting the rural economy. Building on the work of the pre-war Development Commission, the 1918 Agricultural Policy Sub-Committee of the Reconstruction Committee recommended proposals to expand agricultural research and education, including technical advice to farmers, and a ring-fenced sum of £2 million was set aside for this expansion over a five-year period.[3] Part of the price which the state was also willing to pay for the repeal of the Corn Production

3 *Report of the Committee on Post-War Agricultural Education in England and Wales* [The Luxmoore Report], Cmd. 6433 (1943), p. 37. The Development Commission provided £325,000 for funding farm institutes, including 75 per cent of capital building costs, 50 per cent of annual maintenance costs and 53 per cent of staffing costs. Source: F. L. C. Floud, *The Ministry of Agriculture and Fisheries* (1927), pp. 129–30.

Act was a further £1 million earmarked for agricultural education and research, including the provision of scholarships and bursaries for farmers' children.[4] A more robust partnership between local government and central government emerged, therefore, by which, in return for expanding agricultural education, counties could receive up to two-thirds of their operating costs and four-fifths of the salaries of agricultural organisers.[5]

THE NATURE AND FUNDING OF PROVISION

In planning for expansion, LEAs were required to submit schemes for agricultural education covering a ten-year period, which observed national and local requirements.[6] Each scheme was to be comprehensive, encompassing the establishment and maintenance of a farm institute or an institution for higher agricultural education, although counties could group together if necessary. Each county was responsible for the provision of agricultural staff, where these did not already exist, and in particular, the appointment of a county organiser. He and his staff were expected to provide up-to-date technical advice to farmers, offer regular courses of instruction at approved centres, and organise local courses, lectures and practical demonstrations.[7] Further expansion took place between 1925 and 1929, when LEAs were pressed to review existing provision, particularly that relating to short, day and evening courses in agriculture and horticulture, and were offered further grants towards the salaries of new staff.[8]

In 1919–20 the total grants in aid made by MAF to LEAs for agricultural advisory work and education amounted to £120,968. An additional £46,332 was provided by county councils themselves. The overall total expenditure amounted to £213,602. By 1938–9 the sums had risen to £277,642 and £176,990 respectively, the total expenditure being £606,385 – almost triple the original sum.[9] Similar expansion can be seen in the numbers of staff involved in agricultural education. Of the sixty counties in England and Wales, there were

---

4   This was later extended in 1926 to cover the children of agricultural labourers.

5   MAF Circular to LEAs regarding agricultural education, Jan 1919; PRO/MAF/33/59 File TE942/1922.

6   Board of Education Circular 1119 to LEAs, Nov 1918.

7   C. J. Holmes, 'Science and the farmer; the development of the Agricultural Advisory Service in England and Wales, 1900–1939', *Agricultural History Review* 36/1 (1988): 77–86; Board of Education Circular 1119.

8   Circular to County Authorities for Agricultural Education, 7 Nov 1929, PRO/MAF/33/61.

9   Luxmoore Report, p. 32. These figures include the grants for the Provincial Advisory Service, the support of the WI and the National Federation of Young Farmer's Clubs movements, Rural Community Councils, the National Council of Social Service and the Rural Industries Bureau.

thirty-two county organisers of agriculture with a staff totalling 166 in 1919, but the numbers had increased to fifty-five and 468 respectively by 1938–9.[10] Seventeen farm institutes were administered by county councils (thirteen in England and four in Wales) in 1939, as opposed to five in 1914. A steady growth can also be discerned in lectures and demonstrations in agriculture and horticulture, particularly in evening classes and student numbers, both of which more than doubled between 1921 and 1938.[11] Rural students could also apply for one of the 140 annual scholarships awarded through MAF's educational and research scholarship scheme. (See table 2.)

TABLE 2 MAF scholarship scheme, 1922–37

Scholarship holders	No.
Sons or daughters of agricultural workmen	533
Sons or daughters of working farm bailiffs	168
Sons or daughters of smallholders	465
Sons or daughters of other rural workers	299
Qualified on their own account as *bona fide* workers in agriculture	528
Total	1,993

Source: *Journal of the Ministry of Agriculture*, 12 (1938–9), p. 248.

Over 80 per cent of scholarship students progressed to farm institutes, of whom almost 40 per cent returned to farming or smallholdings. An additional 15 per cent were employed in a supervisory capacity in farms or dairies, and a further 8 per cent became teachers, researchers or advisors in agriculture.[12] Although the figures represent a small proportion of the agricultural population, such opportunities had not been available previously, and some rural families were clearly willing to partner the state in investing in their children's further education, particularly in the developing branches of agriculture such as dairying, market gardening and poultry husbandry.

For the purposes of local democratic accountability, each county council was required by the 1920 Agriculture Act to create an Agricultural Committee, or Sub-Committee with a specific remit for agricultural education. These included members of the council's Education Committee, appointees of the ministry and, ideally, two women who represented small producer's interests.[13]

[10] Luxmoore Report, p. 17.

[11] Luxmoore Report, pp. 17–19.

[12] *Journal of the Ministry of Agriculture* 12 (1938–9): 250.

[13] Federation of Women's Institute Archives (FWI), the Women's Library, London Metropolitan University. The WI movement was represented on committees in

Most committeewomen were members of the county federations of the Women's Institutes movement, a voluntary body responsible for the education of countrywomen, whose numbers reached over 300,000 by 1939.[14] The extent to which the National Federation of Women's Institutes (NFWI) contributed to agricultural education during the interwar period and how their members benefited from state and other funding is now considered, together with a brief survey of the education provided by Young Farmer's Clubs.

THE CONTRIBUTION OF VOLUNTARY BODIES

To the NFWI, women were the 'Cinderellas' of the agricultural industry, whose education had much to make up for when comparing that available to country-women elsewhere. They argued that 'Happiness in the countryside depends on women', who, if not catered for, would encourage their families to move out of agriculture altogether.[15] Although the Development Commission withdrew most of its financial support for the movement after 1925 since it was felt that the services of county council agricultural staffs sufficed, the NWFI insisted that its 'agricultural side' continued, not only in the interests of the many small women producers it represented, but also because of the propaganda value of a WI presence at agricultural shows.[16] Thus, opportunities afforded by the publication of the Hadow Report on the education of the adolescent in 1926 were seized upon by the NFWI, since it enabled them to argue for more technical, agriculturally based education for young women and girls in rural areas. Under the recommendations of the ensuing Denman Report, the NFWI redefined agriculture in such a way as to encompass rural domestic economy, arguing that women aspired to a reasonable home life, provided with 'skill in the management ... not only in the house or cottage, but in the garden, with ... poultry, and very often the farm as well'.[17] Moreover,

forty-five counties in England and Wales by 1926, although not all served on Agricultural or Agricultural Education Sub-Committees. File 5/FWI/E/E/1/2/31.

14 *Annual Report of the National Federation of Women's Institutes* (1938).

15 Report of a deputation to the Minister of Agriculture by members of the NFWI Executive, Nov 1929. File 5/FWI/H/8.

16 During 1917–25 the NFWI received grants from the Development Commission totalling £25,058. During 1921–39, it received £14,192 for education in handicrafts from the Commission. 5/FWI/ B/1/2/46.

17 The Interdepartmental Committee of the Ministry of Agriculture and Fisheries and the Board of Education; *Report on the Practical Education of Women for Rural Life* (1928), chaired by Lady Denman, the President of the NFWI; NFWI Deputation to the Minister of Agriculture.

Any separation of instruction to women in the growing of food from instruction in its subsequent use must be both artificial and absurd; any scheme of agricultural education for women which ignored household management was disastrously incomplete.[18]

The Denman Report also showed the unsatisfactory situation existing in some counties, whereby Agricultural Education Sub-Committees were negligent in exploring the needs of women – 'a visit from a dairying school once in ten or twelve years can hardly be thought to be satisfactory'.[19] However, fresh from the positive reception of her report, and supported by both MAF and the Board of Education, Lady Denman and her Executive were in a position to exercise influence on the County Councils Association (CCA).[20] They sought models of local co-operation whereby WIs would raise the consciousness of countrywomen as to what kinds of agricultural education were possible. Regular courses for WI speakers in Agriculture were held with this aim in mind, which would then enable more advanced instruction by county staffs to follow. In 1930, therefore, the CCA advised LEAs to co-operate with the NFWI wherever possible in the provision of appropriate technical and adult education and it appears that a 'marked' expansion took place in WI production and utilisation of home-grown food.[21]

Other than providing lectures and demonstrations in poultry-keeping and horticulture, for which there was steady demand, county staffs advised on the development of WI Market Stalls, their participation in county council egg-laying schemes, and the co-operative buying and distribution of fruit trees, seeds and potatoes.[22] In the early 1930s WI competitions and cookery classes were also organised in order to trial National Mark Flour. In March 1939 the Development Commission finally funded the services of an Agricultural

---

[18] I. Jenkins, *The History of the Women's Institute Movement of England and Wales* (1953), p. 110.

[19] *Report on the Practical Education of Women for Rural Life*, p. 18.

[20] The NFWI Executive Committee included Lady Trevalyan and Miss E. Pratt (both from the Ministry of Agriculture) and Miss Grace Hadow (National Council of Social Service). Lady Denman was also able to enlist the services of Sir Percy Jackson, a CCA Committee man, who was also on the Board of the Carnegie UK Trust, and the Executive Committee of the National Federation of Young Farmer's Clubs.

[21] File 5/FWI/H/8; Jenkins, *The History of the Women's Institute Movement*, p. 111.

[22] For example, in Cumbria, when Cumberland Poultry Farmers Ltd. joined with the county Federation to form a marketing co-operative, *Cumberland News*, 27 Oct 1928. For a regional case-study on WI poultry-keeping and horticulture, see L. Thompson, 'The promotion of agricultural education for adults: the Lancashire Federation of Women's Institutes 1919–45', *Rural History* 10/2 (1999): 217–34.

Organiser for 'encouraging the production and proper treatment of fresh foodstuffs' in anticipation of wartime shortages. This entailed the recruitment of WI members already skilled in food preservation, who were required to train and lead groups of WIs in jam-making. The NFWI also influenced decisions to approve a college curriculum for instructresses in Rural Domestic Economy, enabling women who had studied agriculture or horticulture for two years to complete a final year in a domestic science training college in order to be similarly qualified.[23] By integrating agricultural and domestic science, this new subject offered countrywomen practical instruction on a sound theoretical base. In addition, a series of Board of Education refresher courses for domestic science teachers in Rural Domestic Economy were offered by various farm institutes, as a result of the NFWI identifying shortages of specialised teachers.

These initiatives suggest that the governments of the 1930s valued the contribution which women made in developing rural economies in the context of protecting home industries, sustaining the family life of the 'small man', and in preparation for war. Writing to Lady Denman in 1930, the Minister of Agriculture assured her that 'We shall and do require your assistance more and more as time goes on, not only for publicity and propaganda but also for detailed local arrangements made by or through county staffs.'[24] But, however welcome this assurance, it was not accompanied by funding other than as a means of pump priming. Thus, the NFWI's need for additional resources to support a rapidly expanding movement impelled them to further their links with networks of rural voluntarism, in aid of its agricultural educational agenda.

One example was the Horace Plunkett Foundation, which aimed to promote co-operative marketing and similar endeavours between small producers. It recognised that WI Market Stalls were already in existence selling produce grown or prepared by members, and that, by the early 1930s, the NFWI had commenced regular schools in grading and packing. In 1932 it offered the services of its research assistant to assist county federations who wished to organise stalls as Provident Societies.[25] This offer was made since the NFWI had obtained £1,000 from the Carnegie UK Trust, which helped to fund the

---

[23] At Swanley Agricultural College for Women. Minutes of the NFWI Executive Committee, 1 Apr 1931; 11 Jun 1931; 13 Jul 1932; 13 Dec 1933. By 1947 nineteen counties in England and Wales employed thirty Instructresses in Rural Domestic Economy. File 5/FWI/ F/1/1/5. See also *Journal of the Ministry of Agriculture* 6 (1933).

[24] File 5/FWI/H/8 Letter from Dr Addison to Lady Denman, 7 Oct 1930, promising to appoint a second MAF woman inspector in 1931.

[25] File 5/FWI/F/3/04.

services of a Marketing Organiser, and meet her travelling expenses in educational and propaganda work. By 1937 the annual turnover of registered WI markets reached over £22,000, of which approximately £20,000 was returned to the producers.[26] A Produce Guild was also formed which incorporated the work of registered WI markets, and whose members were encouraged to gain NFWI certificates in food production, preservation and judging. Thus the movement was able to demonstrate publicly the standard of its foodstuffs resulting from improved cultivation, skills acquired from county agricultural staffs, and its own educational programmes. Moreover, since WI Market Stalls also sold the produce of non-members, they could be seen as benefiting the community at large.

Agricultural education provided by interwar Young Farmer's Clubs (YFCs) focused largely on calf-, sheep- and pig-rearing, but the broader aims of the movement were to mobilise youth in rural areas, and to consolidate allegiance to the land. Further aims were to provide a more positive attitude amongst the farming community in embracing the benefits of science and technology.[27] In each club young people aged between ten and twenty-one were allotted an individual project whereby they kept a baby animal or cultivated an allotment for a year, during which time scrupulous records were kept on the scientific feeding and rearing of animals, or fertilisers used. A statement of accounts was required, after which the animal or produce was sold for profit. Animals, or the rent of an allotment, were originally purchased by club benefactors, to whom the original price was returned, and the difference went to the Young Farmer, or the club involved. The gain, however, was not intended to be purely financial, but rather an exercise in character development. It was argued that a concern for animal welfare would be transferred to a concern for the community, whilst the sacrifice of spare time could be transmuted into creative and rewarding endeavour. Individual competition was encouraged, although reservations did exist: 'The system is open to abuse in that it leads to a somewhat unhealthy rivalry and that participation must of necessity be confined to well-to-do members.'[28] This led many clubs to undertake less expensive rabbit, bee and poultry-keeping.

Although nearly fifty YFCs were in existence by 1928, with fewer than 1,500 members overall, they lacked direction and organisation.[29] The Carnegie UK Trust stepped in to provide additional resources, in collaboration with the National Council of Social Service. Further grants were supplied by the

---

[26] File 5/FWI/ B/1/2/4 76.

[27] F. E. Shields (ed.) *Fifty Years Not Out! A History of the Young Farmers in England and Wales* (1970), p. 1.

[28] Shields, *Fifty Years Not Out!*, p. 2.

[29] G. P. Hirsch, *Young Farmers' Clubs: A Report on a Survey* (1952), p. 2.

Development Commission, administered by MAF, on condition that the educational side of the movement was emphasised. In 1935 Somerset became the first local authority to make a direct grant to the NFYFC, an example followed by other LEAs.[30] By 1939 412 Clubs had been formed, with a total membership of 15,000, and the Board of Education began to provide grant aid.[31] In the aftermath of the Munich crisis, it called the attention of LEAs to the potential of YFCs as a means of stimulating interest in agriculture for children, leading to a growth of clubs in schools.[32]

The average length of YFC educational programmes was between six and eight months, rather then the ten to eleven months available in WIs. A typical YFC curriculum would include instruction in rural crafts, more popularly known as manual process classes. This category embraced a wide range of agricultural skills which were often at a premium, such as sheep-shearing, ploughing, hedging and ditching, thatching, poultry-trussing, hurdle-making and wall-building. Talks on more general subjects considered to be of interest to YFCs were also available, including cookery and domestic science for girls. As with WIs, each club designed and agreed its own programme, which aimed to take advantage of the free technical lectures and demonstrations provided by local experts and county staffs. As an intended consequence, new contacts were made between the latter and farmers as a result of their childrens' membership. Of increasing importance were educational visits paid by YFC members to other UK regions and, where funding allowed, to the White dominions in order to compare farming systems and practices. Later in the 1930s, however, emphasis was placed on village surveys and local history projects which were conducted on a group basis, and even sports. The reasons may be attributed to the competition afforded by the Scout and Guide Associations, other significant recruiters of rural youth, who, in addition to providing leisure pursuits, also awarded badges for proficiency. Further source of competition were part-time rural science and gardening 'continuation classes' available to school leavers from the age of fourteen.

RURAL BIAS

Continuation classes in agricultural education were formed to address the need for more advanced instruction and vocational training for boys and girls in post-war society. In 1925 a circular to LEAs was produced by MAF and the Board of Education which dealt with stimulating the interest of young persons in agricultural education, followed by a joint memorandum in 1927 which

[30] Hirsch, *Young Farmers' Clubs*, p. 10.

[31] Shields, *Fifty Years Not Out!*, p. 5.

[32] Board of Education Circular to LEAs, Nov 1938.

suggested the curriculum to be followed. A wide range of subjects were identified, from agricultural crafts and rural domestic economy to practical and elementary science, all of which could be offered on a flexible basis. In order to provide such instruction, a prototype system of agricultural training of teachers in rural schools was also devised. MAF thereby 'obtained administrative jurisdiction in the curricular "grey area" between ages of thirteen and fifteen, an issue which had arisen as a consequence of the Education Act of 1918, and which increasingly involved county agricultural and horticultural staffs'.[33]

This Act called for the reorganisation of rural elementary schools in particular and raised the school-leaving age to take effect from 1921.[34] Since the Hadow Report called for a further rise in the school-leaving age, much LEA activity was involved in planning and budgeting for both eventualities. Since there was 'no settled policy for agricultural education' to which LEAs had to adhere, continuation classes for young school-leavers were dependent on the commitment of well-placed agricultural enthusiasts.[35] By the mid-1930s twenty rural English counties provided such facilities for fourteen- to sixteen-year-olds.[36] Those which did not may have been daunted by conflicting demands on LEA budgets, the lack of facilities for scientific instruction in elementary schools or insufficient numbers of suitably trained teachers. Others did not wish to be perceived as influencing vocational choices at an early age by the National Union of Teachers, for example, who argued that all children, regardless of location, should benefit from a general, 'liberal' and free secondary education up to the age of fifteen.[37] In addition, it was anticipated that tensions might arise between qualified teachers and better-paid

33 PRO/MAF/33/61 Circular letter to LEAs on Rural Continuation Classes, 22 Mar 1927. An Interdepartmental Committee between MAF and the Board of Education was set up to identify and resolve anomalies in funding and overlaps in provision. Originally, lines of administrative demarcation were at age fifteen.

34 Rural elementary schools were to phase out 'single stream' classes, and replace them by infant (five to seven years) junior (eight to eleven years) and senior sections (twelve to fourteen or fifteen years, although the normal age for leaving was fourteen). This reorganisation called for the closing down of many village schools and their centralisation into bigger units. Some senior schools became known as secondary modern schools, but it depended on the finances of LEAs as to whether they could afford to fund schooling up to the age of fifteen. Most elected to offer part-time education after the age of fourteen.

35 Luxmoore Report, p. 44. See also the *Final Report of the Agricultural Tribunal of Investigation* (1924), p. 204; *Report on Agricultural Policy* (1925), p. 5; *Agricultural Policy* (1926), p. 3.

36 PRO/MAF/33/61.

37 The NUT, the National Union of Agricultural Workers (NUAW) and in some instances, the National Farmers' Union met during the interwar period to explore contesting views on rural schooling. A distillation of the NUT's views can be

but unqualified agricultural staff entering school premises in order to instruct young persons.

Nevertheless, the data illustrates some growth and interest in agricultural education. In Shropshire during 1927–8, for example, Junior Agricultural evening courses lasting twenty weeks during the winter months were provided for fourteen- to seventeen-year-olds at local schools. The first course of thirty-five boys and twenty-one girls included approximately 50 per cent of farm or smallholders' children, the remainder being children of agricultural labourers. The curriculum for both sexes included English, rural lore, elementary agriculture and horticulture, poultry management and agricultural mathematics. One third of the time was spent on gender-based activities such as woodwork, elementary farriery and the care of implements for boys, and cookery and domestic science for girls.[38] Other evening continuation classes took place in Somerset, Staffordshire, Durham and Hertfordshire, and classes comprising one day a week for farmers' children were organised in Yorkshire. In the West Riding fifty children aged between thirteen and sixteen attended continuation classes in 1933–4. Two years later, 129 similarly aged children attended fourteen centres, and in 1936–7 160 attended sixteen centres.[39] Kent recorded eighty-nine students attending continuation classes at four centres whose average age was fifteen, whilst in Monmouthshire, forty-four students under the age of sixteen attended classes in agriculture, poultry-keeping, dairying and rural domestic science between 1934–5. During this year *c.*21,000 students aged fourteen to sixteen in England and Wales attended classes related to agriculture and horticulture. Some counties also offered similar instruction to children still at school.[40]

Attendance at rural continuation classes, therefore, appear to demonstrate more positive attitudes towards the practice and future of agriculture, in which at least some young people acquired skills for employment. In the context of the 1930s, and certainly so far as many parents were concerned, that sufficed. Although the performance of some counties left much to be desired, particularly in the mainly arable regions of England, others showed promise. One of these was Devon, which utilised pastoral forms of agriculture, and had a developed infrastructure for the supply of dairy or horticultural produce to urban markets.

found as reported in editions of the NUAW's journal, the *Landworker*, May 1925, p. 7, and Jun 1929, p. 12.

38 'Junior agricultural courses in Salop', *Journal of the Ministry of Agriculture* 9 (1929–30): 115.

39 PRO/MAF/33/61, File on Rural Bias.

40 N. M. Comber, 'Agricultural research and education in Yorkshire farming', *Journal of the Ministry of Agriculture* 22 (1948–9): 150.

DEVON CASE-STUDY

Devon was the second largest single administrative area in England, and the third-largest county in England and Wales, encompassing over 1,600,000 acres. Like many counties which did not possess a farm institute, Devon County Council (DCC) utilised a peripatetic model of agricultural education. Travelling farriery, dairy and poultry schools had been established, and instructors in agriculture appointed from the late Victorian period onwards.[41] DCC originally intended to provide Seale Hayne Agricultural College with a substantial grant once it became operational in the early 1920s, so that its research should benefit local farmers whilst functioning as a MAF advisory centre. However, due to lack of managerial and financial expertise, the college never realised its full potential during the interwar period whilst its presence was inimical to the establishment of a farm institute.[42] It was left to DCC agricultural organisers and their committee structures to conduct a realistic appraisal of what could be done in the absence of such facilities.

In 1921, therefore, Devon was subdivided into four organisational districts, and a Lecturer in Agriculture was appointed to serve in each, under the agency of Area Committees, whose members (mainly farmers and landowners) represented the farming community. Their role was to identify and provide for the agricultural educational needs of their areas, supervise experimental work, allocate prize money at local shows, organise manual process classes for agricultural workers, and generally act as 'connecting links between their districts and the county Agricultural Education Department'.[43] DCC also created its own Joint Standing Sub-Committee, a body reporting to the Agriculture and Education Committees, and able to co-ordinate agricultural education in all its manifestations under a single chairman and secretary. A new county organiser was appointed, whose annual salary of £600–750 reflected the wider

---

[41] Minutes of the Devon County Council Technical Education Sub-Committee, 5 Apr 1898. From 1907 to 1914 the complement of staff employed by the county ranged between ten and fourteen, some of whom were part-time. This included two dairying instructresses, and instructors in manual process, farriery, bee- and poultry-keeping, and horticulture. This framework of delivery was enhanced in 1910 to include two more instructors and a further assistant instructor in agriculture, two of whom also performed the tasks of district and assistant analyst. Their appointments were a result of the Devon Agricultural Education Committees' (DAEC) decision to keep milk records, but their key function remained in providing farmers with technical advice. Minutes of Devon County Council Technical Education Sub-Committee, 19 Mar 1908.

[42] A. Kennerley, 'Seale Hayne', in *The Making of the University of Plymouth*, first draft (Plymouth, 1999), p. 12.

[43] Devon County Agricultural Committee, *Scheme of Agricultural Education and Agricultural Experiments* (1926).

responsibilities required.[44] The appointment of Colin Ross in 1925 proved to be an inspired choice, and through his efforts DCC was to gain a national reputation for its agricultural education provision. On his appointment Ross produced a scheme of work for Devon according to MAF guidelines, which informed the remainder of the interwar years. Given the lack of direction at Seale Hayne, emphasis during the interwar period continued to be placed upon peripatetic adult agricultural extension, field trials and experiments, and (free) routine advisory services. An impression of what could be achieved by county agricultural staff and supportive committee structure during the interwar years is now described.

DCC aimed to improve and develop dairy farming, horticulture, egg-production, rural crafts and products. Thus Ross and his team developed a new travelling cheese school, revived farm orchards and cider-making (overseen by a new Orchards Sub-Committee) and initiated field experiments in crop and plant production in different geographical locations.[45] A Milk Supply Sub-Committee was formed in tandem with the council's decision to provide milk in schools during the early 1930s, the mobile dairy school was extended to include advisory work with farmers interested in clean milk production, and the farriery school taught oxy-acetylene welding. A fifth administrative area was created, and by December 1938 the complement of staff involved had risen to twenty, of whom eight were women.[46]

Their students could progress to Seale Hayne College after taking a three-year part-time Certificate course which prepared them for the examination in Agricultural and Rural Economy.[47] This curriculum included biology, agricultural chemistry, crop and plant diseases, the use of manures and fertilisers and their effects, livestock feeding and breeding, the management of dairy cows, sheep and horses, and orchard management.[48] Correspondence courses in aspects of agriculture were also available. Students were encouraged to take advantage of MAF, county council and United Dairies agricultural scholarships, and a travelling subsidy of 1*d* per mile was available for those who lived more than two miles away from seven centres of provision.[49]

44 Minutes of Devon County Agricultural Education Sub-Committee (DCAESC), 28 Jun 1921.

45 Scheme of Agricultural Education; R. M. Ferguson, *A Centenary of Agricultural Education and Training* (Bicton, Devon, c.1973).

46 Minutes of DAESC, 5 Dec 1938.

47 The examination in Agricultural and Rural Economy, offered by the Union of Agricultural Institutions. 140 scholarships to Seale Hayne were awarded to Devon students between 1920 and 1934. Minutes of DAESC, 14 Jun 1934.

48 I am grateful to Mr Hubert Snowden, of Totnes, for this information.

49 A fund of £30,000 was made available by United Dairies in 1924 for promoting

However, Ross appears to have had an uphill struggle in convincing farmers to increase herds and specialise in dairying, due to the increased capital outlays involved, which were prohibitive for the 'small man' who populated Devon agriculture. His efforts in achieving change through agricultural education were often compromised by the caution of farmers reluctant to abandon their multi-purpose herds of South Devons and Dairy Shorthorns, or to improve grassland and abandon turnip culture.[50] Thus Devon's approach to agricultural education for all members of the agricultural community included an emphasis on the technical development of children, achieved by the inclusion of rural bias in the curriculum of Devon's elementary schools from 1929 onwards.

This system involved four peripatetic instructresses, four of whom taught in Devon schools for two separate hours a week, one hour being associated with science and poultry-keeping and the other focusing on science and dairying. The head teacher of each school involved had complete authority over the instructresses, who liaised with school staff to create an appropriate syllabus, and appeared to meet little opposition. In addition, a free ten-week methods-of-teaching course arranged for school staff earmarked for teaching rural science was organised in collaboration with the University College of the South West.[51]

This innovatory scheme, by which children employed a mixture of mathematics, mensuration, woodwork, elementary biology and nutrition in order to house, rear and sell the products of their labours, also reflects the extent to which scientific education was developing in Devon, including that privately available at Dartington Hall.[52] Here Leonard Elmhirst encouraged

practical and scientific education in dairy farming, including research and travelling scholarships to travel abroad. They were open to the sons and daughters of farmers and smallholders in Somerset, Cornwall, Devon and Dorset, and students could progress to Reading University, Seale Hayne College and Somerset Farm Institute, Cannington. Eight scholarships were awarded annually. *Journal of the Ministry of Agriculture* 11 (1937–8). But girls and women who wished to study for Certificates and Diplomas in Dairying or Poultry Husbandry, for example, had to travel to Cannington. Minutes of DAEC, 10 Feb 1932. Prior to cuts, the subsidy was 1½d per mile for those living over 2 miles from a centre, *Scheme of Work 1926*. Devon, like many other rural authorities, also reduced fees for the children of farmers and farm workers living in the county.

[50] For a survey of the expansion of dairying in Devon, see V. H. Beynon, 'The changing structure of dairying in Devon since the 1930s', *Devon Historian* 11 (1975), pp. 35–40.

[51] This was provided by the Board of Education, part taught by a member its divisional staff, and including lectures and demonstrations by Professor Watkins of the University College. Minutes of DAESC, 28 Aug 1933.

[52] After two and a half years practice, HMIs made favourable comments on Devon's instruction in rural science and gardening in elementary schools. In 1932, for

the agricultural and horticultural education of children so that they learned directly from their environment. However, it appears that there was an element of competition between Ross and Elmhirst. This may have arisen since Elmhirst ran profitable short courses in rural science for teachers for the Board of Education, thus duplicating provision which Devon and Seale Hayne staff already offered.[53]

Elmhirst's experience of agricultural extension work in the USA, his views on progressive education and his insistence on scientifically informed practice seems to have affected his judgement on what Ross was attempting to achieve in Devon, and this led him to question the capacity of county council staff. He commented on the 'compartmentalised' system whereby one member of the advisory staff rarely communicated with another, and had neither the time or inclination to develop their science further. He argued, for example, that poultry husbandry in many cases was the same as it had been for fifty years, and that improvements in county performance in this respect depended on the calibre of staff employed.[54] W. K. Slater, his colleague at Dartington, also discounted the expertise of county agricultural staff as being 'stereotyped and perfunctory', thus appearing to corroborate some of MAF's underlying concerns.[55] Perhaps both did not take into consideration the immense work-load which agricultural staff were shouldering. For example, with their assistance, the poultry population of Devon had increased by 92 per cent, worth £2,500,000 by 1934.[56] Moreover, the sheer size and diversity of Devon farming presented challenges which science was only beginning to address. Even allowing for gaps in the data, the figures in tables 3 and 4 suggest that Ross and his team could not be faulted for effort.[57]

example, thirty-six schools were visited over a six-month period, at these 119 children attended dairy and poultry sessions out of a total of 1,048 (16 Oct 1932). By 1934 1,600 children aged eleven and over had participated in poultry-keeping and dairying classes. Minutes of DAESC, 3 Mar 1934.

53 The Elmhirst Archive, Dartington Hall, Devon, Files T Ag. Econ 1 and T Ag. Econ 2. Minutes of DCC, 18 Nov 1931; Kennerley, 'Seale Hayne', p. 13.

54 Elmhirst Archive, File T. Ag. Econ 3.

55 *Ibid.* Evidence to be placed before the Luxmoore Committee by the Dartington Hall Trust by W. K. Slater, Bursar, 21 Oct 1942, p. 15.

56 Minutes of DCAESC, 13 Dec 1934.

57 The rise in visits to WIs in 1934 may be accounted for by a severe outbreak of poultry disease. (Note, too, the high number of advisory visits to farmers etc. in that year, for the same reason.) The decline in the number of WI classes in subsequent years does not necessarily suggest a decline of interest, but the increasing numbers of rural science classes in school and school gardening, together with campaigns in clean milk, and ploughing-up took up most of staff time during the later interwar period.

TABLE 3 Types of classes, visits etc. by county agricultural staff to Women's Institutes, YFCs and other student bodies/clients

	1931/2	32/3	33/4	34/5	35/6	36/7	37/8	Total
WIs	136	170	242	174	157	80	26	985
YFC/ Manual Process	74	110	137	181	197	169	121	989
Certificate classes in Agriculture / Rural Science for teachers/ schools	213	336	537	659	460	779	847	3,831
Beekeeping / farriery		4	2	12	n/d	6	n/d	24
Demonstrations / Lectures	485	798	539	848	549	532	400	4,151
Advisory visits to farmers, interviews etc.	6,654	5,979	6,800	10,273	7,194	6,154	7,006	50,060
Attendance at shows, meetings	n/d	1,027	1,349	1,748	971	1,451	1,651	8,197

Source: Minutes of DAESC, 1931/2 to 1937/8

TABLE 4 Numbers participating in classes

Type of class	1931/2	32/3	33/4	35/6	36/7	37/8	Total
YFCs	751	1,146	1,448	1,315	797	866	6,323
Certificate Classes etc.	631	643	n/d	713	349[*]	780	3,116
Lectures/ Demonstrations	13,904	16,015	15,230	15,660	n/d	n/d	60,809

Source: Minutes of DAESC 1931–2 to 1937–8   [*] Teachers only

Note: Attendance figures for lectures and demonstrations were not kept after 1936, and the numbers in classes from 1935 represent those for teachers and/or children studying rural science. WI records do not appear to have been kept on a regular basis.

A COLLABORATIVE NETWORK

By 1938 Devon County Federation of Women's Institutes (DCFWI) was a flourishing organisation of 201 clubs with over 11,000 members.[58] It collaborated closely with DCC in a variety of experiments, such as slug-testing trials on potatoes, and the Joint Standing Committee reciprocated by publishing DCFWI leaflets on fruit-bottling, jam-making, milk and poultry. The Federation supplied trained judges for local produce shows whilst Ross's staff organised small fruit and potato competitions. In addition, DCC provided free instruction (normally six to twelve two hour classes per week) to WI clubs in all branches of horticulture, the preservation of fruit and vegetables, poultry-keeping, dairying and bee-keeping.[59] Short courses in rural domestic economy were also offered at minimal fees.

DCC and DCFWI also shared personnel, as characterised by Miss Gunnell, the organiser of domestic subjects in Devon schools, and an ex-officio member of the Federation's Executive Committee. Lady Clinton, the President of the Federation, became a member of Joint Standing Committee in 1931, and she and Mrs Shapland, another member of the Executive Committee, also represented WIs in East and South Devon Area Agricultural committees respectively. Miss Gunnell was permanently seconded to work with WIs in 1929, her additional responsibilities being to promote soft fruit production and preservation for small growers. She assisted in raising the profile of DCC educational work by addressing the NFWI Consultative Council on 'Co-operation between county councils and the Women's Institutes' and co-ran schools and tests for methods of teaching in WI preservation schools with the Royal Agricultural College at Cirencester.[60]

The strengthening of links between county councils, educators and voluntary bodies represented in the NFYFC Executive Committee was reflected in Devon, where a network of men and women representing agriculture were involved in both YFCs and WIs.[61] For example, Mrs Luttrell, a dairy farmer's

[58] Annual Report of the National Federation of Women's Institutes, 1938; Minutes of DAESC, 5 Mar 1936.

[59] FWI/5/E/1/1/2/31.

[60] Minutes of DCAESC, 20 Jun 1935 and 11 Oct 1933.

[61] As in Devon circles, the Executive Committee of the National Federation of Young Farmers Clubs comprised farming, state, educational and voluntary bodies and interests, including amongst others, Sir Merrick Burrell, Chairman of the Royal Agricultural Society of England, Professor W. G. S. Adams (Warden of All Souls (and Executive Committee Chairman), Miss E. Pratt and J. G. Stewart (Ministry of Agriculture), J. Scott Watson (National Council of Social Service),

wife and member of WI county and National Federation committees, donated a challenge cup to be awarded to YFCs annually, and Mrs. Shapland's husband was vice-president of Devon YFC (DYFC) and chairman of the South-West Devon Area Agricultural Committee.[62] By 1936 DCFWI was requesting DCC for expenses of £60 accruing from visiting villages where YFCs might be established.[63] This provides a useful example of the movement's strengths in agricultural propaganda work at local levels, whilst acting in self-interest. Collaboration in recruiting rural youth might pay dividends for both voluntary organisations, and girls who joined YFCs might become active WI members later on.

Although the first Young Farmer's Club originated at Hemyock in 1922, under the auspices of United Dairies, and a further forty-nine had been formed with a membership of over 1,000 by 1938, there appear to have been problems in sustaining interest.[64]

As table 3 illustrates, manual process classes characterised the educational activities of Devon YFCs, but an attempt to broaden their appeal and observe MAF's insistence that a wider sphere of topics should be covered was introduced through inter-club spelling bees and brains trusts during the later 1930s. Devon was also the first county federation to pioneer the very popular Efficiency Tests, which were devised as a means of enabling youngsters to demonstrate expertise in a variety of skills. If five tests were completed successfully, the student received a badge, and a certificate produced by the Joint Standing Committee was awarded for nine successful tests. Shields has argued that such awards 'lifted their status' and began the 'professionalisation' of the farming community due to the standards set by Efficiency Tests.[65] After the Second World War the NFYFC set about standardising the practice pioneered in Devon, which became enshrined in National Proficiency Tests emulated by other industries. By these means, more young people may have been persuaded to stay in farming, or have the confidence to succeed than might have otherwise been the case. Certainly self-esteem was fostered by demonstrating hard-won skills and winning the approval of peers:

Mr N. Salter Davis and Sir Percy Jackson (CCA and the Carnegie UK Trust) and G. H. Garrad (Agricultural Education Association, of which Colin Ross was also a member). Minutes of the NFYFC Executive Committee 5 May 1932, NFYFC, Stoneleigh, Warwickshire.

[62] *Western Times and Gazette*, 18 Apr 1958.

[63] Minutes of DCAESC, 5 Sep 1936.

[64] Devon Record Office, Young Farmer's Clubs files. W. R. Wilson, *Devon Federation of Young Farmers' Clubs: 50 Years, 1932–1982* (1982).

[65] F. E. Shields, quoted in Wilson, *Devon Federation of Young Farmers' Clubs*, p. 3.

Members acquired a great art in turning out ... beasts to perfection ...
The best ... was getting these animals halter trained since very often at
a show, a nine cwt. steer might go madly out of control.[66]

Although Devon's example shows what was possible to achieve in agricultural education during the interwar years, it might be argued that farmers
learned as much from each other. Ross himself organised popular farmers' and
horticulturalists' discussion societies – over twenty were in operation by 1939
– whilst 'hobby' farmers were catered for by visits to other regions.[67] Although
some 'sneered' at 'interfering' by DCC, its 'over-funding' by government, or the
expense involved in order to adapt, farmers began to obtain advice from those
who had taken it from Ross and his team. According to one farmer, 'people
came from far around' to see the bumper crops of wheat, barley and mangolds
which his father had grown in a DCC trial plot on his land.[68] Agriculturalists and WI members also learned from dedicated BBC regional programmes,
in addition to their regular journals and MAF's *Yellow Book* acknowledged
the contribution of commercial travellers when selling agricultural feeds and
machinery, whilst having reservations as to the objectivity of their advice.[69] By
these means, together with the methods of agricultural education and propaganda work described in this chapter, farmers and horticulturalists were in a
better position to face the exigencies of war than their forbears were in 1914.

Initiatives introduced during the interwar period bore fruit after the
war. The 1944 Education Act provided for rural science or rural studies to
be included in schools and teacher training curricula and the Burnham salary scale for teachers in all areas was rationalised. Meanwhile, the NFYFC
was incorporated into the national Youth Service, WIs enjoyed their highest-
ever memberships and obtained further Development Commission funding
for their own Denman College, although their contribution to agricultural
education was to be associated with jam-making in the public mind.[70] Not all

---

[66] W. R. Cook, *Braunton Young Farmer's Jubilee Book* (n.d.).

[67] Minutes of DAESC 14 Jun 1934.

[68] H. N. Snowden, *Born to Farm in Devon: By Horse and Hand Tool at Thurlestone,
1918–1939* (Totnes, 1998), p. 51.

[69] Also autobiographical accounts of successes in farming, *Farmers Weekly, Farmer
and Stockbreeder, Home and Country* (for WI readers) and the plethora of leaflets
and booklets published by MAF, many of which were circularised to WI county
federations.

[70] In 1949–50 there were 7,505 WIs in England and Wales, with a total membership
of 446,500. There were 310 WIs in Devon. *Annual Report of the National Federation
of Women's Institutes, 1949–50.*

county council staffs were incorporated into the National Agricultural Advisory Service in 1946, but their experience was required to address the increased demand from technical colleges and other areas of further and adult education in agriculture delivered by LEAs.[71]

It has been argued that the voluntary bodies described in this chapter were 'serving the ends of an (interwar) government which was parsimonious in its dealings with social services' particularly so far as agricultural education was concerned; indeed, the amount of expenditure on this and relevant research was far less than that spent on elementary and secondary education.[72] Even so, it should be remembered that the state had to negotiate trade-offs within the education system and manage 'contesting interests in policy formation and debate'.[73] Moreover, most educational legislation enacted during the interwar period was permissive. Thus, rural regeneration via agricultural education depended largely on human agency, in the form of those with formidable networking skills such as Lady Denman, and pioneers such as Ross in Devon. Given that human agency seems to have made a difference, we cannot, however, assume that its absence was a reason for the vagaries of provision elsewhere. As Douet states, further research is required on the work of county agricultural committees during the interwar period before the complete picture emerges.[74] For the moment the evidence suggests that far more was transpiring at the 'grassroots' than might be assumed.

---

[71] This was particularly the case during the years of austerity and rationing 1945–50, when the training and education of small producers in country and towns was seen as an essential component of LEA provision.

[72] W. E. Williams, *The Auxiliaries of Adult Education*, Life and Leisure Pamphlets 1 (1934), p. 13.

[73] G. McCulloch, *Educational Reconstruction: The 1944 Education Act and the Twenty First Century* (1994), p. 14.

[74] A. Douet, 'Norfolk Agriculture, 1914–1972' (unpublished PhD thesis, University of East Anglia, 1989), p. 85.

5 Cold Comfort times: women rural writers in the interwar period

Marion Shaw

A T the end of Flora Thompson's *Lark Rise to Candleford* trilogy, the teen-age protagonist, Laura, comments on the arrival in the village of Candleford Green of a new kind of resident, 'clerks and shopmen from Candleford town', earning at least £2 a week, who live in newly built villas 'run up of old oddments of second-hand stuff, without proper foundations'. She is recording the early twentieth-century movement of town dwellers into the country, and the growth of suburbia on the outskirts of towns. Laura is impressed by the life-style of suburban dwellers, their cleanliness and social pretensions, and most of all by the fact that they practise some form of birth control. Laura knows she will spend much of her life amongst such people, and that she will leave behind what they are replacing, which is the rural communities of her late nineteenth-century childhood. The book ends on an elegiac note; as she pushes away the gossamer threads on the autumn bushes, she thinks that 'The threads which were to bind her to her native country were more enduring than gossamer. They were spun of love, and kinship and cherished memories.'

Part-fiction, part-autobiography, part-social history, the Candleford trilogy was published between 1939 and 1943 and was immediately and enduringly popular. It evoked for a nation at war an image of a vanished England, but one that was only just out of reach, not beyond the possibility of recall. Its level-toned, first-person narrative, its childhood perspective, its meticulously detailed descriptions and its known autobiographical basis, credit it with a formidable authenticity. Though not itself a rural novel, it summarises the golden age of the rural novel, and it also points to its demise. Afterwards, it is the documentary that will record rural matters for the ordinary reader, such as Ronald Blythe's *Akenfield* (1969) or Raphael Samuel's *Village Life and Labour* (1975). There are exceptions, of course: a writer like John McGahern may be classed as a rural writer, but he is Irish; there is also the continuing popular-ity of *The Lord of the Rings*, which in some respects is a rural text, though one replete with horrors and extravagances undreamed of in Candleford. Perhaps also during the last few decades, there has been the emergence of a kind of anti-pastoral in works like Graham Swift's *Waterland* (1983) or Christopher Hart's *The Harvest* (1999).

What do we mean by the rural novel? In his 1977 study, Glen Cavaliero does not offer a definition, but rather an apology. Noting their neglect by critics, he explains that the achievement of rural novels 'seems, in a derogatory sense, provincial', in that a precise, circumscribed, recognisable rural locality is evoked.[1] Because of this, such writers are more valuable to historians than are greater ones: 'They reflect the taste and outlook of their time precisely because they lacked the major writer's capacity to transcend it.' The assumption here about the timelessness and universality of great writing is debatable, and so too is the question of whether a canonical writer like Thomas Hardy escapes the classification of 'rural novelist'. It seems more profitable for the purposes of this chapter to define the rural novel, as opposed to the novel that happens to have a rural setting, as one in which the land and the earth, the rural environment, have an importance equal to, if not greater than, the characters in the novel, and in which the plot is inextricably linked to rural conditions. Such a definition would, in fact, find the apotheosis of the rural novel in the work of Thomas Hardy, although Emily Brontë has also perhaps some claim to its lineage. The heights in *Wuthering Heights* or Egdon Heath in Hardy's *The Return of the Native* are as powerful 'characters' as any human figure.

Hardy's novels presage a fictional concentration on rural life that begins around the 1870s and coincides with a decline in agriculture, one which, with some upturns, has continued ever since. England in the first third of the twentieth century was ceasing to be an agricultural nation, and the fiction of the period records this decline, much of it with a deep nostalgia for things past. As A. J. P. Taylor has argued, 'rarely avowed, was a belief in the superior quality of country life. The rural communities were supposed to enshrine historic England.'[2] The point is endorsed in G. E. Mingay's comment that throughout the nation during the interwar years, 'Country life became a special interest, a kind of escapist cult.' But the reality of rural life was very different; a 'deep, persistent poverty which helped feed the rural exodus' culminated at the end of the interbellum in 'depression among the farmers, rootlessness among younger workers, deficiencies in the conditions of life, in social relations, in education'. Agricultural prices declined by 20 per cent between 1929 and 1931 and then by a further 16 per cent in 1933.[3] The resulting unemployment amongst farmers and particularly farmworkers brought devastating hardship, not least because agriculture was not covered by unemployment insurance, and agricultural workers had to apply for relief under the Poor Law. It was a bitter irony that a traditional occupation was reduced to traditional remedies. Nevertheless, as agriculture declined as a percentage of the gross national product, and as

[1] G. Cavaliero, *The Rural Tradition in the English Novel, 1900–1939* (1997), preface.

[2] A. J. P. Taylor, *English History, 1914–1945* (Oxford, 1965), p. 342.

[3] G. E. Mingay, *A Social History of the English Countryside* (1990), pp. 227, 222.

agricultural workers left the industry at the rate of 10,000 a year, the imaginative significance of the countryside increased.

There were other factors to intensify the sense of loss. In a post-Darwinian world, nature had been deprived of its divine revelatory power, and in this newly scientific understanding of the world, it had been stripped of its magical properties too. In an age of increasing industrialisation and mechanisation of agriculture, nature was also losing its practical potency; seedtime and harvest, ploughing and harrowing were becoming less a contest with nature than with forces outside the farming community to do with world trade and money markets. As Winifred Holtby's *South Riding* (1936) points out, traditional farmers, represented by Carne in the novel, are failing to manage changing conditions:

> The Carnes of Maythorpe were like ... a tree – rooted deep in the earth ... their leaves and branches were uplifted and all men saw them, a conspicuous growth, proud, decorative. What they could not see ... were the winds that blew from all the ends of the world, Canada, Argentine, Denmark, New Zealand, Russia ... taxes and tariffs and subsidies and quotas, beef from the Argentine, wool from Australia, economic nationalism, fashions and crazes – all those imponderable influences of which their slow, strong, rigid minds took no heed – these would destroy them ... The tree must be cut down.[4]

The legacy of the Great War and the encroaching shadow of the next war served more than any other factors to intensify nostalgia for a rural way of life. In psychological terms nostalgia is a longing for home, and from the Bible story of the Garden of Eden onwards, a pastoral life has always been imagined as a lost ideal, a home from which we are expelled by forces beyond our control. The wreckage of human lives in the war is reflected in images of a wrecked nature, in the broken trees and ruined fields depicted so vividly in landscape paintings like Paul Nash's *We are Making a New World* (1918) or in images of the 'withered stumps of time' of Eliot's *The Waste Land* (1922). The desire to reclaim what had been lost, even if only in the imagination, to return to a kind of prelapsarian landscape – 'never such innocence again' as Philip Larkin put it – is strong in much of the writing of the period, alongside a need to assert a national identity which has to do with notions of tradition embedded in a perception of a landscape which is immemorial.[5] As Hardy wrote in 1915:

---

4 W. Holtby, *South Riding* (1988), p. 424.

5 P. Larkin, *Collected Poems*, ed. A. Thwaite (1988), pp. 127–8. Larkin's poem is titled 'MCMXIV' and was written in 1960.

Only a man harrowing clods
In a slow silent walk ...
Only thin smoke without flame
From the heaps of couch grass ...
Wars annals will cloud into night
Ere their story die.[6]

As many of the medical practices of the period testified, a return to the continuities of nature was perceived as bringing healing to those psychically dam-
aged by the effects of the Great War. The identification of Englishness with
rurality – that somehow the real England was one of village greens, country
churches, haymaking, maypole dancing, and communication with nature – was
a powerful motivator of patriotism by the outbreak of the Second World War.
But, as Howard Newby has written, 'the attention lavished on the aesthetics
of landscape contrasted sharply with the public indifference to the plight of
agriculture ... the Leavisite elision of elitist cultural sensibility and organic
rural community allowed an idyllic version of rural life to be elevated to the
status of quintessential England and Englishness.'[7]

An extreme form of the elitism Newby describes was the writing of Mary
Butts, not so much in her experimental novels, which are not 'rural', but in
some of her non-fiction essays, such as two short works published in 1932,
Warning to Hikers and *Traps for Unbelievers*. A passionate conservationist,
Butts believed that English territory, having survived foreign invasion, was
now in danger from the spread of democracy, which would encourage the
intrusion of the urban working classes into the countryside: 'The enemy is
the democratic enemy, in a country where people have lost their stations and
like badly-trained children can neither keep to their own places nor respect
other people's.'[8] Even town-bred intellectuals, who appear to enjoy hiking, are
fuelled by a 'synthetic fire'. To educate these town-dwellers is not an answer;
the true country dweller is not made but born, preferably from aristocratic
stock, or at least from workers who knew their natural place in the scheme of
things. As Jane Garrity has argued, Butts's writing

is concerned primarily with the notion of historical, cultural, and ances-
tral connections to *place*, seeing the advance of suburban housing, commercial developments, American advertising, and Hollywood cinema
as elements of encroachment, signs that English authenticity is being

---

[6] T. Hardy, *Selected Poems*, ed. D. Wright (1978), pp. 282–3. Hardy's poem is titled
'In Time of "The Breaking of Nations"', and was published in 1915.

[7] H. Newby, *Country Life: A Social History of Rural England* (1987), p. 178.

[8] M. Butts, *Warning to Hikers* (1932), p. 36.

endangered … At the heart of *Warning to Hikers* is Butts's conviction that England has compromised her soul because her people 'have begun to breed a race outside … the true nature of things'.[9]

Other conservationists were less extreme, more willing to accede to the growth of an urban population wishing to visit and benefit the countryside. The attention such moderates lavished on 'the aesthetics of landscape' was exemplified by the various movements to conserve and access the countryside, such as the Council for the Preservation of Rural England (1926) and the Ramblers' Association (1935). An indication of how powerful such organisations were becoming is provided by the Royal Society for the Protection of Birds. Founded in 1891 to stop the use in hat decoration of the feathers of the great crested grebe, this society expanded and prospered in the post-war years, buying land to create reserves and successfully lobbying for legislation, such as the Importation of Plumage (Prohibition) Act of 1922 and the Protection of Birds Act of 1934. This growing sense of the affinity between humans and animals is, of course, one of Stella Gibbons's satiric targets in *Cold Comfort Farm* (1932). Old Adam Lambsbreath, who is 'linked to all dumb brutes by a chain forged in soil and sweat', finds the cow Pointless eating the tail of Graceless, another cow. He gives her his neckerchief instead: 'she mumbled it, while he milked her, but stealthily spat it out as soon as he passed on to Aimless, and concealed it under the reeking straw with her hoof. She did not want to hurt the old man's feelings, by declining to eat his gift.'[10]

In terms of literary history and reputation, the novel in the interwar period is dominated by modernist texts – those by Richardson, Joyce, Woolf, Sinclair, the late Lawrence – but the traditional novel sturdily survives, and this is where the rural novel, for the most part, belongs and, like the regional novel, enjoys a popular, 'middle-brow' following. It is also the time of the emergence of the professional woman writer, as journalist, polemicist and novelist. The careers of Vera Brittain and Winifred Holtby, establishing themselves as 'writers' in 1921, are a good example of this. They differ from their great Victorian predecessors in the formal education they had received and in the public nature of their writing, their consciousness of being wage-earning professionals. To them the middle-brow novel was profitable and also a platform for putting across reformist ideas to large numbers of women. If the rural life fell within their expertise, as it most certainly did in the case of Holtby, then this could be a vehicle for their views on the changing society in which they lived. Women's employment and lifestyles were full of change at this time, and

9 J. Garrity, *Step-Daughters of England: British Women Modernists and the national Imaginary* (2003), p. 198.

10 S. Gibbons, *Cold Comfort Farm* (1938), p. 36.

it is worth noting in passing, as did the Women's Employment Committee in 1919, that very little agricultural employment was available to women after the war, except in certain specialised areas, such as dairy, poultry-keeping and fruit-canning.[11] The working life of country girls described by Jennie Kitteringham in *Village Life and Labour* belonged to earlier times, really to before about 1880.[12] The modern fate was more that of Flora Thompson, who left the village to become a post-office clerk.

Were women particularly drawn to the rural novel as writers and readers? Vita Sackville-West's long poem *The Land* (1926) thought they were, describing women's special affinity with trees, animals and flowers. But the picture is more complex than this, with both women and men writing novels of nostalgia and also of sharp critique of the contemporary agricultural scene. What is clear is that women novelists were interested in the plight of rural women, farmers' wives and daughters, the elderly female country-dweller. Perhaps this derives from a sense of women's displacement from the traditional rural scene, and a search for new roles, either symbolic or actual, in relation to agriculture. Rural novels by women are often feminist texts, but of differing kinds, from the 'woman as victim' of Mary Webb's work – the heroine of *Gone to Earth* (1917) is a good example, hunted to death, like the vixen she befriends, by a predatory man – to the 'equal rights', women-as-hero variety of Holtby's novels. Their writing must be seen in the context of a general upsurge of feminist texts by women during this period, the result of increased education, including access to higher education, and the winning of the vote in 1918 and 1928 and a concomitant commitment to the idea of the 'woman citizen.'

In *The Fallow Land* (1932) H. E. Bates, still regarded as the quintessential rural writer of the period, makes a useful distinction between attitudes towards the rural scene, between what he calls the earth and the land:

> The land was something more than the earth; the earth was something vague, primitive, poetic; the land was a composite force of actual, living, everyday things, fields and beast, seed-time and harvest, ploughing and harrowing, wind and weather; bitterness and struggle; the land was an opponent, a master ... The land ate into the body of a man and the land and the man became at last part of each other, bonded together and lost without each other.[13]

---

[11] V. Brittain, *Women's Work in Modern England* (1928), pp. 27–30.

[12] J. Kitteringham, 'Country work girls in nineteenth-century England', *Village Life and Labour*, ed. R. Samuel (1975), pp. 73–138.

[13] H. E. Bates, *The Fallow Land* (1932), p. 71. Cavaliero (*The Rural Tradition in the English Novel*, p. 200) draws attention to this interestingly diagnostic novel.

The Fallow Land charts a decline in a farming family, the men either drunkards or killed in the war, and only Deborah, the wife and mother, to continue the work. When she dies, the farm passes into other hands. The men complain that there is no money in farming, but Deborah claims that 'The land's all right … it's the people on it. The land's the same as ever.'[14] Bates is sharply critical of a romanticised version of the countryside but also of the defeatism of the time, which sacrifices the heritage of 'land' to modern technology, either military or agricultural. The bond between man and land has been broken and no amount of 'earth' worship will restore it.

The contrast between 'earth' and 'land' Bates posits is between the elemental and the practical. Those rural novelists who wrote about the earth, like Mary Webb or T. F. Powys, strove to reinvest it with symbolic, magical and/or religious significance. Those who stayed with the land, to continue with H. E. Bates's formulation, like Constance Holme, H. W. Freeman, Sheila Kaye-Smith, Eden Phillpotts, Doreen Wallace and Winifred Holtby, wrote to varying degrees about the economic problems of the agricultural way of life. The rest of this chapter will address a small number of novels by women, out of many that could have been discussed, which are, to varying degrees, earth or land novels, each in differing ways reflecting the interwar rural environment.

Mary Webb's *Precious Bane* (1924) is an 'earth' novel, set at the time of Waterloo, which allows it both historic license and poetic archaism. It is the first-person narrative of a Shropshire country girl, the hare-lipped Prue Sarn, and uses dialect, folk songs, old spells, superstitions and rural customs to give a voice to 'us women, living such lost and forgotten lives' in this community. It is also highly literary and self-conscious, even disingenuous, about its own fictional processes. After an ecstatic description of the standing corn, Prue says, 'I make no doubt that if any read this book it will seem strange to them that a farm women should look at the things about her in this wise, and indeed it is not many who do.' It has a refracted modernity, however, for its values are those of a hundred years later: there is great concern for and rapport with animals, the central love affair is the product of a century of bourgeois romantic love, the disabled are vindicated (a kind of fictional balm to the many war victims disfigured by fire and gas), and there is an intense, mystical identification with the 'wild' in a culturally determined construction of what constitutes the 'natural'. Consider this description of waterlilies, which involves a resacralisation of nature:

> … they were so lovely you couldna choose but cry to see them. [Their] petals are of a glistening white within, like the raiment of those men who stood with Christ upon the mountain top, and without they are

---

[14] Bates, *The Fallow Land*, p. 312.

stained with tender green, as if they had taken colour from the green shadows in the water …

So the mere was three times ringed about, as if it had been three times put in a spell. First there was the ring of oaks and larches … Then there was the ring of rushes … Then there was the ring of lilies, as I said, lying there as if Jesus, walking upon the water, had laid them down with his cool hands, afore he turned to the multitude saying, 'Behold the lilies!' And if they were not enough to shake your soul, there beneath every lily, white and green or pale gold, there was her bright shadow, as it had been her angel. And through the long, untroubled day the lilies and their angels looked one upon the other and were content.[15]

For the most part, however, the wild in *Precious Bane* is sinister and threatening, and its powers are demonic rather than Christ-like. It is altogether a violent story, with suicide, murder and arson, sin-eating and other superstitious practices. It is also an admonitory tale for the times; those who exploit the earth, and who prize money above a patient working with the earth, are punished by it. It has mythic pretensions and, like a gothic tale, it thrills by its juxtaposition with modernity. But it is also a kind of allegorical tale, with forces of darkness contending with rationality. In the aftermath of war it consoles with its promise of the triumph of love and rationality over satanic and primitive forces. Twentieth-century England does not really believe in the curse of a hare crossing a pregnant woman's path, does it? And it no longer indulges in bull-baiting, which in the wake of the war's horrific slaughter, is some kind of compensatory superiority. Its heightened, romantic descriptions of landscape were, of course, the sort of writing Stella Gibbons mocked in *Cold Comfort Farm*, where she marked purple passages with asterisks for the reader's benefit, indicating that a suitable awe-struck response is required, and also how disconnected these passages are from the main narrative, how implanted to impress a largely urban and suburban audience.

Cold Comfort Farm was serialised in *The Lady*, the genteel journal of country life, with the knowledge that its middle-class readers would have read Webb, whose novels sold in their thousands, and would therefore appreciate her satire. Webb's novels trade in nostalgia, not just for ancient farming customs but for a vivid past of primitive passions and violent deeds, the erotics of antiquity in an increasingly drab and uniform age. In the rather haunting foreword to *Precious Bane*, Webb admits to the nostalgic purpose of her writing, claiming that only the past has romance: 'The past is only the present become invisible and mute; and because it is invisible and mute, its memoried glances and its murmurs are infinitely precious. We are tomorrow's past.' Prime Minister Stanley Baldwin's

---

[15] M. Webb, *Precious Bane* (1956), p. 190.

discovery and promotion of the novel was representative of its huge popularity, and indicates the reasons for this: 'Her sensibility is so acute and her power over words so sure and swift that one who reads some passage in Whitehall has almost the physical sense of being in Shropshire cornfields.'[16]

A novel that seems at first to be more concerned with earth than land is Sylvia Townsend Warner's *Lolly Willowes* (1926). Townsend Warner's life exemplified a pattern of rural displacement and return common in the early years of the twentieth century, in that she was born in 1893 in Harrow-on-the-Hill, at the time a quiet village to the north of London, soon to be engulfed in suburban development. But in her adult life she returned to live in rural locations, sometimes very remote, and though she became politically active, joining the Communist Party in 1934 and writing for a range of left-wing papers, most notably *Left Review*, she never lost her sense of the enduring powers of the countryside. Her early poems, published with her lover Valentine Ackland, record, as Wendy Mulford has suggested, a Wordsworthian sense of the connection between the earth and the people who live close to it. An old woman digging her garden is as fierce and determined as the thorn trees that surround her:

> ... at one
> With them seemed she, wrathful and resolute,
> As though her root
> Went deep as theirs into the ground and thence
> Sucked like a harsh sap the will to be.[17]

All Townsend Warner's work possesses a strong political awareness, even in the guise of a rural novel. Not for her a merely rhapsodic appreciation of the earth but a sense of its relation to human economic and cultural conditions, and she shared something of Mary Butts's contempt for weekend hikers, and for the Council for the Preservation of Rural England for its hypocrisy in ignoring the plight of rural workers. *Lolly Willowes*, her first novel, combines a critique of oppressive bourgeois practices, particularly in relation to women, with an understanding of nature's magical, even diabolical, properties. Lolly (Laura), born in 1874, is the unmarried daughter left at home to care for ageing parents, and when they die she is given a home by her brother. Everyone is kind to her, but her life is constrained and largely useless. Prompted by the smell of a florist's beech leaves from 'dark rustling woods', she takes the last of her savings, and in 1921, when she is forty-seven, goes to live in the

---

[16] Webb, *Precious Bane*, introduction.

[17] Quoted W. Mulford, *This Narrow Place: Sylvia Townsend Warner and Valentine Ackland: Life, Letters and Politics, 1930–1951* (1988), p. 49.

small village of Great Mop, in the Chilterns. The countryside at Great Mop
is animated by ancient powers, both consolatory and terrifying, and Lolly's
immersion in them reveals to her her true nature, that she is, in fact, a witch.
All women are potentially witches; 'even if they never do anything with their
witchcraft, they know it's there – ready!' To become a witch is to escape the
monotonous dependency and busyness that dominates most women's lives.

> … they are like trees towards the end of summer, heavy and dusty, and
> nobody finds their leaves surprising, or notices them if they fall off. If
> they could be passive and unnoticed, it wouldn't matter. But they must
> be active, and still not noticed. Doing, doing, doing, till mere habit
> scolds at them like a housewife, and rouses them up – when they might
> sit in their doorways and think.[18]

Warner had read Margaret Murray's *The Witch Cult in Western Europe* (1921)
and its claim that there is white witchcraft, which 'is a form of nature worship that survived from pre-Christian paganism and was the original religion
of the British Isles', is a powerful presence in the novel.[19] Like others at this
time, Warner was also influenced by the feminist archaeologist Jane Harrison,
who similarly proposed a matriarchal inheritance for human society. Lolly
reclaims this inheritance in an eroticised landscape inhabited by the Devil,
who is the benign master of witches, has hunted her throughout the book, and
is an emanation of nature itself, 'a skilful and experienced naturalist.' His satisfied but profoundly indifferent ownership' of her has been expressed through
the seasonal changes, the creatures and people of Great Mop, and through
descriptions of nature that are sacerdotal, though it is the devil's spirit they
possess. This is the devil of Blake's *The Marriage of Heaven and Hell*, with its
celebration of energy, freedom, sexuality and opposition to authority:

> She felt the wind swoop down close to the earth. The moon was out
> hunting overhead, her pack of black and white hounds ranged over the
> sky. Moon and wind and clouds hunted an invisible quarry. The wind
> routed throughout the woods. Laura from the hill-top heard the various
> surrounding woods cry out with different voices. The spent gusts left the
> beech-hangers throbbing like sea caverns through which the wave had
> passed, the fir plantation seemed to chant some never-ending rune.[20]

The full title of the novel is *Lolly Willowes, or The Loving Huntsman*; it
was a successful and popular book, its feminist message striking a note with

---

[18] S. T. Warner, *Lolly Willowes, or the Loving Huntsman* (1979), p. 236.

[19] Garrity, *Step-Daughters of England*, p. 163.

[20] Warner, *Lolly Willowes*, pp. 133–4.

middle-class women who had worked during the war and had now gained political and professional status, albeit one threatened in the aftermath of war. Its popularity differed from that of Mary Webb's books, its 'cult escapism' used to explore social evils, Webb's to offer a restorative, though not always comfortable, sense of national identity developing in a progressive continuity from more primitive times.

Constance Holme's most popular novel, *The Lonely Plough*, published in 1914, has some affinities with Mary Webb's work. It ends, prophetically in view of the date, with a cataclysmic flood, and nature is in general seen in sublime terms as creator and destroyer. But her post-war novels are 'land' novels, in the H. E. Bates sense of the term. They focus on homely individuals, often elderly villagers, with local concerns and limited lives. But they face modernity in a more direct way than Webb's or Warner's. They are set in a contemporaneous context; cars and the telegraph impinge on the lives of these country dwellers, and there are acute memories of the war. The class dimension, which was pronounced and traditionalist in *The Lonely Plough*, is subdued, and it is the consciousness of these humble people which predominates. The landscape is a subtle although determining context rather than an insistent presence, and its aesthetic qualities are complexly intertwined with the lives of the characters. In *The Trumpet in the Dust* (1921) an old charwoman goes to see the almshouse she believes she will shortly be living in; the lyrical description of a soft September day is a brief interlude of indulgence before her struggle with work and responsibility begins again. In *The Things Which Belong* (1925) the head gardener and his wife have totally opposing attitudes to the garden he tends: he loving it, she hating it, and the descriptions of it are mediated through these respective attitudes. The old wife longs to emigrate to Canada, where her daughters are, but, when the time comes, she is frightened of the sea, and a terrifying dream of shipwreck convinces her that they should not go. She goes to the door and looks at the garden, which up to now has always oppressed her:

> … the choking terror which had sprung on her out of the ocean slowly loosed its grip. The peace of the garden reached her even in the house, making an exquisite stillness where the sea had rolled and rolled. She sat drinking in the quiet, watching the sky fade and the lawn dim as veil after veil was laid upon them.[21]

But this is no consoling resolution; the novel ends uncertainly with her running out to meet her husband in the bitter knowledge that this stasis of tranquillity has trapped and defeated her; its rural dream has destroyed her. The novel

[21] C. Holme, *The Things that Belong* (Oxford, 1949), p. 159.

captures the contradictory nature of the relation between past and present: the lure of the past and the fear of the future, and the fear of the past and the lure of the future. It also captures, in its unemphatic way, the contradictory attitudes to rural life of the interwar period. There is a subdued political sense in these novels of a spatial relation of characters to the land, a relationship that is determined by class and gender and age. This scrupulous attention to lives in a landscape is emphasised by the use of a single day for the action of the novels, a modernist chronology enclosing a traditional style.

Winifred Holtby is the most obviously political of my novelists, and in her rural novels a political approach to the land is more pronounced. Her first and her last novels, *Anderby Wold* (1923) and *South Riding* (1936), chart change in the countryside, the decline of the patriarchal, or matriarchal, farm and the coming of unionised labour to the village in the former, and the decline of the big estate and its dissolution into land for building and public services (a mental hospital, in fact) in the latter. Holtby, who was a wealthy farmer's daughter, drew on actual events affecting her own family in the East Riding. *Anderby Wold*, for example, used her parents' departure from farming, caused largely by a strike of agricultural workers in 1919, to furnish the novel's dynamics. Set in 1912, it gropes towards a fictional understanding of historical change in the post-war period. It acknowledges, even exploits, a romanticised farming landscape in which, for example, the harvest is brought home by contented workers, accompanied by children carrying garlands of flowers.

> From the upland acres came heavy waggons behind great horses that strained and sweated with their golden load … The men wore dark loose clothes, quaintly fashioned, exposing their brown throats and sinewy arms. Thus they had harvested at Anderby since those far-off years when the Danes broke in across the headland and dyed with blood the trampled barley. Thus and thus had the workers passed, and the children waved their garlands following the last load home.[22]

Every stereotype of harvest home is here (although the invading, blood-stained barley introduces an interestingly discordant note), but this is nothing but a moonlight fantasy by Mary Robson, the novel's protagonist, and as her nostalgic vision dissolves it becomes a pre-vision in which the master of the harvest is not the traditional farmer but the union agitator who will bring about her downfall. Mary becomes one of the displaced women mentioned earlier: an ailing husband forces them to give up the farm and become suburban dwellers.

Perhaps it is cheating to include *South Riding* as a rural novel, because the

[22] W. Holtby, *Anderby Wold* (1981), p. 240.

ruination of the gentleman farmer, through incompetence, recession and an outmoded agricultural system, is subordinate to other plot lines, other social concerns, like education, maternal welfare and local government responsibilities. But it is appropriate that farming is pushed to the margins in this highly contemporary novel, for its proponent, Robert Carne, in failing health and fortunes, is representative of a traditional type of landowner whose day has gone. This is a novel very concerned with English society and identity which refuses to endorse the pervasive belief that the real England is a rural one, and that there is a deep continuity between ancient rural practices and the current needs of society.

Every social issue of the early 1930s is mentioned, and the book is an index of progressive concerns during the period, and in this it is perhaps over-determined, too knowing, almost a parody of itself. For example, a smart architect's wife talking to a farmer (Carne) says: 'Well, how are the dear, dark elemental things of the countryside – the cows, aimless, homeless and witless, aren't they? The passionate peasants?'[23] This not only mocks Mary Webb and her kind, but also makes use of Gibbons's satire. In this manner it ranges in its sources from *Jane Eyre* for the mad-wife plot-line to government reports and county council minutes, which Holtby salvaged from her mother's waste-paper basket. But in its register of the decline of traditional agriculture there is a heartfelt seriousness. Carne's death, and the breaking up of his estate, is a kind of elegy for the rural way of life rooted in a particular class structure which has to give way not just to international markets but, as far as the novel is concerned, to more pressing social concerns. Although it is elegiac, it refuses to be sentimental; there is a brisk moving on. Farming is swept aside and its patriarchal practices are replaced by local government schemes, education, welfarism, and entrepreneurial private enterprise. In this new world there is really nowhere for farming to go.

South Riding states more directly than the other novels that the traditional rural world is in decline. The novels that suggest otherwise are either deeply nostalgic, like *Precious Bane*, or escapist, like *Lolly Willowes*. Even those that are equivocal about the future of farming, such as *The Things Which Belong*, recognise the stagnation the rural world has fallen into. It will take another war to revive, however temporarily, the fortunes of farming. At the same time, *South Riding* is the most regenerative of the rural novels discussed here, but, ironically, the regeneration is not linked to the most traditional of rural practices, agriculture. Regeneration in the countryside will come about through improved medical practices, new roads, slum clearance, and, most of all, feminism. Lydia Holly, the casual labourer's daughter, will become a scholarship grammar-school girl, Mrs Beddows (based on Holtby's mother) will succeed

---

[23] Holtby, *South Riding*, p. 277.

as a woman alderman, and Sarah Burton will surmount the disappointments of romantic love to remain a successful headmistress, nurturing other girls like Lydia Holly, and demonstrating that a single women can be happy and fulfilled, an encouraging message for the million and a half unmarried women in the British population at the time.

In 1933, trying to justify writing *South Riding* rather than engage in pacifist activities, Winifred Holtby said that 'I feel the whole world is on the brink of another catastrophic war, & to go and shut oneself up in a cottage writing an arcadian novel ... seems to me a kind of betrayal. ... But I *want* to write this particular novel & the one after.'[24] Though one might not agree that *South Riding* is an arcadian novel, it itself and Holtby herself typify positive qualities at work in the interbellum rural novel. They challenge traditional roles and attitudes relating to marriage, class distinctions and even the role of the countryside in the English novel. In many Victorian and Edwardian novels the countryside is too easily seen as a haven of peace and harmony; this stereotype is interrogated in the interwar women's novels, and the serious rural novel henceforth can no longer take the stereotype on trust. Modernity has come to the world of 'fields and beast, seed-time and harvest, ploughing and harrowing, wind and weather.' That the interwar women's rural novel are cast in a non-modernist form – *South Riding* is almost a pastiche of *Middlemarch* – has much to do with their middle-brow status and readership. A modernist rural novel may have to wait until 1941 and Virginia Woolf's *Between the Acts*.

---

[24] Winfred Holtby to Phyllis Bentley, Dec 1933, quoted in M. Shaw, *The Clear Stream: A Life of Winifred Holtby* (1999), p. 233.

6 Dead chickens: Henry Williamson, British agriculture and European war

Mark Rawlinson

> So now and again poultry casualties remained where they had died
> – perhaps in some remote corner of the Home Hills – and were soon
> reduced to feathered skeletons by maggots of the Bluebottle and Spanish
> Green Fly.[1]

T̲HIS essay reassesses the motifs and rhetoric of decline and regeneration in
the work of Henry Williamson. It focuses on *The Story of a Norfolk Farm*
(1941), but sets this non-fictional book in the context of Williamson's recen-
sion and completion of his narrative of interwar East Anglian agriculture in
the novel sequence *A Chronicle of Ancient Sunlight*, which was published in
fifteen volumes during the 1950s and 60s. Though it remains idiosyncratic,
Williamson's motivation of themes of rural decline and renewal as vehicles
for a heterodox political and historical vision of post-1914 Europe exemplifies
the imaginative charge of myths of agricultural decadence in the mid-century.
But through his serial production of narratives reinterpreting and allegorising
his experience as a farmer in the 1930s, Williamson represented the interwar
years in a way which could scarcely be countenanced after the defeat of Hitler
in 1945. His persistence in these misconceptions is itself a notable dimension
of the broader cultural interplay between rural myth and authoritarian politics
in the interwar period.

When commissioned from Edith Whetham, the eighth volume of the
Agrarian History of England and Wales was projected to cover half a century
from 1914. This happens to be roughly the period throughout which Henry
Williamson reimagined the legacies of the Great War (a project of recupera-
tion which only gave out with the publication of *The Gale of the World* in 1969).
Whetham, however, modified her task, and the volume that appeared in 1978
stopped at 1939. It is, by its author's account, a history of the 'daily round and
common task', taking a perspective governed neither by policy nor econometrics, but by 'what it felt like to be a landowner, farmer or farm worker'.[2]

---

[1] H. Williamson, *Lucifer before Sunrise* (*A Chronicle of Ancient Sunlight*, vol. 14)
(1967), pp. 145–6. Hereafter *LBS*.

[2] E. H. Whetham, *The Agrarian History of England and Wales*, vol. 8: *1914–1939*
(Cambridge, 1978), pp. xxi–xxii.

The volume closes on decades of depression with a description of a celebration, the centenary show of the Royal Agricultural Society of England, held in Windsor Great Park in July 1939:

> the farmers who attended both the centenary show in 1939 and the jubilee show in 1889 were probably using on their farms many of the same implements, either individually or in type, which had survived over the fifty years. As long as horses remained the principal source of power in the majority of farms, the form and weight of the farm implements could not be greatly altered. And the majority of farmers were still operating within fields and buildings which had originated either in the nineteenth century or even earlier.[3]

Undercutting these signs of continuity, Whetham reminds us of the decline in arable acreages since 1916, and notes the disappearance of the plough from some Midlands parishes. But the future is just around the corner, to breathe renewed life into British farming:

> the farmers gathered at Windsor in July 1939 to watch the parade of prize-winning cattle round the grand ring knew what would be required of them, and were ready to start work on the third day of September.[4]

This is the 'moral to this story', although Whetham is at pains to deny such teleology. For the second time in a quarter of a century, British agriculture is rescued from undercapitalisation and foreign competition by national emergency.

Whetham's 'appropriate concluding date' is worthy of consideration not in order to contest her periodisation from a socio-economic perspective, but to ponder the role of the motif of memory in this shaping act, and further to reflect on the cultural representation of interwar agriculture beyond the Second World War. Those present at Windsor in 1939 who had attended the 1889 jubilee would, we are told, remember working the land in the 'deep depression' of the 1880s. But any recall of the pre-repeal 1830s elicited by the idea of the centenary would not have been personal memories, but a socially coded expression of the residual economic ideology that Joan Thirsk has called 'mainstream agriculture'.[5]

In Henry Williamson's recursive fictional and non-fictional writings, the story of interwar farming is similarly distinguished by the perspective of what

---

3 Whetham, *The Agrarian History of England and Wales*, vol. 8, p. 331.

4 Whetham, *The Agrarian History of England and Wales*, vol. 8, p. 333.

5 J. Thirsk, *Alternative Agriculture: A History from the Black Death to the Present Day* (Oxford, 1997), p. 149.

if felt like to be a farmer. But the moral he draws – which has its roots in Mosleyite economics and the iconography of fascism, and which is elaborated by
a protagonist who identifies with Hitler as a pacifist war-veteran – has often
been deemed too controversial to figure as a landmark in the imaginative writing of English rural life. It is an account in which policy and econometrics
– uncritical, simplistic, or plain false – shape the presentation of memory in
both its personal and collective senses. Williamson stopped his first account
at 1939, but then, with the war over, resumed his imaginative historiography
of English soil. And as it turned out, the work that wartime farming readied
him for was telling the story all over again. In contrast to the official story, his
tale was not about how the Second World War regenerated British agriculture,
but about how agricultural decline was a microcosm of the political errors of
Versailles, and of uncomprehending views of Hitler's Germany.

Williamson's decision to become a farmer was taken late in 1935, during a
stay with his publisher Richard de la Mare. *The Story of a Norfolk Farm* would
be published in February 1941 by Faber and Faber, the firm of which de la Mare
was a director. That wartime spring, when estimates of UK shipping capacity
for food imports were lower than the figures for 1917, Williamson's 'prophecy'
of an end to the system of cheap imported foods which had undermined the
profitability of British husbandry seemed to have come to pass. Farming, as
Williamson's fictional cipher Phillip Maddison would say twenty-five years
later, 'will be a respected thing in England for a year of two now'.[6]

By Williamson's own arguments, there was no commercial logic to moving
his family from Devon to a dilapidated granary in Stiffkey in 1937:

> for a long period, the fertility of English land had been slowly diminish-
> ing, until to-day it produced about half of what it produced even at the
> beginning of the twentieth century, when for fifty years or more it had
> been declining.[7]

Economic historians will seize on this misstatement. Since the turn of the century, cereal acreages and farm employment had certainly declined (by factors
of around a fifth and a quarter respectively), but yields of cereals had increased
by up to 10 per cent in the same period.[8] Fertility, in Williamson's writing, is
always a cipher for political and economic policy: his legend of a near ninety-
year fall in output and the exhaustion of English acreages is initiated with the

[6] H. Williamson, *A Solitary War* (*A Chronicle of Ancient Sunlight*, vol. 13) (1966; 1999),
   p. 14. Hereafter *ASW*.

[7] H. Williamson, *The Story of a Norfolk Farm* (1941), p. 29. Hereafter, *SNF*.

[8] P. Brassley, 'Output and technical change in twentieth-century British agriculture', *Agricultural History Review* 48/1 (2000): 64–6.

repeal of the Corn Laws. The historical and economic falsehoods, as well as the rhetorical exorbitance of Williamson's description of agricultural decay, provide the key to his story of farming in interwar England, a story in which nationhood and selfhood are porous terms in an overloaded and ambiguous dialectic of 'decadence and resurgence'.

The Story of a Norfolk Farm narrates the purchase and restoration of Old Hall Farm, Stiffkey, which Williamson disguises as Old Castle Farm, Creek. The farm is taken over at Michaelmas 1937, and the story proceeds to the second anniversary, in May 1939, of the author's arrival on the East Coast to begin reclamation work. We can begin to restore the political context to *The Story of a Norfolk Farm* by sizing up the image of Williamson presented in the first phase of the book, which establishes two themes which will expand into the 6,000 pages of *A Chronicle*: the decline and regeneration of England, and the decadence and redemption of self. The book opens with a journey to London in 1935, in pursuit of the stimulus which Devon, where the Brockley-born Williamson had settled in 1921, no longer supplies: 'My life there was a closed book' (*SNF*, 20). (In fact *Goodbye West Country*, his fascist-minded diary of 1936, would be contracted in March 1937 and published in September, a month before Old Hall Farm was vacated by the then tenant.) The need to *do* something, rather than write, is nourished by a debate about the relation of action and contemplation which rages throughout his work, an opposition resuscitated by English literary modernism, and which Williamson sought to transcend through a fetish of the mechanical.

His model in all of this is T. E. Lawrence, a fan of *Tarka the Otter* since 1927, and whose powerful Brough motorcycles acted as a goad to Williamson's cult of speed and mechanical know-how. Among the literary productions of the Norfolk years was the commemorative selection of Lawrence–Williamson correspondence titled *Genius of Friendship* issued in 1941. Lawrence figures in *The Story of a Norfolk Farm* as leader and an exemplar of the truly strong. Williamson, by contrast, is an alienated amphibian, a townsman amongst countrymen and vice versa. Lawrence's *The Mint*, which recounts going underground in the RAF and the security of living incognito amongst aircraftsmen, is cited here as a prospect of fellowship which 'give[s] one a root in the ground' (*SNF*, 20). This, however, is not sufficiently 'something'. Williamson frequently reprises the divisions between Lawrence of Arabia and Aircraftsman Shaw as a figure for the tension between his own imagined engagement, and retreat from, the world-historical process. In one passage he discovers courage to buy the farm (he will later compare himself, a new farmer at Michaelmas, to a 'soldier before zero hour') in words we are told Lawrence had drafted for *Seven Pillars of Wisdom*:

I meant to make a new nation, to restore to the world a lost influence, to give twenty millions of Semites the foundation on which to build an inspired dream-palace of their national thoughts. So high an aim called out the inherent nobility of their minds and made them play a dangerous part in events: but when we won it was charged against me that the British petrol royalties in Mesopotamia were become dubious, and French colonial policy ruined in the Levant (*SNF*, 51).

These sentences resonate with the pattern of Williamson's myths of selfhood, the prophet of regeneration stymied by international capital and the balance of national power, and misrepresented in his own land.

Norfolk will be the scene of Williamson's own political revolt, a war on the white bread which becomes the author's synecdoche for capitalism: adulterated food poisons the children of peasants uprooted to industrial towns to manufacture the goods to pay for imported wheat. Williamson's dying mother's lack of faith in the son's agricultural experiment is deemed a symptom of degeneracy: 'Was this dread thing that was killing her due to white bread, to wrong values, to industrialism, to unnatural ideas which had come upon European man?' (*SNF*, 48). The lapsing virility of landowning families, the sale of land (like the Mosley estate at Rolleston, which was broken up at the end of the Great War), the wastage of England's fertility – all are rolled up together by Williamson as the calamitous effects of international trade and investment. But fertility operates as a symbol of self as well as of the utopia of mercantilist or autarkic nationalism. Williamson is exhausted as a writer: 'A million braincell impressions had gone out of my head into words, and it seemed my life was finished' (*SNF*, 20). Why write prose, when few appreciated it and when it was 'easier to be uncaring about the slow decline and decadence of the human life about one' (*SNF*, 50)? The answer was that imitating 'the historic Coke of Norfolk' in 'altering the face of England' was a revolutionary act and the source of renewed literary invention: 'What a book I would write of my experiences!' (*SNF*, 51).

Restoration of fertility thus has a triple signification, as the husbandry of soil, nation and self. The narrative that unfolds this project has three corresponding timescales, respectively the recent cultivation and manuring of the farm's 230 acres, together with the maintenance of rotations, drains and buildings; the economic history of Europe since Napoleon; and the memory and imagination of Henry Williamson, particularly since Christmas 1914.

Napoleon is Williamson's chosen exemplar of the mixture in himself of genius – 'the pure expression of natural force' – and its flawed expression (*SNF*, 121). In *The Phoenix Generation* (1965) Phillip Maddison, visiting Germany in 1936, defends Napoleon, and by implication Hitler (another flawed angel or

Lucifer), as an engineer of autarky provoked into defensive economic measures by a system controlled from the vaults of Threadneedle Street. Maddison is, with characteristic immodesty, retailing 'what he had read in Birkin's weekly paper'.[9] Birkin is Williamson's post-war cipher for the ideologue who presides over *The Story of a Norfolk Farm*, Sir Oswald Mosley.

Along with a subscription to the *Farmer and Stockbreeder*, and membership of a farming association which acts as intermediary in the ill-advised purchase of fat stock, Williamson pays his dues to what he describes as the Imperial Socialist Party. This alias for the British Union of Fascists – which acknowledges the sources of Mosley's economic thinking in J. A. Hobson's *Imperialism* (1902) and Joseph Chamberlain's campaign for tariff reform (1903) – was advisable, given the declaration of the BUF as a proscribed organisation on 10 July 1940.[10] Mosley himself was detained from 23 May until his release on humanitarian grounds on 20 November 1943.[11] Although Faber and Faber insisted on substantial cuts to *Norfolk Farm*, the ideological framework of Mosleyite economics shows through. Ridding the farm of thistles and rats is a necessary but not a sufficient step in expelling 'the golden tapeworm … from the body politic', to create a new age in which books like Richard Jefferies' *Hodge and his Masters*, which Williamson revised for Methuen in 1937, 'would have a proper and full appreciation' (*SNF*, 103). He addresses the party's local public meetings, campaigning for the wages Hodge deserved but meeting indifference: 'Nobody cared for Hodge; least of all, Hodge' (*SNF*, 283). He uses a ISP loud-speaker van to broadcast the saving doctrine that 'the land must be fed' (*SNF*, 343). Bled of capital, England is a waste land:

> Rats, weeds, swamps, depressed markets, labourers on the dole, rotten cottages, polluted streams, political parties and class divisions controlled by the money-power, wealthy banking and insurance houses getting rid of their land-mortgages and investing their millions abroad (but not in the Empire), this was the real England of the period of this story of a Norfolk farm.
>
> When I began farming it was nearly the end of that period. (*SNF*, 331.)

The success or otherwise of Williamson's husbandry in Norfolk rests on a number of contradictions. In emulation of Coke, but against the grain of

---

[9] H. Williamson, *The Phoenix Generation* (*A Chronicle of Ancient Sunlight*, vol. 12) (1965; 1967), p. 191. Hereafter *TPG*.

[10] R. Thurlow, *Fascism in Britain: A History, 1918–1985* (Oxford, 1987), p. 198.

[11] R. Skidelsky, *Oswald Mosley*, 3rd edn (1990), pp. 449, 461.

the post-war industry, he is a diligent keeper of accounts.[12] But the management of inputs and outputs is confounded by the beginner's credulity and his mistakes, as well as by the high ideals of a not-for-profit husbandry, 'for England's sake'. The man who 'would put more into farming than I got out of it' is actually replicating, but this time in an idealistic frame of reference, the predicament of those agriculturalists whose margins collapsed and whose indebtedness increased, and those labourers whose wages fell, after the repeal of the Corn Production Act, which Williamson elsewhere misdates to 1923 and makes the prime cause of the encroachment of bull thorns, brambles and thistles into the arable (*TPG*, 294). The 'psychic income element in British farming' may still have been large, but not large enough to make Williamson's principles of selfless husbandry an answer to the structural problems of the industry.[13]

As Williamson admits in drawing up the balance sheet for the first year, a member of the Imperial Socialist Party might 'scorn usury', and therefore decline to enter 5 per cent of the capital in the business in the column of losses, but the overdraft remains. The dream of self-sufficiency on Old Castle Farm – a kind of domestic mercantilist separatism – is further undermined by the business's dependence on the income from Williamson's writing and broadcasting (including, through 1938–9, the reprinting of extracts from his 1930 *The Patriot's Progress* in the BUF journal *Action*).[14] But war changes all of this. Having paid £2,250 for the property in 1936, he would sell out for £9,000 in 1945 in a very different agricultural market. The auction of live and dead farming stock would raise a sum equal to the original purchase price.

Wars, Williamson writes 'were always economic in origin, although by the time of their breaking-out all sorts of human emotions, genuine and otherwise, had usually arisen … and simple men, often in peace-time the victims of the economic system, lost their lives in defence of that system' (*SNF*, 75–6). Wars which waste men raise agricultural prices. Barley and beet net £10 per acre after 1939's 'resumption of the Napoleonic trade war, of blockade and counter-blockade' (*SNF*, 399–400). Williamson's break-even is a distinctly reluctant accommodation with the state.

A quarter of a century later, in *The Phoenix Generation*, where the purchase of the farm follows Maddison's inspirational tour of Hitler's Germany, this same Norfolk farm (named Deepwater, and purportedly a Napoleonic invasion target) is a diagram of the political economy that has brought Europe

---

[12] R. A. C. Parker, *Coke of Norfolk: A Financial and Agricultural Study* (Oxford, 1975), pp. 6, 22.

[13] C. O'Grada, 'British agriculture, 1860–1914', in *The Economic History of Britain since 1700*, ed. R. Floud and D. McCloskey, 2nd edn (Cambridge, 1994), p. 172.

[14] A. Williamson, *Henry Williamson: Tarka and the Last Romantic* (1995), p. 222.

to the verge of catastrophe. Compensation for Great War dilapidations by billeted soldiers has been exported as capital to Kenya, the owner 'believing that England was finished, and that the future of the white man lay in Africa' (*TPG*, 250). East Anglia is a 'wild, remote and betrayed country ... a great arable tradition half-lost in its weedy fields and rotting barns' (*TPG*, 254). The farm 'was a microcosm of the European macrocosm: it was a race between resurgence and death, otherwise another world war' (*TPG*, 257). Maddison's struggle against the conservatism of his farm-hands is a version of the ideological opposition of international capital and nationalism: 'The war of ideas on the farm is like the greater looming continental war of action and reaction' (*TPG*, 293). Where in *The Story of a Norfolk Farm* the 'mental fear and diffuseness of the village mind' is 'symbolized' in thoughtless damage to Williamson's new 'seed-measure', twenty years on the ratio is reversed: 'I try to explain that Birkin is attempting to do on a national scale what I am trying to do on a small scale: a sort of desperate attempt to avoid the coming smash' (*SNF*, 254, and *TPG*, 323).

The epilogue to *The Story of a Norfolk Farm* (curiously mistitled 'epigraph', a detail to which we must return) posits a future at odds with the vision of the peace promulgated in the largely urbanist Second World War reconstruction talk which issued in symbols like Beveridge's Five Giants. Williamson imagines that 'one day the sewage of the cities will cease to be poured into the rivers, and will be returned to the land, to grow fine food for the people', and that 'one day salmon will leap again in the clear waters of London river'. This picks up on an earlier reference to the 'trade in bones after the Napoleonic wars', when wheat was 'nine times' the current price. The organic chemist Justus von Liebig (1803–73) is cited as calling England 'a vampire' on the neck of Europe, turning up battlefields and emptying catacombs, 'removing the manurial equivalent of three million and a half of men, whom she takes from us the means of supporting, and squanders down her sewers to the sea' (*SNF*, 140). Here the management of the economy of waste which dominates Williamson's imagined husbandry is explicitly yoked to the causes and effects of war, a connection he will reanimate in his post-war writing.

Waste, the inappropriate or underemployment of matter, does not simply starve the land – it pollutes it. The vision of a post-war metropolitan waterfront teeming with fish is more than advocacy of the world view of *Salar the Salmon* (1935) against the planners. It resonates forward and backwards in time with the world-historical dimensions of Williamson's political- or managed-ecology. It lies behind the reimagining of *Salar* as Maddison's book *The Blind Trout*: 'we are passing through an age of industrial darkness; but beyond it, I can see salmon leaping again in both the Rhine and its ancient tributary Thames' (*TPG*, 145: a clear redeployment of the language of the 'epigraph').

And, via this revision, it recalls the dedication of the 1930s redaction of the 1920s *Flax of Dream* tetralogy which salutes 'the great man across the Rhine' – a phrase which has unaccountably acquired the status of being 'the main evidence against' Williamson.[15]

What I have called Williamson's political-ecology is the author's restless pursuit of both comprehension and direction of the interconnectedness of biological and cultural processes. It remains to explore ecology as an aspect of his imagination. As the function of the Norfolk farm – a site of struggle between mentalities and ideologies – is developed in response to the Second World War, Williamson's analogical composition of themes breaks down under the burden of history into something at once richer and more testing than the idea of a 'policy of reconstruction' which resurfaced throughout Williamson's career.

The 'epigraph' of *The Story of a Norfolk Farm* is dated 13 June 1940. The sense in which this really is an inscription, not a last chapter, and that the real significance lies in that date, purportedly the date of the last thing written, is suggested by the fact that this was the day before Williamson's 'arrest … under the Defence Act, Section 18 B' on Friday 14 June.[16] The book ends then on the eve of its author being declared (at his, not the authorities', estimation) an enemy of the country he is working to renew. War brings not a recognition of his contribution to the renewal of fertility, but betrayal. The details of Williamson's arrest and questioning, and the issue of the length of his detention in the police station at Wells, remain unclear.[17] No less straightforward, but more readily analysed, is the registration of this event in Williamson's subsequent fiction. A sequel to *The Story of a Norfolk Farm* was incorporated into *A Chronicle* but earlier rewritten as *The Phasian Bird* (1948).

In *The Story of a Norfolk Farm*, the business of husbanding the land back into productivity is a vehicle for speculations about the productivity of the nation and of the artist. But in subsequent versions of the Norfolk experience, the pattern or ratio of analogy is inverted, so that the conduct and issues of the Second World War are played out as problems of farm management, and the question of political and moral leadership is more explicitly dramatised as a struggle for mastery in which the authority or tyranny of the guardian of 230 acres is tested and resisted by family, farmhands, friends, the military and the state.

The Phasian Bird is on the surface an animal fable, but it has a human protagonist through whom Williamson reassembles the symbolic components of

[15] Williamson, *Henry Williamson*, p. 199.

[16] Williamson, *Henry Williamson*, p. 233.

[17] A. W. B. Simpson, *In the Highest Degree Odious: Detention Without Trial in Wartime Britain* (Oxford, 1992), pp. 214–16.

his myth of the decline and regeneration of fertility into a study in victimisation. In Wilbo, a painter and farmer, a fantasy of persecution is set in train, in which both the individual and the land are victims. Protesting that 'I wanted to help create a Greater Britain', he is arrested and detained for 'weeks and months and years'.[18] In a new version of the micro/macro ratio, Williamson's arrest is magnified into Mosley's imprisonment. With his release, the War Agricultural Executive Committee, which has ruined the fertility of his farm by cropping corn without rotation, dispossesses him for not having farmed 'in accordance with the rules and usages of good husbandry'.[19] Wilbo, crushed between MI5 and the WAEC, is subsequently shot and killed by servicemen poaching game.

But it is only in the further recomposition of these themes in *A Chronicle* that the complexity of Williamson's discourse of decadence and rebirth becomes fully apparent. In the three volumes fictionalising the Norfolk years, but also across the sequence as a whole, which opens in the 1890s and ends with a post-war deluge (the North Devon floods of 15 August 1952), the vectors of analogical symbol-making divide the writing against the simplifications of its ethical and political programme. This is most palpable in the way Williamson's overarching fixation on legacies of the Great War becomes entangled with themes of waste and fertility.

For Williamson, the truth about the Great War – and this leads us directly to his imaginative identification with, and wilful misconstruction of, interwar authoritarian ideologies, ideologues and states – lay in the Christmas truce of 1914. Of his many versions of that fabled revolt against adversarialness, the following is taken from *Goodbye West Country*, completed in 1937:

> The usual talk of War in the papers; the usual semi-fearful antagonism to the new Germany. What can one do? Three weeks after my eighteenth birthday I was talking to Germans with beards and khaki-covered *pickelhauben*, and smoking new china gift-pipes glazed with the Crown Prince's portrait in colour, in a turnip field amidst dead cows, English and German corpses frozen stiff. The new world, for me, was germinated from that fraternization. Adolf Hitler was one of those 'opposite numbers' in long field-grey coats. His apprenticeship in the hell of war, his period of agonized meditation, of self-doubt about his nervous power to plant the idea of a new world in men's minds, broke into concrete ideals, and action, five years later. We in England are still pre-war minded.[20]

[18] H. Williamson, *The Phasian Bird* (1948), pp. 225, 248.

[19] Williamson, *The Phasian Bird*, pp. 250, 254.

[20] H. Williamson, *Goodbye West Country* (1938), p. 9.

Down to the late 1960s Williamson was still insisting on understanding the war against Nazi Germany in terms of his repeatedly elaborated myths of the First World War. We can read *The Story of a Norfolk Farm* as his assumption of the role of veteran-saviour, planting new ideas, germinating a new England. Describing Christmas Eve 1937, he recalls how, twenty-three years earlier, 'Hope sank into the mud again' for four years, then was forgotten in a peace 'like pre-war again'; but is now rising again with the morning star he watches across his fields (*SNF*, 225).

The book's other reminder of 'years whose Truth seems incommunicable' (*SNF*, 225) is the farm's malkin or scarecrow, a figure too realistic for its function of watching over the process of germination.

> The legs were rounded, as though swelled. It looked like something that had died in that position, in a warning attitude, its arms spread out, its shattered head thrown back … a reminder of things that had been forgotten, and were likely to happen again, unless men began too think very differently (*SNF*, 270–1).

In Williamson's own copy the frontispiece photo of the malkin is given an autograph speech-bubble: 'I died in Flanders – I am the unknown soldier – I died for ideals which were not of the market place – my voice is gone, but not my ghost'.[21]

A Chronicle is in one sense the story of a writer's forty-year struggle to ready himself to speak for the unknown soldier. But it is also, clearly, the story the soldier of Christmas 1914 would tell, a story of speaking the truth to indifferent ears, and of suffering in the quest to remake the world in the light of that truth. The Norfolk farm figures as the final attempt at a kind of political action before defeat leads to regrouping of the 'creative will' and readiness for a summative act of writing (*ASW*, 85). As a unit of the home front the farm is the scene of a redefinition of war aims, 'to make agriculture an honoured national industry' (*LBS*, 73). Fighting squalor and neglect is a matter of morale, inspiring a 'new spirit': but if Maddison is a leader in this war of production, 'the Potentially Keenest Agricultural Mind in England' as a would-be disciple dubs him (*ASW*, 83), he is also at once tyrant and unacknowledged prophet.

Observing one of his labourers 'flying' ewes, Maddison meditates on the intersection of the life cycle of the blow fly and the indisciplined management of waste on the farm. Rats killed in the corn barn are flung onto the home field, instead of being buried in the dungsteads, and lie alongside the 'poultry casualties' his wife neglects to inter, and which are soon 'reduced to feathered skeletons by maggots of the Bluebottle and Spanish Green Fly':

---

21 Williamson, *Henry Williamson*, p. 237.

Phillip watched Matt, with the back of his stubby fingers, flipping away scores of maggots, each with a red speck showing through an ivory, semi-transparent body. The maggots, falling to the trodden ground, began to hurry away to shelter.

'They won't trouble yar no more, master.'

'Each one of those will pupate and hatch into a blowfly, Matt. They ought to be killed. It's best to dose them with disinfectant, surely?'

'I do,' he replied. 'They won't come to narthin'. That old Spanish bottle-fly is the worst. They always did swarm on these meadows.'

'They also swarm on the rats your terrier kills, which you throw out in the yards, Matt. Those rats are real fifth columnists. So are our dead hens. They're symbols of decadence. They *are* the war! Look at all these maggots running away!' He forced himself to speak quietly. 'All will have wings shortly.'

'Yar birds will pick 'em up, master.'

'Matt! Do you ever listen to anything I say?'

'Too often, master.'

Matt wiped his sweaty brow with a dirty old fragment of what looked like a shirt.

'Matt, *please* listen! If you'd been on the Somme battlefield and seen the swollen faces of the dead men – hundreds lying all together – or a badly wounded man's face, come to that, you'd have seen his face masked by black flies. And if you'd passed by two days later you'd have seen the face all liquid wriggling pale.'

'This harn't a battlefield.'

'It *is* a battlefield! This is part of the war!'

Phillip trod on the maggots he could see, but more legions of the dispossessed were swarming into the cover of grass. 'Our opposed views *are* the war!' (*LBS*, 145–6).

That Matt is based on Jimmy, who makes the scarecrow in *The Story of a Norfolk Farm*, underlines the ironies that enlarge this studied exercise in what Williamson terms writing 'the microcosmic-macrocosmic events of my time and age' (*LBS*, 73). Maddison, the suspected fifth-columnist, identifies the real enemies within as a decadent mentality and a parasitical economy. The farm is a battlefield in total war twice over, as the site of the disciplining of productive forces, and as the arena for a contest of the ideologies which Williamson distinguishes as the pre-war and the Truth. But the somatic casualties of the war, which find their way into the allegorical lecture as an illustration of an undesired ecological system, are revenants like the ghostly presence of the scarecrow in the sprouted barley. They mark the eruption of the traumatic into the diagrammatic patterns of Williamson's programme of ideological reconstruction.

It might be useful at this point to correlate Williamson's political intelligence with his determination, against all the odds, to read a redemptive trajectory into twentieth-century history, a trajectory which is at once the product and exemplification of a creative will conceived in defiance of a will to destruction. With this in mind, we can begin to see how the rhetorical excess which brings human corpses onto the metaphorical battlefield of the Norfolk farm could be understood as a manifestation of the unconscious of Williamson's writing, which cannot be kept at bay by the effort to husband history, society and culture into something analogous to a model farm. The rage for order in the farmer, a tyrannical insistence on tidiness, is matched by a determination to subdue experience to schematic fables. This risks the accusation of coming at Williamson from the wrong end, for his writing is also properly to be described in terms of both its particularity and its prolix, artless indiscipline. But such an approach is warranted because it reveals how the writer's perpetual revision and reordering of his themes binds him in imaginative affiliation to some of the primary cultural symbols of twentieth-century fascist politics.

The link between fertility and war's waste is not original to Williamson, being both proverbial and a recurrent trope in Great War writing. But where in Hardy and Owen the recycling of human organic matter is the vehicle of fatalism or irony, in Williamson those overtones are often at odds with the practicalities and ethics of good husbandry. Surveying a handful of examples from across the second half of the sequence, it is evident how complexes of imagery function in excess of either the local argument of the fiction, or its overall plan. Thus a young Phillip Maddison rewrites Rupert Brooke in contemplating the enrichment of Flanders by The Fallen:

> Westy said, 'the slums have died in Flanders'. Donkin is dead and millions like him. They arise as flowers from an enriched soil that is forever England and Germany; but also very good manurial dressing for Flemish and French farmers. Were not the bones of Waterloo dug up and collected and ground into phosphates for the wheatfields of East Anglia, only five years after Napoleon was finally defeated?[22]

When we met these ground bones before, they were a contested resource (another justification of autarky); here they correct an immature mind in its too sudden leap from a pacificist idealism to a sardonic registration of civilian indifference expressed in a kind of war-profiteering. Later, however, in his

---

[22] H. Williamson, *A Test to Destruction* (*A Chronicle of Ancient Sunlight*, vol. 8) (1960; London, 1964), p. 352.

cousin Willie's article about war cemeteries (a reuse of material from *The Wet Flanders Plain* of 1929), signs of such fertility are figured as the designs of a 'spirit of vengeance', not an echo of fraternisation:

> The bones of the slain … may lie side-by-side at peace in war-time; but in peace-time they are religiously separated into nations again, each to its place: the British to the beautiful cemeteries, fragrant with green turf and flowers one sees in cottage gardens, 'that are forever England', and the others to – the Labyrinth.[23]

This perspective is recalled in Phillip's observation, at the beginning of the Second World War, that Germany is a 'great nation on a scalt soil' (*ASW*, 38), an ecological apology for Hitler's expansionism. The terms of these transactions between the quick and the earth just will not stay in place. This is not just because the times are changing (and of course it is implicit in Williamson's historiography that they aren't, or at least not yet). It is because their implications breach the confines of the geo-political landscape into which Williamson would order them.

In the post-1945 phase of the sequence, the maggot-infested corpses summoned to the Norfolk farm in Maddison's upbraiding of Matt's superstitious fatalism are revived and, indeed, doctored by the same ecological cycle that had represented dullness in the unending war of ideas:

> Flies were merciful on the summer battlefields. The Yorkshireman with arm blown off in wide no-man's land between Croiselles and Bullecourt in the Hindenburg Line. Wound cleaned of suppurating flesh by maggots.[24]

Worn-out by his farmer's war Maddison is crossing Salisbury Plain in his imagination (retracing the journey by car with which *The Story of a Norfolk Farm* opens) when it turns into the Somme country:

> Machine gun nests on the landsherds of those wider downs above the Somme, Moonrakers and Back-to-Fores – Wiltshire Regiment and Dorsets – mucking the aerated wheat-fields of Piccardy. Six-foot sub-soiling, all free – Somme cornlands in heart for a century, the composted lost heart of England (*GOW*, 93).

---

[23] H. Williamson, *The Innocent Moon* (*A Chronicle of Ancient Sunlight*, vol. 8) (1961; 1965), pp. 66–7. The Labyrinth is a former German redoubt, described by Willie as acres of black crosses 'planted in the bare chalk', a burnt landscape of war.

[24] H. Williamson, *The Gale of the World* (*A Chronicle of Ancient Sunlight*, vol. 15) (1969; 1999), p. 91. Hereafter *GOW*.

The writer Maddison's failure to speak for his generation has shifted the meaning of this cluster of images yet again: comrades are just extra-territorial mulch, the symbolic cross-territorial fraternisation of 1914 contradicted now not just by Versailles but by the Nuremberg Trials too.

Roger Griffin has defined ideal-type or generic fascism as a 'political ideology whose mythic core … is a palingenetic form of populist ultranationalism'.[25] Myths of regeneration are not confined to fascism. But there are clear correlations between the economic, historical and patriotic framework of Williamson's palingenetic vision of England, and the myth-making and the culture of the 'generation of 1914' in which fascism found adherents. It is important to register not only Williamson's errors of judgement, but also the congruence between elements in the working up of his myth of regeneration and symbols and values circulating more widely in interwar and post-war culture. Williamson's constellation of motifs from husbandry, authoritarian politics of renewal, and war is perverse in its appeals to logic. In the form this takes in *A Chronicle*, it is as undisciplined and immature as is the juxtaposition of empathy and egotism in the narrative's voice and structure. But it is evidence of the imaginative resonance of representations of British agriculture which emerged in the interwar period. As is the case with post-war discourses of declinism – Britain's loss of great power status, economic competitiveness, social and moral cohesion – the motifs and narrative forms through which heterogeneous data is mediated as knowledge readily lend themselves to further acts of composition into potent symbols. The ruin and regeneration of Williamson's Norfolk farm, microcosm of the battlegrounds of two world wars, is the metaphorical ground of a redemptive fantasy of European politics. The only licence for these projections is Williamson's imagination. This imagination is, in a sense, exemplary, in the way it draws out again the linkage between land, nation and war to attempt the transformation of a story of personal defeat into a political myth.

---

[25] R. Griffin, *The Nature of Fascism* (1991), p. 26. Palingenesis: 'A new birth; a re-creation; a regeneration; a continued existence in different manner or form': *Webster's Revised Unabridged Dictionary* (1913).

7 Drama in the villages: three pioneers*

Mick Wallis

BETWEEN the wars amateur theatre was perceived and practised as a privileged means to regenerate village life; and to deliver adult education in rural areas. This terrain will be explored by tracing three interlocking narratives. One of them, the career of Mary Kelly, intersects the other two: the doings of the Drama Committee of Gloucestershire Rural Community Council and the adult education work of F. G. and D. Irene Thomas.

MARY KELLY (1888–1951): CONTINUITY AND SCHISM

When, in 1919, Mary Kelly extended the modest theatricals of Kelly House to include tenant-farmer and labouring families in and around the Devon village of Kelly, she caught a moment. Not only did the Kelly Players and their barn theatre quickly become famous, but many villages followed their example or made similar beginnings. Inundated with requests for advice, Mary founded the Village Drama Society (VDS) later that year.

Mary's initiative – as her sister's, in founding the Kelly Women's Institute – was part of a continuum and of a schism. It drew on the spirit of service that her father, squire and elsewhere parson, himself inherited from the movement since the 1850s to reform church and squirearchy. But it was also the result of the Great War, when, in the course of voluntary work, Mary's perspective was both broadened and democratised.[1]

Village theatre and, less extensively, historical pageantry, became Mary's life work. In her book *Village Theatre* (1939) she figures her own work as part of an international folk-theatre movement, and drama as the key means to recover an alienated potential in British culture. Through generations, country people have lost their vital expressivity. Village theatre can help restore it, and thereby enrich the national culture. Much of the book tells the history of the agricultural labourer, exploited and silenced by her own class. Her great-great-grandfather had imprisoned supposed wrongdoers in the windowless and

---

* Primary research for the second section of this chapter was supported by an AHRC Research Grant and that for sections 1 and 3 by AHRB Research Leave and a travel grant from the Society for Theatre Research.

[1] For a full account, see M. Wallis, 'Unlocking the secret soul: Mary Kelly, pioneer of village theatre' *New Theatre Quarterly* 64 (2000): 347–58.

airless cellar of Kelly House. Even her father's generation were touched by the assumption of inbred superiority. The book also tells a history of theatre from a rural perspective. Contemporary vestiges of folk ritual and drama point to the origins of all theatre in rural life and vegetative religion. But, by late medieval times, urban centres had absorbed theatrical culture, leaving country-folk bereft. Yet, due to their contact with the earth and natural rhythms, country people retain an ability to immerse themselves in otherness, including theatrical parts. Town-bred actors who witness their playing are stunned by their direct honesty. Community and religion are key principles for Kelly. Village theatre must belong to the community. And villagers retain a strong sense of religion, more through daily contact with the mysteries and forces of nature than through organised Christianity. This gives their playing a natural gravity, a sense of ceremony shared by the village audience.

Two forces had run in counter directions since Victorian times. On one hand, print culture, elementary rote-learning and urban culture threatened finally to extinguish truly rural culture. On the other, the 'benevolent autocracy' of the late Victorian village had been 'a slow revolution' that restored neighbourliness, community and the self-expression of the labouring class.

The book is founded, then, on a sense of urgency: this is a last chance, though a magnificent one. Kelly was aware of the contradiction at this cusp: her class had ushered in reform but was fast losing hegemonic control. Convinced that other agencies must take the lead, she actively supported efforts by the NCSS to rationalise and promote provision for amateur theatre-making.

The VDS grew rapidly, first through promotion in church newspapers, and then through the infrastructures of the WI movement. Mary set up office in Camberwell, London in 1926; and in 1932 the VDS was absorbed into the British Drama League – also founded in 1919 – as its Village Drama Section. By 1939 over 600 villages had affiliated. The VDS established a lending play library and costume store; organised 'schools' to train amateurs, especially producers (now 'directors'); promoted the writing of village plays. And Mary travelled the country to train, give advice, adjudicate competitions, and curate events. The leading proponent of amateur theatre in Britain, the BDL proselytised, curated training events, inaugurated an annual Community Drama Festival with local heats in 1926, and published the journal *Drama*. County reports on village theatre appeared annually, and a special 'Village Drama Double Issue' appeared in February 1932. Caitlin Adams records that VDS's merger with the BDL was urged by the NCSS and Carnegie United Kingdom Trust (CUKT); that Kelly found the relationship difficult; and that the BDL was 'very slow to meet local needs'.[2]

---

[2] C. Adams, 'The Idea of the Village in Interwar England' (unpublished PhD thesis, University of Michigan, 2001), chapter 3.

If there is a narrative to be traced of the VDS, Mary's own professional career points to a broader narrative of rural arts provision and education. She begins as a gentrywoman exercising class patronage; works in the 1920s and 30s for occasional stipends in the nexus of state, charitable and other independent agencies increasingly brought into collaboration by the NCSS; and ends in the 1940s as a wage-earner in a publicly funded institution.

GLOUCESTERSHIRE RURAL COMMUNITY COUNCIL DRAMA COMMITTEE – FACILITATION VERSUS BUREAUCRATISATION

Oxfordshire, Gloucestershire and Kent were pioneers of the Rural Community Council movement. Gloucestershire RCC was formed in 1924, with Sir Francis Hyett, chairman of Quarter Sessions, its chair. A drama committee (hereafter GRDC) was established in 1928, with Hyett's daughter Lucy as secretary. The inaugural membership determined that all village drama societies be invited to elect one representative; the committee affiliate to the VDS; and 'classes and courses in dramatic work' be organised for the winter season. There would be a lecture course on production; and a drama festival in spring 1929. A calendar of village productions would be compiled and distributed; and a list of books on drama in the county library be issued. In correspondence, the Village Drama Society offered 'any assistance'. In 1931 the committee were satisfied that they were adhering to the lines laid down at the national RCC conference at Cambridge.[3]

In 1927 CUKT had placed funds with the NCSS to be administered by it and the National Federation of Women's Institutes through a Joint Committee for Music and Drama in the Villages. Grants were to support activities encouraging local leadership and the establishment of independent drama societies. These means might include single lectures or courses, short schools, advisory visits, bursaries to drama schools run for example by the British Drama League, and festivals. Organisation of the work was to be at county level, based wherever possible in the RCC. County committees increasingly formed panels of music and drama advisers working either voluntarily or for a small fee. In 1935 a welcome to the expansion of 'experimental work' was signalled. By 1939 nearly every county in England had some kind of rural drama committee. George Taylor remarks that the 'County Drama Movement' 'did

---

3 Gloucestershire Rural County Council Drama Committee minutes 1928–45, Gloucestershire Record Office D3168. Unless otherwise specified, references in this section are to this source, here quoting GRDC, 1 Jun and 28 Jul 1928.

much to raise standards of drama to the level at which it could be taken seriously by the educational authorities'.[4]

At Gloucestershire as elsewhere, dramatic activity was seen as a direct means to redress social decline in the village. The committee was principally concerned with two interlocking activities – competitive festivals and education. The festivals were a celebration of village life and culture, taken to a principal venue in the county or other large town. They also stimulated the desire for education in dramatic arts. As was argued at national government level (see below), this was itself seen as a means to stimulate a more general educational interest and to nurture the capacity for sympathy – co-requisites for democratic participation.

A key contemporary theme linking both education and festivals was bureaucratisation. As Nora Ratcliffe put it in her own account of village theatre, *Rude Mechanicals* (1938), the interwar years saw a 'craze for organization':

> Whether we like it or not, we live in an age of centralisation and control. The most spontaneous of nature's expressions are regimented, improved upon, exploited … a group of innocent villagers, who decide it would be good fun to act a play, find that all unwittingly they have become part of something known as the VILLAGE DRAMA MOVEMENT'.[5]

The record in Gloucestershire exemplifies that, nationally, rural regeneration by means of amateur drama involved mediation between facilitation and bureaucratisation.

Entries to the 1929 festival could be made under three junior and eight senior classes. Seven of these were for twenty-minute scenes, for instance by girls' or boys' organisations, or mixed teams from village schools; or by senior teams acting fewer or more than six parts. Presumably to accommodate the WI, there was a class for women players only; and in line with a national drive, another for new plays by villagers. A planned class for mime persisted, but one for recitation was dropped. Designs for décor and costume were given a class, as were model stages applied to village halls. All performances had to be dressed, but makeup was optional. From 1932, marks were given for acting (25 per cent), general production (50 per cent) and choice of play (25 per cent). In 1933 class divisions were discarded. In 1932 an official time-keeper was appointed – teams faced 'penalty of loss of marks' for overrunning.

The planned 1929 festival was soon being minuted as a Countryside Drama 'Competition'– until a specific minute corrected this silent drift. The *Cheltenham*

---

4 National Council of Social Service, *The Music and Drama Fund for Villages* (1935); M. Kelly, *Village Theatre* (1939), p. 153; G. Taylor, *History of the Amateur Theatre* (1976), p. 127.

5 N. Ratcliff, *Rude Mechanicals: A Review of Village Drama* (1938), pp. 14–15.

Chronicle and Gloucestershire Echo duly heads its press report, 'Drama in the Villages / Non-competitive festival at Cheltenham'. The threat that competition posed to festive spirit became an issue nationally.

The need to accommodate a number of plays in quick succession had occasionally bizarre outcomes. For the 1935 final:

> As the scene required was in every case but one (*Richard III*) a room, it was decided that a box set should be erected to serve for every team. Mrs Walker offered to lend her own set together with a fireplace and carpets. The offer was gratefully accepted.[6]

Campden WI was presumably not doing one of the battle scenes.

The RCCs were not alone in mounting drama festivals. The 1932 festival, at Cheltenham, was institutionally reframed, according to a national agreement made between the NCSS and the BDL, whereby the BDL would adjudicate a one-day county festival as part of its own national festival, provided the RCC concerned was affiliated to the League. This duplication of competition infrastructures resulted in various knots and conundrums. The fact that county-level scheduling had to wait on the BDL caused frustration, for instance. And in October 1934 the committee questioned the rubric that only one team could be put forward to the BDL's national festival from their own, even though another team belonging independently to the BDL might also be good enough to qualify. The BDL ruled that such a team must appear at some other festival if they desired to be sent on, but might enter the RCC festival on a non-competitive basis.

In 1935 Miss Hyett moved for disassociation from the BDL festival, because (1) 'village' plays were neither encouraged nor appreciated by the BDL; (2) publication of marks made the festival competitive; (3) the Music and Drama Fund had withdrawn support. Arguments for continuation were that (1) the door should not be shut on further progress; (2) marks were valuable indicators for improvement; (3) 'Dramatic Art was one and it was not in the interest of the villages to segregate "Village Drama" from the National Amateur Dramatic Movement.' Hyett's proposal was eventually defeated, but in the meantime prompted approval at the national Village Drama Conference of Gloucestershire's proposal, 'That unusual emphasis is being placed on sophistication in adjudication and that at least an equal place be given to sincerity.'[7]

The committee agreed to co-operate closely with the WI Drama Committee on both festivals and drama advisers. But potential clashes persisted.

---

[6] GRDC, 4 Mar 1935.

[7] GRDC, 3 Jun 1935 – 4 Nov 1935, *passim*.

In March 1939 the County Federation of WIs was planning a drama festival for Institute members only at five centres in 1940. The committee was assured that this would not injure the RCC festival, as it was for elementary teams, who might indeed graduate to the county festival. Asked in February 1940 by Miss Dawson if she could act in both the Painswick Players and the WI team for the county festival, the committee ruled that she should stand down from one, advising her that their preference was always for mixed teams.

Whether officially framed as competitive or festive, art or education, the festivals generated a discourse and practice of improvement as much as communal celebration. The contribution and status of the adjudicator played an important part in this. Both preliminary heats held at around five regional centres and the final were externally adjudicated.

On the recommendation of the VDS, noted Shakespearean actor and producer John H. Moss was appointed adjudicator for 1929. His emphases were sincerity, propriety and technical skill. Moss regretted that women had played so many men's parts in the Shakespeare scenes; and that Bourton-on-the-Water had chosen *King Lear*, Shakespeare's 'worst and weakest play'. In the *Merchant of Venice* scenes, he criticised Shylock's very mobile accent and the historical inaccuracy of Portia's costume – one detail had been red rather than gold. However, 'the exits were some of the best he had ever seen'. And while in *Banns* 'a real, human parson was impersonated', rather than 'the stage specimen' regularly given, Mrs Seeley's team's *Loaded* 'went with an ease and slickness' that suggested this was not the first performance it should have been. Moss generously returned his fee.[8]

Care was taken to ensure that adjudication was constructive. In 1932 it was recommended that 'kind and instructive criticism' be given to those not selected for the final, adjudicators negotiating the most sensitive arrangement for feedback. In 1935 entrants were divided into categories A and B, to give less-experienced teams encouragement. Marks were awarded by the same criteria but according to a different standard, and communicated privately. The categories were dropped in June 1939, adjudicators being advised of novice actors so they might be more lenient.[9]

Nonetheless, the adjudicator's basic status as an outsider sitting in judgement sometimes raised hackles. One issue was impartiality. In 1934 Mrs Seeley was accused of corrupting the adjudicator by offering them hospitality, while also entering teams to the competition. The producers conference agreed that 'If anyone's sportsmanship, integrity and devotion to the cause for its own sake was unquestioned it was our chairman.' The conference was held at her residence. When, in January 1937, Mrs Peters reported that the Newent

8 GRDC, 19 Oct 1928; 15 Apr 1929; *Cheltenham Chronicle*, n.d.
9 Quoting GRDC, 23 Mar 1932.

Players objected to her entertaining the adjudicator; it was resolved that they be invited to do the same.[10]

Another issue was value judgements and manner. The committee regretted 'unfair criticism' of Kelly and Moss in 1931. In 1936 a complaint was sent to the BDL that their adjudicator had 'seriously failed to give constructive criticism and that his comments were valueless to the teams'. In 1938 the secretary wrote personally to Mary Kelly that she had been accused by some team leaders of causing 'great distress' to certain players when adjudicating 1937 preliminaries. But the committee resolved to discourage further correspondence from teams to Dora Salaman, challenging her judgements. Salaman was soon criticising a fall in standards. Considering a fall in entries, the chairman enquired whether members were 'doing their best to arouse interest and encourage entries or were merely sitting in judgement on such as happened to come in'. Several members countered that Mary Kelly had caused offence last year. But 'it was not fair to put all the blame on Miss Kelly. It seemed that to receive criticism cheerfully and gracefully was still a difficulty with many teams.'[11]

Adjudication reflected judgement on the committee's educational provision as much as on the teams. After adjudicating the 1932 and 1933 finals, Mrs Penelope Wheeler – selected under the new arrangements by the BDL – advised that, while a few teams were of national standard, the rest were well below average. Thus prompted, the chairman, Mrs Seeley, inaugurated the regular producers' conference at her home, Boddington Manor, in May 1933; attendance was over twenty in April 1935.

The first course for producers and players had run on four Saturday afternoons in 1928. Topics covered were: management and organisation; choosing the play; the theory of 'make believe'; stage construction; casting; 'assisting' versus 'directing'; speech and gesture; getting 'inside' a part; polish and confidence; costume and makeup; décor and lighting; Shakespeare; educating your company. In July 1931 seven mostly unpaid drama advisers were appointed, and in July 1932 two paid professional advisers subsidised by the Joint Committee. Each village hall could pay for two visits. Any amateur advisers still requested by villages could continue if they wished. In both 1934 and 1936 the committee noted that most of the teams participating in courses had gained much and had entered festivals, in most cases regularly.[12]

An early high-profile educational initiative was the nine-day Cirencester Drama School in 1931. The VDS played a key role in its design and delivery – Mary Kelly was by now adept in their organisation – and the Gloucestershire Federation of Women's Institutes played an active part. Specific recruitment

---

[10] Quoting GRDC, 10 Jul 1934.

[11] Quoting GRDC, 23 Mar 1931, 16 Mar 1936, 10 Feb 1938.

[12] Quoting GRDC, 30 Jun 1928.

approaches were made to all branches of the WEA and nine individuals, all women. The WIs were encouraged to pay for one student each.

Finding venues for both preliminaries and finals was an abiding problem. For the first two festivals Madame Irving gave her Little Theatre, making 'such stage properties as chairs, tables, couch' – and in 1930 dressing tents – available to the teams, and providing teas. The basic requirement was a hall with proscenium, scenery and blackout. Size, cost, acoustics, convenience and availability were also factors. In 1932 the number of preliminaries had to be curtailed for lack of suitable halls. In 1936 the final was confined to two evenings, open only to companies and supporters. This retraction into the immediate drama community counters a continuing thrust for propaganda and dissemination, when for instance a selection from the 1931 Festival was displayed in a Drama Enclosure at the County Exhibition and Fete.[13]

From 1937 the final was held at Painswick Institute, organised by the Painswick Players under Miss Hyett. That year, the Players had built a new proscenium and begun acquiring modern electric lighting. The trustees allowed free use of the Institute, in exchange for access to the lights; the WI – founded by Lucy's sister – lent its piano free. The Players were formed by Lucy in 1923, following her success with three friends in mounting scenes from *As You Like It* and Congreve's *Way of the World* outdoors the previous summer, to aid a district nursing association. Noted productions in the grounds of the family home, Painswick Hall, followed. The progress from a core of genteel amateurs to a company including villagers is typical for the period – though at Painswick as elsewhere, it is not yet clear how many of the villagers involved were 'locals' and how many middle-class incomers – 'residents'. Lucy Hyett directed until her death in 1961.[14]

ADULT EDUCATION IN RURAL DEVON: CONFLICTING IMPERATIVES

Three government reports argued for the importance of drama as a mode of recruitment to, and delivery and assessment of, adult education – and its particular pertinence to the rural context. Producing *Adult Education in Rural Areas* (1922) and *Drama in Adult Education* (1926), the Board of Education's Adult Education Committee developed the perspective of the *Final Report* (1919) of the Ministry of Reconstruction Adult Education Committee.[15] There were 'good grounds for hoping that the drama is sufficiently deep-rooted in

[13] Quoting GRDC, 11 Mar 1929.

[14] *Painswick Players* album, Gloucestershire Record Office D2161.

[15] Ministry of Reconstruction Adult Education Committee, *Final Report*, Cmd 321 (1919).

the instincts of the people to ensure that the recent dramatic revival … will substantially enrich our national life'.[16]

There was a wealth of initiative by independent benefactors and young rural touring companies – like the Arts League of Service – to build on. And if drama had the virtue of instilling human sympathy, it had particular pertinence in the rural context, since 'the necessity in adult education of proceeding from the informal to the formal applies with particular force to the countryman'.[17] Pioneer educators were needed, working in the context of local and national collaboration between agencies.

Waller notes the 'rare optimism' of the 1919 *Final Report*, the persistence in it of the 'dominant liberal and radical spirit' that had developed in England especially since 1873. Waller contrasts this residual belief that only 'wise engineering' was needed to realise a vast and enlightened national potential, with general post-war cynicism.[18] We see below how some pioneers carried the liberal torch of progress into the 1930s.

The 1918 Education Act made each county authority responsible to the Board for making public education available to all capable adults, typically through evening classes. The close association of universities and WEA districts as 'Responsible Bodies' for the delivery of Board-funded classes was formalised in 1924. While grant-aid was principally reserved for the three-year tutorial class, there was some provision for one-year, terminal and shorter classes, to stimulate the growth of extension work and lead on to the tutorial class. One important datum for debate about rural adult education was the notion of 'the university standard'. The fundamental principle of the WEA was that university-level education should be available to working-class people. To offer them a lesser goal was to deny this.[19] In this section, we witness a tension between two progressive principles: the imperative to open up rural areas through 'pioneer' work and the 'university standard'.

From 1927 until 1935, CUKT funded the WEA nationally to develop rural adult education. F. G. Thomas was appointed tutor organiser to the newly established Devon Extension Scheme (DES) under this initiative in 1927.

---

[16] Adult Education Committee, *The Drama in Adult Education*, Adult Education Committee Paper 6 (1926), para. 50.

[17] Adult Education Committee, *The Development of Adult Education in Rural Areas*, Adult Education Committee Paper 3 (1922), p. 36.

[18] R. D. Waller, '1919–1956: the years between', in *A Design for Democracy* [abridgment of *1919 Report*] (1956), pp. 15–45.

[19] HMSO, *The Education Act* (1918), 8 and 9, c.39, section 1; HMSO, Board of Education, *Grant regulations, No. 33, Adult education regulations*, 1924; T. Kelly, *A History of Adult Education*, 5th edn (Liverpool, 1992), p. 273; W. E. Styler, *A Bibliographical Guide to Adult Education in Rural Areas, 1918–1972* (1972), *passim*.

The principal institutions involved in the DES were University College of the South West (UCSW), Devon County Council, WEA (South-Western District) and Dartington Hall.[20] Between the wars, power and responsibilities with respect to adult education provision shifted between WEA, county authorities and universities. In Devon the course of this institutional drama was influenced by Leonard Elmhirst, who, with his wife Dorothy and her inheritance, founded Dartington in 1926.[21]

Thomas and Leonard Elmhirst both insisted that, since adult education had evolved in urban contexts, its practices needed revision for rural ones. This was for two principal reasons. First, market conditions differed. In a town, a subject-specific class could be advertised and might recruit a small percentage of the population – enough to make it viable. This was not an option in a village. Challenging the WI definition of a village as a settlement of less than 4,000, Thomas characterised those with more than a thousand people as 'town villages'. Where the population was under 500, conventional delivery of the terminal course was entirely unworkable: the whole village must be interested. Second, villagers think differently from urbanites: they 'ruminate' rather than think consecutively. In 1928 Thomas commented: 'this does not imply either standards or judgement; but it does imply methods, and what those methods will be we cannot say yet.'[22]

Thomas experimented with film and with innovatory science classes, and participated in a national radio-listening scheme. But most significant is his work with his wife, D. Irene Thomas, using drama. Play-making acted as the necessary focus to recruit numbers, and as a platform for other educational content; it also provided a community focus around which a village might regenerate. In a two-part article published in 1931, the Thomases reflected on their developing practice. Drama appealed to the countryman's latent sense of symbolism and his dislike of the meretricious; provided a willed and controlled activity, especially for the young; demanded patience and mutual respect. Such community effort was necessary for any pioneer educational work. Drama not

[20] Rural extension work was also funded by the Cassel Trust. By 1931 seven resident tutors had been appointed nationally. 'Organising tutor', 'tutor organiser' and 'resident tutor' are synonymous.

[21] For a full account, see M. Wallis, 'Drama and the new learning for villages: F. G. and D. Irene Thomas, Dartington and rural adult education, 1927–33' (forthcoming).

[22] References hereafter identified as 'DHTA' are to materials held at the Dartington Hall Trust Archive under LKE Education 1–9. Unless otherwise specified, references in this section are to this source, here quoting F. G. Thomas, 'Notes on the village centres', in *First Annual Report* (1928). Quotations are by kind permission of the Trustees.

only involved contact with good works but also required understanding and sympathy with human nature and motive.[23]

Of the twenty-five villages in the scheme by 1929, Liverton was central to the Thomases' drama work. For the 1927–8 session D. Irene taught a terminal class on 'Merrie England' and offered a production of scenes from *A Midsummer Night's Dream* as a supplementary activity. It was eventually performed on Midsummer Eve 1928 in a copse close to the village, as were productions in succeeding years. In 1928–9 the play itself – Beaumont's *The Knight of the Burning Pestle* – became the central activity of the thirty-week terminal course. Men disinclined to act worked from contemporary sources to convert the village hall stage into an Elizabethan one. This collapsible set then toured to other village halls. A group of women, again working from contemporary sources, designed and made costumes. The educational content was not dressmaking but costume as social history. The performers were encouraged to apply 'intelligent thought' to questions of plotting and character. Both the determination of the Elizabethan playhouse on playing and the translation of Renaissance conventions into the twentieth century were discussed. The whole play was studied before being cut for production. In order to develop the villagers' skills in self-government, a committee was established, to encourage 'group intelligence and collaboration'.[24]

In 1931/2 the work was a reduced version of *Peer Gynt*. Fifty of the village's population of 300 – twenty-five adults and twenty-three young people – took part, all of the adults being members of the Liverton branch of the WEA.

D. Irene wrote that to villagers, a lecture is merely the expression of another's mind, and a discussion something that silences them. The drama production method worked because the villager expressed his thinking and his knowledge as adequately, and perhaps with more sincerity, through craftsmanship. Here she clearly echoes the discourse of the 1919 *Final Report*.[25]

Unexplored in 'Fresh woods' is the Thomases' institutional struggles to defend and promote their perspectives. In the *WEASW Monthly Bulletin* of March 1930 D. Irene assaulted the perspective that drama's function was merely to entertain other class members or secure publicity for the movement; and 'the mental attitude that distinguishes "higher and lower" subjects of educational activity … In education, as in art, our values are absolute.'[26]

23 F. G. and D. I. Thomas, 'Fresh woods and pastures new: adult education in rural Devon', *Journal of Adult Education* 5/2 (1931): 164–74; 5/3 (1931): 259–81.

24 DHTA: F. G. and D. I. Thomas in *First Annual Report* (1928); D. I. Thomas, 'Tutor report', 1929; and quoting Thomas, 'Fresh woods', p. 272.

25 DHTA: D. I. Thomas, 'Tutor report', 1929.

26 DHTA, Workers' Educational Association South Western District. *Monthly Bulletin* 14 (1930): 2, 8–9.

At the launch of the DES at Pinchaford in 1928, Professor Stanley Watkins of UCSW described adult education as 'a joint voyage of discovery into the realms of the spirit; a quest for the "eternal verities" of life'. The gathering agreed that, in 'community drama', where process is more significant than product, 'the play is bigger than the individual, and for one moment in the play is symbolised the effort of the community.' Here dramatic effort figures as a local embodiment of the universalising and transcendent ambitions for adult education. In this sense, drama figures in the Thomases' practice as a centripetal principle. But as one of the new ways of learning for rural contexts – along with radio and film – it acts centrifugally, challenging orthodoxies and institutions. Thomas himself was a centripetal actor in a multi-institutional drama, scattering established structures in order to negotiate more adequate ones.[27]

Carnegie funded Thomas's post for three years on the basis of an agreed progression from pioneer to grant-earning work. But intrinsic to that progression is a tension between those two priorities. Thomas and WEA District Secretary Travena took up opposing positions. In his first DES Annual Report, Travena specified that pioneering work was to be funded by grant earned from new terminal courses. But in his own tutor-organiser's report Thomas advised that, unless its very nature was recast, a tutorial class in a village within three years was extremely unlikely:

> on all hands there are villages waiting and folk keen … this is not a demand that can be organised into classes. It demands careful personal guidance into channels of social activity and progressive thinking which shall contribute something to the welfare of the community.[28]

In 1930 Travena reported imminent success in the aim to make the scheme self-sufficient: income from grant-earning classes almost met the cost of Thomas's salary. But Thomas insisted that the pioneer work had both depended on his working extra hours and had anyhow suffered.

Thomas locked horns, and first Travena and then the WEA bureaucracy came down on him. Travena had introduced Thomas to Elmhirst in 1927; they quickly formed a close ethical relationship. At Pinchaford, Elmhirst had insisted that 'No one movement has the sole prerogative of claiming itself the only educational movement.'[29] Elmhirst now set about pulling the necessary institutional strings. He invited Captain Ellis of the NCSS to review the situation, accusing the WEA, University Extra-Mural Department and County of

---

[27] *Mid-Devon and Newton Times*, 26 Nov 1927, p. 7.

[28] DHTA, F. G. Thomas, 'Tutor-organiser's report', in *First Annual Report*, 1928.

[29] *Mid-Devon and Newton Times*.

having failed to co-operate. Only Thomas had the necessary vision, but might resign. Might he run a Devon Rural Community Council, or an independent educational settlement? And Elmhirst wrote to Watkins at UCSW: 'The WEA will have to decide whether the work that Thomas is doing can legitimately be called WEA work or not.' If necessary, an 'REA' should be invented instead, 'on which various friends and authorities may be represented'. Negotiations with UCSW Principal Murray ran into financial sands. Meanwhile, Elmhirst made a pitch to J. F. Young at Devon LEA: 'I suppose the day will come when the valuable work of such mediating bodies as the WEA will be incorporated in the programme of the county council or local university.'[30]

During 1929 Thomas had, in consultation with Murray, developed proposals for an Adult Education Committee for the South West: 'The unit of all this would be the GROUP and not the class … The village is the unit not the WEA.' Thomas was convinced that the proper future of adult education in Devon was with the university – except that the principal lacked perspective or initiative. Thomas insisted that revitalisation could be achieved 'without destroying the autonomy of any voluntary group'. But his final infrastructural model offers no representation to the WEA. Thomas merely suggests that some of its tutors might deliver a class just as they might for the WI. The WEA was being sidelined.[31]

In July 1930 CUKT extended the Extension Scheme grant for three years, and the WEA won similar funding for Cornwall. In April 1933 Thomas won a Rockefeller Foundation scholarship to get more experience in films and education, extra-mural organisation, and rural problems in a year's study leave – joined by D. Irene – to the United States. Travena's opposition to Thomas was clearly partly personal and partly principled. It also had an economic imperative. In 1929 the WEA had requested Board of Education grant towards the salaries of full-time tutors delivering pioneer work as well as tutorial classes. This was refused. Instead, under Article XI of the amended Regulations of 1931, the universities were afforded such funding. When Thomas returned from the USA, it was as an Article XI tutor employed by UCSW.[32]

AT THE END

Geoffrey Whitworth, founder of the BDL, had introduced Mary Kelly to Dorothy Elmhirst in 1932. They got on well. While Hyett and Seeley in

---

30 DHTA correspondence: LKE/SHW 28 Mar 1928; LKE/JFY 13 Mar 1929.

31 FGT/LKE 22 Feb 1929; 23 Oct 1929.

32 HMSO, Board of Education (1931) *Amending regulations, No. 11, SRO, No. 605,* chapter 3, article XI. For an overview of pertinent legislation, see S. G. Raybould, *The English Universities and Adult Education* (1951).

Gloucestershire maintained class patronage through the new institutions, and the Elmhirsts arguably reinvented the gentry for the modernist age, the Kellys were losing their wealth to death duties. In 1939 Mary came to Dartington to work for Thomas's UCSW Rural Extension Scheme. The institutional nexus changed rapidly with the war, as it had done with the peace. Seeing Mary increasingly sick and impoverished, Dorothy unsuccessfully recommended her to CEMA in 1940 to lead community theatre nationally. Instead, she was appointed Director of Drama for the new Devon County Committee for Music and Drama – the first such post in the country. In the meantime a new broom was sweeping through Dartington. Chris Martin, who took over the Arts Department in 1934, found Mary's product an old-fashioned embarrassment. By 1944 the Dartington Trustees were considering pulling funds; and in 1947 Mary accepted the option of retirement.[33]

In Gloucestershire the war brought an end to the festivals. Four repertory companies were formed in 1942 out of the best players remaining in the depopulated village teams – to mount full-length plays in their Base Towns and surrounding towns and villages. The scheme would provide first-rate if limited entertainment; 'give interest and the opportunity for service' to the players; and have valuable effects on village drama after the war, with a pool of trained players to lead and set the standard. Chairman Guy Pemberton wrote, 'The time for learning is over, the time for action is here.'

[33] DHTA.

8 Dartington Hall – a landscape of an experiment in rural reconstruction.

David Jeremiah

WITHIN ten years of the beginning of its reconstruction in 1925, the Dartington Hall Estate had undergone an unparalleled scale of redevelopment and restoration. Transformed from dereliction to a modern estate, it generated national interest, and has remained a popular destination for the tourists and lovers of the arts. Yet with the impact of the post-1945 building programme and the incremental demise of the departments of its experimental years, the meanings of Dartington as a modernised landscape have been obscured. This chapter seeks to identify and evaluate the key elements of the reconstruction of a country house estate.

THE DARTINGTON EXPERIMENT

Clustering the departments around the Great Hall, the Rex Gardner[1] cover design for the 500th edition of the estate *News of the Day* (13 March 1934) imaginatively illustrated the scale of change that had taken place on an English country house estate since it had first been discovered by Leonard Elmhirst in March 1925.[2] (See illus. 1.) Representing the spirit and work of Dartington, from the restoration of the hall to the modernist architecture, domestic appliances to telephone exchange, the industrialisation of textiles to the mechanised milking parlours of the farms and factory farming of poultry, education, and support of the arts and crafts, it was a portrait of a modernised country house estate which within a decade had achieved a national reputation and was attracting international attention.

Dartington was not without its critics, but in general it received a good press, particularly from the architectural journals, amongst which a series of four articles in the *Architect and Building News*, June/July 1933, were comprehensive and adulatory. Headed 'The New Rural England', it identified the Dartington experiment as something more than 'a millionaire's plaything'.

---

[1] Rex Gardner: worked for Gimson; commenced work at Dartington in October 1927; responsible for building design.

[2] From May to September 1925 Leonard was negotiating the purchase of the Hall and farms.

The present low state of English agriculture and of rural life is variously attributed to the ineptitudes of Government, lack of protective tariffs, the leasehold system, inefficient marketing, the conservative outlook of farmers and their inability to cooperate, migration of labour to towns, and even to such incidentals as hunting, foot-and-mouth disease, and uncertainty of the English climate. It therefore comes as a welcome surprise to find that, in spite of these things, a very flourishing rural community exists on an estate of 2,400 acres in South Devon.[3]

At a time of anxiety over the effect of commerce, ribbon development and speculative building on the countryside, Dartington was seen as an ideal model of a modernisation that showed respect for the character of rural England, with the sensitive introduction of new building materials, the careful restoration and repair of old buildings, and buildings that conformed to the 'landscape contours and colour harmonies'.[4]

To drive off the Exeter to Plymouth stretch of the A38 into the country road running down the side of the River Dart, and hear the panting and whistle of the steam train on the Dart Valley railway line, offers a glimpse of the sounds and sights of a landscape that first captivated Leonard Elmhirst as he searched for a place where he could begin a new family life and engage in a social experiment. Leonard was thirty-two, from a Yorkshire family of moderate means, the son of a parson, educated at Cambridge and then, after the First World War, at Cornell. He had been out of the country for eight years, and remained without any clear professional ambitions, although in time he came to see himself as an agricultural economist. Idealistically he wanted to contribute to the reconstruction of England, believing that through research and experimentation the country house estate could achieve a programme of social and economic regeneration that would be a model for the nation. His wife-to-be, Dorothy Straight, was thirty-eight, wealthy, radical, well travelled, a member of New York society. She had been widowed for seven years, with three children aged fourteen, twelve and ten, and in personal terms the move to Dartington was of epic proportions. Twelve months after the discovery of Dartington, Dorothy had her first child by Leonard; a year later she had a miscarriage; and then in February 1929, when she was forty-two, her last child was born. For Dorothy, Dartington was part of a continuing search for a purpose to her life, and her own spiritual identity. So together, Leonard and Dorothy marked the ideological extremes of the Dartington regeneration.

At the end of the nineteenth century Dartington, with its ruined Great Hall and Victorian gardens, was part of the picturesque tour of Devon. By the

---

3 'The new rural England', *The Architect and Building News*, 30 Jun 1933, p. 404.

4 'The new rural England', p. 405.

ILLUS. I Rex Gardner's front cover of the 500th edition of
News of the Day – Dartington Hall (13 March 1934)

time Leonard discovered the estate it had been dismembered in three separate
sales in July 1919, October 1920 and June 1921, and the contents of the Hall
were sold off in December 1921. The Hall and estate, with its two surviving
farms, had subsided into further decline, and was a prime example of rural
depression. However, for Leonard Elmhirst with his vision and money, it had
the location and all the necessary ingredients to instigate his programme of
modernisation. Writing for *The Countryman* (1937) Leonard recalled that he
had seen in Dartington a beautiful landscape for family life, arts and education, the land for economic farming and industry, and a history that provided
a continuum of the values associated with medieval England. Over a ten-
year period Dartington considerably added to its land and property holdings,

extended the Hall estate, increased its forestry and implemented substantial speculative housing developments on coastal sites in Devon and Cornwall. But it is the reconstruction of the Hall estate that Leonard first discovered that is the focus of this chapter.

Dartington had good communication links. The Great Western Railway station at the adjacent town of Totnes linked the estate with London, Plymouth and beyond, as well as the local Ashburton branch line. Electricity had not reached the estate, but Leonard saw the River Dart as a potential source of hydro-electricity. This scheme was always problematic, and, while Dartington found it necessary to link into the national grid when it arrived in the 1930s, it was an important indication of the scale of Leonard's planning for the estate to be economic and self-sufficient. From the outset Dartington had welcomed visitors to the estate, and in 1931 a semi-formal permit system was introduced, accompanied by Rex Gardner's illustrated map (illus. 2). Informing its visitors that the estate had been 'developed for the purposes of education and rural research', the landscape was now filled with buildings, the track from the Hall to Totnes had been made into a road for motor access, while the nursery with arable land had been turned into an open-plan field for the Parsonage Farm (known on the estate as 'Sneezle's Prairie'). In terms of restructuring and new buildings it showed how farming, rural industries and education were at the core of the initial plans, with related housing developments for the estate workers and its professional class. The broader remit for the arts came later.

Cushioned from the economic constraints of the interwar years, Dartington was unique in having the finance to embark on a comprehensive programme of new initiatives and buildings. But it was not alone in its thinking on rural reconstruction. From the beginning of the twentieth century there had been various schemes to introduce the urban unemployed to the healing qualities of country life. At the same time there was a recognition that, if the rural working-class exodus from the countryside was to be halted, it was not just industry that had to be revived, but housing had to be improved, along with provision for the social and cultural life of the communities The new industrial villages, notably Port Sunlight, had offered a model of the social, cultural and educational provision for the workers, and the same was now wanted for the agricultural villages.

Craft industries were seen to be a fundamental part of this process of revival, but had only limited commercial success. Even so, there were some interesting role models for the Elmhirst's to take note of, such as Godfrey Blount's 'Gospel of Simplicity' and work at Haslemere, and the Russell furniture business at Broadway that in the early 1920s had grown out of the early twentieth-century restoration of the Lygon Arms into a flourishing cabinet-making company. As for leisure in the countryside, the developments were proving

ILLUS. 2 Rex Gardner's illustrated map of Dartington Hall estate (1932)

to be more productive and enduring. The setting up of Women's Institutes in 1915 had been a success: by 1918 there were 800 institutes, and by the following year, with the publication of its monthly journal *Home and Country*, it was evident that the WI was exercising an increasing influence on community activities, particularly in the areas of crafts and drama. Over the same period the Village Club Association had moderate success in encouraging communities to acquire premises for the social life of everyone, irrespective of class, sex, religion or politics.

The idea that the cultivation of country life would play a major part in the national recovery gathered momentum, and was perceived as being a key part of the post-First World War reconstruction. This climate stimulated the formation of the Arts League of Service in May 1919 that was intent on bringing the arts into everyday life, with its touring theatre group visiting remote villages across England and Scotland. At the same time there was a growing interest in the potential of the countryside to heal the war-wounded and act as a lung for the unhealthy cities. Mrs Annabel Dott, writing in February 1919 on 'The Disabled Officer in Rural Reconstruction', had anticipated much of Dartington's agenda. She saw the value of mechanisation, electricity, intensive farming, better transport, amusements, sports and new housing.[5] Comprehensive in her vision, she wrote about the need to encourage craft industries, notably weaving, and poultry-farming, fruit-growing, fish-breeding and tree-planting. She also identified the need for a village green for cricket and other activities, a village hall for lectures, dances and plays, and the construction of an open-air theatre. As well as making this general statement on rural reconstruction, she had specific plans for a settlement at Goathland on the Yorkshire Moors, a recognised beauty spot for the summer visitors to whom she anticipated selling local products. There was an increasing interest in the potential of factory farming, and a general discussion was emerging on the educational needs of children and adults, giving rise to Henry Morris's ideas on 'The Village College'. As W. R. Lethaby wrote in his republished articles from the *Home and Country* journal, 'The country and country-life are and must be the basis of national life.'[6]

These were the ideals that Leonard sought to put in place on the Dartington Hall Estate, not in collaboration with the neighbourhood, but as a self-contained estate community. Ideologically the Dartington Hall experiment was a twentieth-century interpretation of the social and economic function of the medieval manor house. In 1934 Gerald Heard, writing for the estate's newsletter, referred to the Dartington experiment as a nucleate process out of which it would be possible to build a planned nation, generating a social revolution from the English countryside. This popular opinion of the time was part of a widespread national interest in the idea of a revitalised village life that would provide an antidote to the displaced sense of community in modern society and the possibilities of political revolution.

A core ambition of the Dartington experiment was to show that it was possible to establish a harmony between rural and urban life, and demonstrate that the creative pleasures more readily associated with cities could be fostered in a country setting. But in setting this agenda, it produced a cultural conflict, for it seemed impossible to balance the approach towards those experiments that could be measured and made accountable, and those that defied such

---

5 A. Dott, 'The disabled officer in rural reconstruction', *The Nineteenth Century and After*, Feb 1919, pp. 359–76.

6 W. R. Lethaby, *Home and Country Arts* (1923), p. 16

forms of economic accountability. From the outset all aspects of Dartington were subsidised, but, in the case of the commercial ventures and agriculture, the question was for how long should they be supported before they demonstrated their viability or were closed? The tensions that this situation created between the social, practical and spiritual ambitions of the experiment were issues that Dartington struggled to answer, but never comfortably resolved.

In the process of its reconstruction and modernisation, Dartington's programme of new building and restoration moved from arts and crafts, through neo-Georgian and modernist to municipal domestic architecture styles and ideals. At times it showed conflicts of interest, but under the initial influence of William Weir[7] Dartington retained its belief in the importance of achieving a harmony between the restoration and the new, respecting the heritage while being prepared to bring old and ruined buildings back to life and in good repair. As an amalgam of the rational and the spiritual, Dorothy believed that every site contained in itself the elements of the design most suited to it.

The most notable achievements of the decade were the reconstruction of the courtyard, great hall, and private house and garden by William Weir, and the garden landscape including the courtyard by Beatrix Farrand, American garden designer and friend of Dorothy. Yet, just as important to the understanding of its ideological and class structure are the building designs of Rex Gardner, Oswald Milne,[8] Louis de Soissons[9] and William Lescaze.[10] Taken as a whole, the estate acts as a paradigm of the tensions between reconstruction and modernisation; without undervaluing its unity of purpose, the most useful way of understanding this relationship is to consider how the Elmhirsts provided for agriculture, arts, education, housing and commerce.

[7] October 1925, first contact between William Weir and the Elmhirsts. He had a national reputation for restoration work and involvement in the activities of the Society for the Protection of Ancient Buildings. William Weir made his first visit to Dartington August 1926. He selected timbers for Great Hall roof November 1928; completed in December 1932.

[8] Oswald Milne (1882–1968): October 1929 recommended for work at Dartington. Articled to Blomfield, assistant to Lutyens, set up own practice 1903, well-established reputation for domestic and education design. Milne made his first visit to Dartington April 1930.

[9] Louis de Soissons (1890–1962): architect to the Welwyn Garden City development.

[10] William E. Lescaze (1895–1964), architect in partnership with George Howe, Philadelphia, introduced to the Elmhirsts by the new headmaster W. B. Curry.

AGRICULTURE

One of the most dramatic changes to the landscape came about through the reconstruction of the farms. At the time of purchase, the estate had two farms, Barton Farm in the courtyard of the Hall, and another at Shinners Bridge. From the outset Leonard was intent on reclaiming the courtyard for arts and education, and determined to find an alternative farm site for Shinners Bridge with its fragmented land holding. The problem of relocating the Barton Farm was easily answered by building a new farmhouse and farm buildings on adjacent land. The Barton Farmhouse, designed by Alfred Fincham, was completed by September 1927, with the farm buildings ready a year later. Four farm cottages, by Milne, were finished by March 1931.

It was July 1926 before the estate acquired the necessary land on which to construct the new farm, and it was not until the October that the process of creating the Old Parsonage Farm began. Twelve months later work started on digging up the hedgerows to create what became known as 'Sneezles Prairie'. It was another three years before Milne prepared designs for the farmhouse and its buildings. The farm buildings, completed in September 1931, were strictly functional in layout and appearance. Four farm cottages were completed in January 1932, and the farmhouse in a restrained eighteenth-century style was finished in the following March. With two new farms, orchards, nurseries, forestry and poultry, the estate had embarked on a comprehensive package of agricultural planning for rural economy, but it was the Old Parsonage Farm that was the primary attraction, and its new field structure a permanent reminder of how Leonard set out a comparative study of a modern and traditional farm.

ARTS

With the removal of the Barton farmhouse in September 1927 the courtyard could seriously begin to be reclaimed for the Hall. On the other side of the Hall the Victorian formal gardens were to be dug up, and the open-air theatre created, which, with the restructuring of the private house and the reroofing of the Great Hall, gave Dartington Hall a stylistic coherence, and an air of authenticity.[11] (See illus. 3 and 4.)

Work on the house involved the removal of the gothic revival entrance porch, replacing the conservatory with a loggia, introducing new windows in

---

[11] February 1927, first visit of Henry Avray Tipping (writer for *Country Life* since 1907 on craftsmanship and English homes; garden designer and wrote important work *The Garden of Today*). Advised on the first phase of clearing the formal gardens, and opening up the tiltyard.

ILLUS. 3 The Victorian formal gardens at Dartington Hall, before their
conversion to an open-air theatre (from a sales brochure, 1925)

ILLUS. 4 The Ballet Jooss, who arrived at Dartington in 1934,
practising in the open-air theatre

the basement to create a library, and the restructuring of the main windows with three mullions. Planning for the restoration of the Great Hall began in November 1928, with the selection of timbers for the roof, a year later Weir inspected the arrangements for the roofing, but it was not until April 1931 that work commenced, and the roof was finally finished in December 1932. The task of selecting suitable furnishing and decoration could then begin. The Elmhirsts took on this responsibility, and in what proved to be a defining moment in the positioning of Dartington's modernism, they commissioned Elizabeth Peacock to create a series of banners for the Great Hall.[12] Started in 1933, six of the banners were completed by the end of 1934, and four more between 1936 and 1938. They were instantly recognised as embodying the spirit of Dartington, providing the link between ancient and modern. (See illus. 5.) To compare the Great Hall with High Cross House (illus. 6) provides a further opportunity to directly confront the restoration and modernisation axis of the Dartington experiment. Further confirmation of how the restoration work was part of the modernisation process can be seen in the photograph of the Victorian garden at the time of purchase in 1925 and the Ballet Jooss practising in the open-air theatre (illus. 3 and 4). Dartington was not only modern but also international in its profile.

With the building of Milne's design for the Dance School in 1931, on a site adjacent to the courtyard, the identification of the Arts with the Hall was confirmed. But the possibility of aligning the experiment with the international design movement was rejected. Gropius had made his first visit to Dartington in the week commencing 29 June 1933, and in December 1934 he was commissioned to redesign the Barn Theatre. There was opposition to this association, particularly from Lescaze, and in October 1935 Gropius received his final and unrealised project for redesigning the Open-Air Theatre. The possibility of Dartington becoming the new Bauhaus had been lost.

EDUCATION

Establishing a school in a beautiful landscape was a key element in the location of the experiment at Dartington. Initially identified with the courtyard, the scale was essentially domestic. However, in 1928 Dorothy decided that she wanted the educational experiment to be involved in child development from the earliest years, and demanded a purpose-built school for nursery education that through scientific study would bring inspiration in homes and the nursery school. The outcome was Aller Park School, 1928–31, designed by Ides van der Gracht, from the New York architectural practice of Delano and Aldrich.

12 Elizabeth Peacock, weaver, had first visited Dartington in October 1929 to run a textile workshop for two weeks.

There was much attention to detail, wonderful mosaic bathrooms, sensitive tiled fireplaces by Jane Fox-Strangways, yet it had a ponderous manor house scale that was ill suited to the intended purpose.

As an educational philosophy took shape that believed that all life could be learning and all experience education, the search was on for a suitable architectural expression for a progressive education. But, by giving the task to Milne, Dartington again had failed to get the building that it needed. Although set within its own copse, it was collegiate in its aspirations, eighteenth-century in its proportions and detailing, with modern equipment and internal fittings. Its progressive quality was emphasised by the four mixed boarding houses,

ILLUS. 5 The Great Hall at Dartington, restored by William Weir.
Note the reconstructed roof and Elizabeth Peacock's banners.

ILLUS. 6 High Cross House, designed by William E. Lescaze
in an *avant-garde* modernist style (1931)

all furnished in good taste from Heals, but the design was bitterly opposed by
the new headmaster, W. B. Curry, who wanted a modernist school designed
by Lescaze. As it was, the Lescaze proposal was little more appropriate for
the education, the design unsuited to the site and rightly rejected by the Elmhirsts. More than any other of the building projects the two school buildings
demonstrated the limitations of the utopian dream. Even the new modernist
boarding houses adjacent to the Aller Park school by Lescaze, Blacklers, 1933,
Chimmels, 1934, and Orchard, 1935, while received by the architectural press
as the fearless expression of the Dartington Experiment, had institutionalised
the romantic idealism of a child-centred learning.

HOUSES AND HOUSING

The very first cottages to be built on the estate were to be boarding houses
for the girls, on a site chosen by Dorothy when walking the estate in October
1925 with Alfred Fincham, the first head of the building division.[13] Fincham

---

13 In September 1929 Dartington leased Staverton Bridge Mills as workshops for
the Building Department. July 1930 the Building Department became Staverton
Builders Ltd, a company of Dartington with its own share issues. A. E. Malbon,
previously of Welwyn Garden City, was appointed as the Managing Director, and
Dartington became involved in a wide range of speculative housing schemes and
commercial building.

designed the cottages and began the process of constructing Park Lane, the first new road on the estate. In November 1927 Gardner continued this development with arts and crafts designs for cottages that were completed in 1929. Just as significant were the building conversions, also by Gardner. The first, in September 1928, was the outstanding arts and crafts redesign of the Shinners Bridge Farmhouse, followed by the conversion of farm buildings into three cottages at Lownard, and a highly original barn cottage conversion at Yarner in May 1931.

In 1928 the estate had consolidated its land holdings around Shinners Bridge with the purchase of the adjacent Orchards Park, Staple, a spectacular hill site looking back over the farm towards Dartington Church. With little concern for the debates on ribbon development, the site was commandeered for three executive neo-Georgian houses, designed in the early summer 1930, by Oswald Milne. More sympathetic to the rural idyll were the nearby pair of thatched bungalows by Soissons.

Modernism came in 1931 with the Lescaze High Cross House for the headmaster. Provocatively located on a rise overlooking Foxhole and Milne's farmhouse at the Old Parsonage, the architectural press chose to interpret the juxtaposition of the buildings as the beginning of a new harmony in a changing landscape. Dartington's new headmaster was convinced that in High Cross he had a house that would almost rival the Hall as a showplace. A house for the car lover, the design presented a catalogue of problems in its design and construction, and an uneasy compromise was reached over the design of the kitchen and the internal finish. The building took over a year to complete, almost doubled the original budget, and cost three times that of a Milne house. It may have looked minimal but it was luxurious in its fitments and materials, and with the wing for servants and guests painted blue, and the family accommodation white, its social status was visible for everyone to see. The house became an icon of Dartington's modernity, and exercised considerable influence on its thinking over the next five years.[14]

Soissons, with his involvement in the development of Welwyn Garden City, had identified Shinners Bridge as the ideal location for creating a new village for the estate workers, but on reflection it was decided that its close proximity to Dartington village, with its school, shop and village hall, would challenge the loyalty of the estate workers. The outcome was the building of two housing estates designed by Soissons at Huxhams Cross and Broom Park. As experiments in cheap housing, the building materials and plans were modified, reducing costs per house to just over £500, which compared favourably to

---

[14] The modernist housing development in Warren Lane by Lescaze started in 1934 with a pair of cottages, and followed in 1934–5 with the house for Kurt Jooss, whose ballet company had arrived at Dartington in 1934.

the national framework shaped by the 1926 Housing Rural Workers Act and the 1930 Housing Act. The development added little to the national debate on municipal housing, and, while Dartington Hall did operate its own bus service, the housing estates were isolated, inconveniently located, and failed to encourage the sense of worker loyalty that Leonard had hoped for.

COMMERCE AND COMMUNITY

With its textile mill, craftsman's studio, central office and saw-mill, Shinners Bridge became the commercial and industrial focus of the estate. Architecturally it brought arts and crafts reconstruction alongside the vernacular, neo-Georgian and modernism, as the designs of Gardner, Milne, Lescaze and Soissons claimed attention. In November 1930 work began on building the Textile Mill, and the following month construction of the Saw Mill commenced, both designed by Milne. The Textile Mill in an informed vernacular style highlighted one of Dartington's recurring problems. It was too big for the craft-based production with which they had started, and not large enough for the industrial-scale output that they were to move towards.

The Craftsmen's Studios designed by Gardner in autumn 1930 became known as Shinners Bridge Studio, and then as the Retail Shop. While this marked the beginning of the identification of Shinners Bridge as the retail centre, it is important to note that it was here that the Elmhirsts provided the much-needed patronage for the craft pottery of Bernard Leach. By 1935 Shinners Bridge was well established with its own tearoom and car park, selling its own products alongside those of the Rural Industries Bureau. Two years later such was its success that there was a request for the building of a new and larger showroom and tearoom. Although national events were to overtake this proposal, it was evident that the culture of the craft experience in a beautiful landscape, enjoyed by the middle-classes in their new family motor cars, had been established.

It was the design and building of the Central Offices by Lescaze in 1934–5 that in style, scale and place radically turned a rural corner of Devon into a twentieth-century centre of commercial enterprise. Modernism now overwhelmed Dartington village, and not even the Beatrix Farrand garden designs for the Central Offices could minimise its impact. Monuments to social and economic power, they contrasted uncomfortably with the crumbling nineteenth-century village school and the prefabricated village hall with its corrugated iron roof.

The first school prospectus (1926) had said, 'If Dartington Hall is to keep true to its ancient tradition it must form a dynamic centre for the hamlets and villages of the immediate neighbourhood.' But in the first instance their concern had been the challenge of building up its own sense of community, hence the dancing classes, choir practice and performances for the estate families of the early years. Dartington provided much-needed work both on the land and through the highly successful Staverton Builders, but it had no interest in challenging the established social order of the great house in relation to the surrounding villages.

With the building programme coming to an end in the mid-1930s, over the next four years Dartington enjoyed and encouraged a range of innovative projects, particularly in the arts. Having become home to a number of dispossessed refugee artists, Dartington had become, in the view of Christopher Martin, the recently appointed arts administrator, a completely international community – part English, part Russian and part German. By the beginning of 1938 its set-up was complete. The following year the development abruptly halted, and as the momentum and vision of these experimental years was lost it is only possible to speculate on what might have happened without this break.

POSTSCRIPT

In the period after the Second World War many country houses have been themed, and their histories and gardens packaged for the modern day tourists. The landscape of Dartington Hall reflects these changes. Today, at the entrance to the Dartington Hall courtyard and the Cider Press Centre at Shinners Bridge, an information board introduces the visitor to the founders of the modernised country house estate, declaring their commitment to a programme of 'regeneration of the countryside and the rural economy' as a vision of providing the abundant life for its inhabitants. Marketed as a place of escape for a weekend break, it is the arts, the beautiful landscape and the wholesome shopping that Dartington now offers the visitor, a popular model of Devon for the tourist.

Dartington had reopened Shinners Bridge in 1950 and made an immediately significant contribution to the revival of the crafts in post-war Britain with its outstanding 1950 exhibition 'Made in Devon', its 1952 influential international conference and travelling exhibition 'Craftsmen in Pottery and Textiles', and its support for the formation of the 'Devon Guild of Craftsmen' in 1955. As part of a national movement it ensured that Devon developed a particular identification with the crafts.

Twenty years later Dartington made the move that has fixed its cultural representation. Dorothy Elmhirst had died in 1968, Leonard died in April 1974, and a month later attention turned to the ways in which their vision of Dartington could be best represented. Looking back to the 1920s Dartington in the 1970s perceived that it was the crafts associated with wholesome food and heritage that could best define the continuity of the founders ideals. So, in 1974 David Cantor, the founder of the Cranks vegetarian restaurant chain was invited to manage the initiative that resulted in the opening of the Cider Press Centre in March 1977. It put Dartington at the forefront of the heritage interpretation movement, and took crafts retailing into a new age, a model of the good healthy life.

With not a car or modernist building in sight, the John Lawrence illustrated site plan introduced the Cider Press Centre as the modern commercial medieval experience. Dartington had been secured as a modern paradise. Assured by its history that stretched back 400 years, and its twentieth-century reconstruction, it was able to describe itself as a small world in its own right and a microcosm of the larger world. What had resurfaced was the importance of the arts and crafts idealism in establishing a vibrant rural England. To cross the road into the Cider Press Centre garden or step into the Hall courtyard is to experience at first hand the effectiveness of these principles and to understand why Dartington has continued to market itself as a combination of beauty, history and commerce, a reminder of an interwar experiment that played a significant part in shaping the idea of a new rural England.

9 Rural industries and the image of the countryside

Christopher Bailey

THE consensus about the rural industries in the English countryside is that they form a kind of index of continuing rural decline. In many representations, such as the collections of physical 'bygones' made and written about by H. J. Massingham, as well as a major genre of fictional writing in the mid-twentieth century, a range of visual and literary tropes appear to make this case. Such a view oversimplifies by minimising the diversity of circumstances in the regions of England, the complex interrelatedness of the agents and mediators of rural regeneration and urban progress, and by underestimating the power of the ideology of modernism, both in the construction of histories of the period, and in policy-making during it.

The archives of the regional community councils are a rich source of evidence of differential growth and change, while the Rural Industries Bureau's papers, and its magazine *Rural Industries*, when compared with similar publications for urban audiences, provide insight into the construction of the 'modernist' view of the 'traditional' countryside and its demise. This chapter, drawing on archival sources and on a range of popular publications, argues that the products and images of rural industry worked both to support a picture of the countryside as England's lost past, and, when the occasion required it, as a seedbed of reinvention and regeneration.

THE IMAGE OF INDUSTRY

The report of the Scott Commission on Land Utilisation in Rural Areas in 1942 influenced the look of the English countryside for decades.[1] It also cemented in place a literary, visual and popular discourse, so that anyone proposing economic development in rural areas would necessarily seem to be striking at the heart of the national heritage. This much was evident on the day of its publication. Why then, did the many organisations whose objective was the well-being of rural communities, rather than their preservation, not make their voices heard more widely during the report's preparation? Why was it the majority report, rather than the minority report prepared by the

---

[1] Lord Justice Scott, *Report of the Commission on Land Utilisation in Rural Areas,* Cmnd 6378 (Aug 1942).

economist Professor S. R. Dennison, that was endorsed by *Rural Industries*, the journal of the Rural Industries Bureau?[2] Why did the many progressive individuals not succeed in creating a network that could deflect the preservationist consensus?

The dissent between the points of view of the preservation-minded Scott and the development-inclined Dennison did not emerge so clearly that we can trace the affiliations of either party to particular ideological positions. The press was mostly impatient with Scott by the time the report appeared, and felt that his commission had done little to address the large questions about the location of industry and population raised by the Barlow Report.[3] John Sheail, in his summary of the report and its reception, notes that Dennison was drawing on the views of Sir Daniel Hall, a prominent member of the Development Commission and author of *Reconstruction and the Land* in 1941, that farming must modernise to overcome competition from foreign food-producers, while also arguing that the majority exaggerated the impact of additional building and development.[4] Sheail also insists that Dennison, far from being excluded from the discussion of the commission, was repeatedly invited to submit his views but failed to do so.[5] Nonetheless, there can be no doubting the drift of Scott's chairmanship when he summarised his recommendations as 'constituting a body of doctrine', and warned his colleagues even as early as his opening remarks that the 'land of England and Wales is no blank sheet of paper on which the urban claimant is free to draw what he will' and the question was 'whether manufacturing industry should have priority as of right to turn out agricultural industry'.[6] The narrow definition of 'agricultural industry' enshrined by Scott not only ruled out the relocation of large-scale manufacturing concerns, but also marginalised the prospects for growth of smaller-scale craft-based production located in the countryside.

Of course, if the decline of rural society were simply the inevitable result of technological advance, then no further explanation would be needed. If the forms of economic activity in the countryside, from hurdle-making and thatching, to potting and quilt-making, were beyond the reforming reach of modern business methods, then decline must surely follow. And it does seem

---

2 Prof. S. R. Dennison, *Minority Report, Commission on Land Utilisation in Rural Areas* (1942), as an adjunct to Scott (1942).

3 The report of *The Times*, 1 Dec 1943, headlined 'A Long Wait' looked forward to Lord Woolton and the Ministry of Reconstruction taking a rather more decisive position.

4 J. Sheail, *Rural Conservation in Interwar Britain* (Oxford, 1981), pp. 206–8.

5 In discussion at the conference, *Regeneration or Decline?*, Dartington, Devon, 9–10 Jan 2002.

6 HLG 80/9, Scott Committee Papers nos. 1–41, National Archives, Kew, Surrey.

to ring true. If the narrative of decline is a familiar one, it is because it is embedded in much of our literature, and also because historians and other academics, being literate people, often reach for it as a readily comprehensible framework for their own arguments. When needing a ready reference point for the process of change as a result of agricultural policy and new agricultural technology, one recent study, edited by Joan Thirsk, refers to 'Massingham's down at heel landscape', as if the romanticised narrative that the author laid over his observations were a transparent window onto the facts beyond.[7]

In a second example Howard Newby, in a book that is sympathetic to those who live in, and create, rural society, writes off the Council for Small Industries in Rural Areas, as

> ... a half-forgotten backwater of the Civil Service, considered by many to be an agreeable and well-meaning joke. It had a reputation for supporting quaint rustic crafts which, while suitably picturesque, were hardly a dynamic force in transforming rural employment opportunities. Basket weavers and blacksmiths might apply, but an engineering factory was likely to be frowned upon.[8]

This is a witty and acute summary of the standard position on the rural industries development organisations expressed by W. M. Williams in his influential 1958 report on the Rural Industries Bureau.[9] Despite some well-publicised successes in locating successful light industry in rural areas, CoSIRA continued to be tarred with the rustic brush for the remainder of its life. It is all too easy to ignore the distorting effect of representations of rural life, especially when written with satiric or political intent. But failing to examine the construction of the image is as serious an error as taking rural society, rather than ruralism, to be Stella Gibbons' target in *Cold Comfort Farm*.

This is not to underplay the effect of agricultural decline on the trades and crafts allied to it. As the research reports of the Oxford Agricultural Economics Research Institute in the 1920s demonstrated, the evidence of decline in rural industries was clear well before Dennison's minority report might have paved the way for the relocation of industry. These pioneering socio-economic studies, discussed by Paul Brassley elsewhere in this volume [chapter 16], provided encyclopaedic coverage of traditional industries, and were positive about the potential for mechanisation. The research project from which they resulted

---

7 L. Hepple and A. Doggett, 'Stonor: a Chilterns landscape', in *The English Rural Landscape*, ed. J. Thirsk (Oxford, 2000), p. 277.

8 H. Newby, *Green and Pleasant Land: Social Change in Rural England* (1993 reprint), p. 242.

9 W. M. Williams, *The Country Craftsman: A Study of Some Rural Crafts and the Rural Industries Organisations in England* (Dartington, 1958).

was, however, motivated by the widespread concern that the effort of documentation might have come too late to inform attempts to save the economy.

At around this time the Secretary of the Cambridgeshire Rural Community Council, E. R. Vincent, had some sharply pointed and subtle questions about the new realism that would be required. In an address to a meeting of craftsmen that is remarkable for the modernity of its content in view of its date of 1927, Vincent acknowledges the decline both of the demand from agriculture for the country craftsman, and the inroads into their markets made by mass-produced goods sold in the shops on market and county town high streets.

> If the village blacksmith will not adopt modern methods, will not make the best use of modern machinery, will not meet a changing market, he will disappear, and no amount of sitting under chestnut trees and singing in the choir will save him. And we should not want to save him. The rural industries movement we favour today is not based, as some people seem to imagine, on a desire to bolster up the romantic, though decrepit, in its losing fight against the unromantic and efficient. The decrepit must not be bolstered up, it must be changed or abandoned.[10]

The debates about mechanisation and standardisation would be familiar territory to an administrator attuned to the thoughts of the Design and Industries Association, and to developments in avant-garde art. Vincent was also highly perceptive about the role that lifestyle plays in the success of what we would now call the 'rural SME'. Almost fifty years later, the Bolton report on small firms starts from the same premise, that small but uneconomic businesses should not be supported. Cutting through the anti-industrial high politics of the Arts and Crafts Movement, Vincent asks, rhetorically,

> Is it necessary to be fighting a losing battle to be charming? Is machinery fatal to our sentiment? Of course not. Some of the most significant expression in modern art is concerned with the machine and its aesthetic effect.[11]

The 'vested ignorance of the forge', the inherent conservatism of the craftsman, plays a part in perpetuating failure, but the greater problem is cultural – the will and opportunity for country craftsmen to communicate, with one another and with their customers. His description of the reaction to his ideas at a recent meeting of fifty rural craftsmen would immediately be recognised

---

[10] E. Vincent, 'The village craftsman', in Notes of a Conference of Rural Community Councils held at Cambridge in 1927, ACRE, Box: RCC History, p. 1.

[11] Vincent, 'The village craftsman', p. 1.

by anyone working in the crafts today – once the initial isolation is overcome, cooperative networks seem to spring to life.

Again foreshadowing the recommendations of later reports, Vincent takes the example of a French government report from the eighteenth century, to show that in the crafts, then as now, it is the situation that is eloquent, not the craftsman. To be effective in supporting the rural industries, the Community Councils must 'adopt the methods of the psycho-analyst rather than the surgeon'. They should understand the mind of the consumer. Marketing co-operatives and imaginative selling techniques were a more appropriate response than crudely amputating living craft skills. If a wholly new product could be made fantastically popular, as had been demonstrated by the recent success of chewing gum manufacturers in building a market from an apparently useless vegetable material, then why should not the blacksmith create a demand, by setting up a collectors' club for horseshoes, as amulets or as table decorations?

Vincent's audience might be expected to have heard some of these arguments before. And so, not surprisingly, the cautious but positive discussion that followed this visionary presentation adopted his broadly 'modernising' position on the rural industries. But what of the opposition to this progressive stance – those determined to see rural industries as no more than a form of industrial archaeology?

Here we have to reckon with underlying changes in the way historical knowledge is transmitted and structured. The shift to photographic illustration in mass circulation publications at the beginning of the twentieth century made it easier to grasp the present, but at the same time released an enormous potential for realising the past. As Lowenthal puts it,

> While relics yield to print's superior powers to preserve and convey information, *images* of artifacts have become more and more consequential (…) Photography made such images accurate and ubiquitous, replacing not only the tangibly antique but history and memory as well.[12]

The press made increasing use of photographic images of the countryside, but recognised the greater immediacy of depictions of people at work in rural settings. The national papers, as well as magazines such as *Country Life*, regularly turned to Rural Industries Bureau (RIB) photographers to supply the demand. In general, the purpose of these photographs of rural life was not to instruct the reader, or to convey specific information about technique or material, as the RIB intended, but to provide a memento of the 'living relics' the reader might be expected to encounter on trips into the countryside. This preference for the picturesque is evident in a comparison of pictures made and published

---

[12] D. Lowenthal, *The Past is a Foreign Country* (Cambridge, 1985), p. 257.

ILLUS. 1 Modernized smith's shop, interior showing modern equipment,
installed on the recommendation of the RIB, at Tunbridge Wells, Kent
(photo: Cattling; not dated; Museum of English Rural Life,
University of Reading, MERL SR RIB PH2/8/1)

in the interwar years. Let me admit openly that this is not a balanced sample of the many volumes of photographs held in the RIB picture archive, which are remarkably diverse in subject, purpose and authorship. The RIB retained their own photographer, Victor Shafer, over a long period, but a number of freelance photographers seem to have sent pictures that they deemed suitable to the London office. When pictures were published, the details of place and date of publication are often included in the archive record, but many have no such details, suggesting that they remained unpublished. They may, however, have been used as an illustration in one of the RIB's booklets for craftsmen and women, for the instruction of trainees on a course, or simply kept for archive purposes.

In the first, undated, image we see a workshop that has clearly been in use as a smithy for some considerable time (illus. 1). Despite the antiquity of the building, a range of modern equipment, including oxy-acetylene cutting and welding gear, has been added to the traditional forge. The grinding, drilling and cutting equipment would have enabled the smith to take on the sort of work that a farmer might need to have done on mechanical, as well as horse-drawn, machinery. As one of Vincent's questioners asserted in the discussion following his 1927 speech, many a smith had chosen to add to his skills at the forge those of a mechanic and fitter. Although not empowered to invest in businesses, the RIB could give expert advice on the right equipment to install, as it did for this smithy in Tunbridge Wells. For many smiths this updating of equipment in the name of flexibility and efficiency represented the way forward.

With such a range of modern machine tools at his disposal, the smith's business could also encompass a wider range of 'lines', including the 'fancy' work that was disparaged by some traditional craftsmen, but on which the RIB was determined to impose higher standards of design. (See illus. 2.) In an undated photograph of the workshop of F. Tamkin in Chelmsford, subsequently published in an RIB booklet, a purpose-built workshop is laid out on the principles of rational factory design, and with a view to safe working practices. The 'transferable' skills of the smith are displayed in the wrought iron, or more probably mild steel, grate and firedogs, just the right size for the smaller hearths then being installed by the tens of thousands in suburban homes on the edges of English towns. Meanwhile, the same householders' lawnmowers are making their annual trip to the workshop for maintenance. While new machinery was often advertised as a way of saving labour – 'an all-round man' – the five men in this workshop could presumably only be kept on by a shop run as a diversified business.

The opportunity to portray rural industries as using appropriate mechanisation was clearly present from the 1920s. Circulation of this kind of image

ILLUS. 2 Modern workshop, F. Tamkin, Chelmsford,
example of a workshop equipped and layout to RIB design
(Photo: unknown; not dated; MERL SR RIB PH2/8/9)

was, however, constrained by the editorial filtering of the picture editor. Given
the choice of two pictures of the process of manufacture, the picturesque value
of an image no doubt played its part in the selection process. The making
of furniture was still a craft-based industry at this time, but the methods of
urban manufacturers were based on a considerable degree of specialisation
and division of labour. The country chair, on the other hand, became a kind of
paradigm of traditional craft, endlessly narrated by commentators such as H. J.
Massingham. The closeness of the craftsman to his material and the limits of
mechanisation form a constant theme in the narrative. A photograph taken at
the premises of E. Goodchild, in High Wycombe, shows a worker checking
one of a stack of chair seats set out for weathering (illus. 3). The considerable
scale of the enterprise is indicated by the sheer number of seats being proc-
essed in a batch.

A photograph of a man boring the holes for the legs in a chair seat depicts
the worker and his work in more direct communion (illus. 4). This was made
by the same photographer, and also shows part of Goodchild's works. It is the

sense of direct engagement with the act of making that might explain why *Country Life* chose to publish the second, on 22 February 1942, while the first carries no details of publication.

The national press regularly used photographs from the RIB in the 1930s, and often tended to use images of work to provide a reassuring backdrop of continuity against which the decade unravelled to war. Typical of the genre is illus. 5, a picture taken not by Shafer or his colleagues, but by *Times* photographers. No details of the location are given, but this idyll of unalienated labour, published in May 1938, shows three men using draw knives to form willow hoops, while a colleague ties and stacks them to harden and dry. Here is outdoor or half-sheltered labour under the 'spreading chestnut tree', making for pleasant working conditions, at least during a summery season. The rhythm of

ILLUS. 3 Chair-making, E. Goodchild, High Wycombe
(photo: C. F. Snow, Braywood, Windsor; not dated; MERL SR RIB PH2/4/34)

ILLUS. 4 Chair-making, Mr Goodchild
(photo: C. F. Snow; published *Country Life*, 22 February 1942; MERL SR RIB PH2/4/5)

work suggests a slowly evolving order in which man and nature are in complete harmony.

A further *Times* picture is in striking contrast with this sylvan scene (illus.6). Three men are shown in this picture published in August 1941, but this time in a dark interior. Finishing scythe blades at large belt-driven grindstones, these workers appear grimly determined, the speed of their work governed by the spinning stones. Safety goggles further harden the facial expression, evoking *Rock Drill*, the man-machine hybrid mounted atop a pneumatic mining drill created by the Vorticist Wyndham Lewis immediately before the First World War. The dominance of the scythe grinders, like that of Lewis's sculpture, is further emphasised by the viewer's position, looking up at the subject. This gang of skilled workers must have consisted of service-exempt men who might otherwise have been considered to be well out of harm's way in a country workshop. Instead the photograph presents a disciplined rank of combatants equipped as if for battle.

The attitude of the countryman, in tune with, if not the victim of, climate and the seasons, is exchanged for one is which courageous individuals play an

ILLUS. 5 Cutting hoops
(photo: *The Times*; published *The Times*, May 1938; MERL SR RIB PH2/6/41)

ILLUS. 6 Scythe-making – grinding of scythes
(photo: *The Times*; published *The Times*, 13 August 1941; MERL SR RIB PH2/6/29)

active role in the survival of society. There is an obvious parallel with the well-known wartime imagery of Londoners' resistance to the blitz. The rural crafts could be conscripted into warfare after all, but when they were, they were treated as an honorary form of heavy industry. Like the women who did men's jobs in the munitions factories, they often found that the sudden respect was a temporary deception, and that peace brought a return to the old stereotype of quaint and ineffectual anachronicity.

There are limits to the claims that can be founded on such a limited sample, yet there is some corroboration here for Vincent's view of a renewed impetus to innovation and independence in the rural industries in the interwar period. We also see how a range of lived experiences were fitted to the available forms of conventional representation, creating an inertial force in the minds even of those for whom 'progress in the countryside' was not a contradiction in terms.

RURAL ORGANISATIONS

In is clear that the distinctions applied to photographic imagery can also apply to literary productions, and by extension to the official documents passed to and fro from the RIB, the National Council of Social Service, local authorities and the Rural Community Councils. This new constellation of organisations brought a different set of discourses to rural affairs, which parallels the potential of the visual image to transform understanding.[13] In E. R. Vincent's county of Cambridgeshire it was Henry Morris, subsequently the instigator of the Village College movement, who, having become Secretary of the Local Education Authority, set up the Rural Community Council.[14] The range of interests he brought to the organisation, in recreation, adult self-improvement and education was typical, not only of the RCCs, but also of the participants at the series of Rural Life conferences promoted by the National Council of Social Service during the interwar years. Participants in these discussions felt it was natural to talk about village life in terms of 'cultural deprivation' and that it fell to them to 'give the initial prescription and supervise the treatment'. Management of rural communities by the professions thus brought in its wake the new terminology of 'latency' and 'development', borrowed from the social services. The new language found expression in a voluminous and unprecedented literature, consisting of reports and minutes, memoranda and

---

[13] For a longer discussion of the main sources relevant to this section see C. Bailey, 'Progress and preservation – the role of rural industries in the making of the modern image of the countryside', *Journal of Design History* 9/1 (1996): 35–53.

[14] W. G. S. Adams, *Formation of Rural Community Councils*, typed notes presumed to be by W. G. S. Adams, ACRE, Box: RCC History, *c.*1948.

correspondence, the purpose of which was to secure funds from local and central government.

It would be unwise to press too far the case that the RCCs represent a consistently radical strain of thought about the countryside. Generally they saw their role as the support of the individual craftsman or woman, in the context of the 'well-being' of the community. As David Matless points out, the new voluntary action tends less to usurp old authority than to intertwine with it.[15] In doing so, the RCC might go some way to emphasise marketing rather than production standards, women's 'leisure' crafts over 'men's work', and local autonomy over central policy.

Furthermore, as Howkins reminds us in the final chapter of *Reshaping Rural England*, 'responses were different in different regions, and experienced differently by different classes and groups ....'[16] The RCCs were diverse in constitution and their members acted from a range of motives. However, the men and women who sat on their boards were, in the case of many counties, fairly described by James Noel White as, 'landed and wealthy, ... able to assist financially [and] did so in a way which remains unrecorded, personal and private'.[17]

A network of well-connected and like-minded people spread the pattern of community councils across the counties of southern England and the Midlands. Between 1922 and 1942 a total of twenty-four Rural Community Councils were created, covering twenty-nine counties in England and Wales. The education network, especially adult education, provided a useful pool of able and energetic evangelists for the cause. A key figure, both in Oxfordshire and in the formation, in 1923, of the Gloucestershire RCC, was Miss Grace Hadow, the Secretary of Barnett House, and the Vice-Chairman of the National Federation of Women's Institutes. She was also a member of the RIB's Women's Advisory Committee. Her husband, Sir Henry Hadow, assisted in the establishment of the RCC in Leicestershire in 1923 where the Adult Education Committee formed a nucleus of activity.

The stimulation of rural industry was only one weapon in the armoury, and was unlikely to be deployed solely on narrow economic grounds. In most cases, the RCC set up a Rural Industries Committee, often with representation from the County Councils and from locally respected craftsmen or women. In Gloucestershire the Rural Community Council included the noted

---

15 D. Matless, *Landscape and Englishness* (1998), p. 44.

16 A. Howkins, *Reshaping Rural England: A Social History, 1850–1925* (1991), p. 293.

17 H. Tebbutt, 'Industry and Anti-Industry – the Rural Industries Bureau – its Objects and Work' (unpublished dissertation submitted for the MA History of Design, V&A/RCA, London, 1990), p. 114.

silversmith George Hart, who was described as coming 'from an interesting colony established in the Cotswolds where rural handicrafts were practised'.[18]

By 1928 demands for advice and support were such that the RIB thought it was time to take a hand in controlling the work of the Community Councils. In its *Memorandum on Rural Industries*, the Bureau argued that all Councils should take responsibility for rural industries' work. It defined these industries rather narrowly, as the trades ancillary to agriculture, country crafts, dependent on 'local conditions or supplies of materials', and 'occupations which may help to increase the standard of home life' – in other words, the 'domestic crafts'.[19] The 'anti-industry' charge laid against the Bureau by Williams has some substance. It undoubtedly applied an unscientific and romanticised definition of industry, it was too small a body to be able to encourage economic strategies such as relocation of industry to rural areas, and it certainly lacked the resources to conduct much in the way of proper surveys or research.

As the Rural Industries Committees proliferated, the Bureau became ever more reliant on the County Industrial Organisers for reports of activity and often found itself in conflict with the approach and values applied at County level. Whenever they were confronted with demands for conformity, the county organisations insisted, with NCSS support, that there was 'no blueprint' for an RCC. They successfully resisted attempts by the Development Commission to 'grade' their performance by a common standard. As a Rural Community Council Chairman bluntly informed the Rural Industries Enquiry set up in 1930, he was against the imposition of Bureau 'standards' in workmanship.

> As for keeping people up to the mark, we have not insisted on too high a standard because the men have suffered badly and must not be too hardly used … we want to get the men's confidence.[20]

Just as contact with rural craftsmen in the 1950s convinced W. M. Williams that very few of them were concerned with high-minded debate about design standards, as the Bureau might have wished, so there was a mood of realism in the RCC-sponsored group discussions held around the country. As Williams soberly observed, the rural crafts worker, like his urban equivalent, was 'more interested in collecting outstanding accounts than in the poetry of Nature'.[21]

[18] W. G. S. Adams, *Formation of Rural Community Councils.*

[19] Rural Industries Bureau, *A Memorandum on Rural Industries Containing a Suggested Programme of Work for Rural Community Council* (Sep 1928).

[20] Evidence given by Colonel Swayne, President of Hertfordshire Rural Community Council, quoted in Tebbutt, 'Industry and Anti-Industry', p. 92.

[21] Williams, *The Country Craftsman.*

ILLUS. 7 Chair-making, Edward Gardiner, Priors Marston, Rugby
(photo: *Leamington Spa Courier*, published *Leamington
Spa Courier*, 17 June 1938; MERL SR RIB PH2/4/3)

In the 1920s, as their basic trade declined, the RIB's first advice to craftsmen had been to diversify. Through this strategy crafts workers could scrape
through hard times by making toys, ornamental scrollwork or decorative baskets. By 1936 the Gloucestershire County Annual Report shows this policy
declining in favour of support directed to industries for which there was a
predictable market.[22] Thus basket-making was supported because there was no
mechanised competition. Instead the focus was on an improvement in marketing methods supplied through a federation of makers and an agent.

In some cases the connection between maker and retailer worked remarkably well. The Secretary of Gloucestershire RCC, J. Madox York, assisted
Edward Gardiner to revive the making of Gimson chairs. (See illus. 7.) Gimson himself had brought the vernacular designs back from extinction in the
late nineteenth century. After Gardiner's death, Neville Neal took over the
workshop, and found that York's successor, T. G. Castle, could arrange expenses
for him to attend several shows, including the County and Royal Shows and
Olympia, each year to promote his work.[23] Distribution through well-known

[22] Gloucester Rural Community Council, *Annual Report for 1936*, ACRE, Box:
Gloucestershire, 1936.

[23] Neville Neal, in conversation with the author, Stockton, Northants, 2 Jul 1994.

retailers was then arranged. According to Neal, Barrow's Department Store in Birmingham 'took everything Gardiner made before the War'.[24]

In many cases county administrators and producers proved extremely able to take their commodities to new markets, whether they were innovators or revivalists. Yet the last two counties to form RCCs were precisely those we might have expected to see in the vanguard – Northumberland and Devon. While Northumberland, which was home to philanthropic families such as the Dowers and Trevelyans, possessed sufficient voluntary expertise and will, local authority structures remained relatively weak. In the second case, the Dartington experiment ought to have been able to inject hard evidence into the debate as it progressed. Yet, despite Leonard Elmhirst's service on the county council in the interwar years, the conjunction of the estate's initiatives and the economic development of the county seemingly did not bear fruit. Perhaps, as Michael Dower has observed, that is because Elmhirst saw each business initiative at Dartington as an isolated experiment on a notional laboratory bench, and therefore no more or less applicable in Devon than anywhere else.[25] Personal relationships inevitably also played a part here, as they did in the extended negotiation through the 1920s and 1930s, in which Henry Morris entreated the Elmhirsts to support his initiatives in Cambridgeshire.[26]

In general the broader social agenda of the RCCs contrasted with the design-focused view of the Bureau. But there are too many variations of philosophy and approach on the part of both organisations to justify this generality as a principle. While some county organisers complained of a prescriptive approach by the London-based officers, most devoted themselves to setting up marketing networks and put on training courses, saving many businesses from extinction in the process.

The Bureau's declared aim was not to propagandise to the public but to engage in successful economic intervention in rural communities. At one point the Bureau even criticised the CPRE for its faith in 'the old, forlorn process of educating the public'.[27] Contributors to *Rural Industries* were conscious of the pitfalls of the sentimental view of handwork. In August 1933, while the Bureau was seeking ways of instructing Durham women in the neglected craft of quilting, Minnie McLeish raised serious objections to an indulgent acceptance of the spiritual value of craft, especially in the domestic sphere. In a 'Note on Cottage Industries in India' she wrote,

---

[24] Neville Neal, in conversation with the author, Stockton, Northants, 2 Jul 1994.

[25] Michael Dower, in conversation with the author, 3 Mar 1997.

[26] Documented in correspondence in the Dartington Hall Records, LK Education 10, Henry Morris, at High Cross House, Dartington, Devon.

[27] 'The rural boom', *Rural Industries* 6 (1927): 1.

Did the handicrafts ever keep us from becoming automatons, or is that simply a human tendency? Does machine minding really stultify the mind (as some aver) any more than doing too much of any one thing would? Did that Indian and his boy take any more pleasure doing the actual work than the Lancashire mill-hand?[28]

Inspired by the example of Sweden's revived glass industry, the Bureau and the University of Wales conducted a survey of the Welsh woollens industry. As a result McLeish was invited by the Bureau to act as a design adviser. Like the planners whose outlook accommodated the rationalisation of the English open-field system into the enclosures of the eighteenth century, many modernists were anxious to find in the forms, rather than in the manufacture, of earlier work, parallels with industrial design.

The contributors to *Rural Industries* might almost be writing with Herbert Read's *Art and Industry* open on their desks as they find precursors, in 'primitive' or foreign artefacts, of the best products of mass production. In 1932, for instance, we find the modern window manufacturer W. F. Crittall as the co-editor of a 'Kitchens' issue of *Design in Industry*.[29] In an issue of *Rural Industries* three years later, he appears as a putative shop-owner prospecting for peasant pottery in Europe.[30] In another case of convergence the DIA magazine *Design for Today* reprints, without any revision, an article by J. R. Brooke on the Welsh tweeds revival that had appeared a year earlier in *Rural Industries*.[31] Here is a way of having your cake and eating it. Tradition is absorbed into an unbroken chain of progressive design, a narrative deployed to great effect by writers on 'industrial art' such as John Gloag.[32]

CONCLUSION

Conventionally, we assume an alliance of the modernists with the socially progressive left and the preservationists with conservative landowning interests. Analysis of the positions and interactions of organisations in the countryside subverts some of these assumptions. In the interwar period the broad brush strokes of house journals such as *Rural Industries* necessarily simplified the contrast between progress, which comes over as a Whiggish optimism, and

---

[28] M. McLeish, 'A note on cottage industries in India', *Rural Industries*, Aug 1933, p. 48.

[29] A special kitchens issue of *Design in Industry*, Autumn 1932.

[30] W. F. Crittall, 'Peasant pottery', *Rural Industries*, Summer 1936.

[31] J. R. Brooke, 'Survival and revival', *Design for Today*, May 1933.

[32] J. Gloag, *Industrial Art Explained* (1934, 1946 reprint), pp. 124–7.

post-lapsarian decline resulting from the unthinking devotion to traditional ways.

As suburbia spread to encompass many of the districts from which the rural crafts were disappearing, middle-class practitioners of the crafts imported a new, consciously aesthetic approach to their work. The heritage of the nineteenth-century Arts and Crafts movement finally resulted in a reincarnation of many of the crafts the RIB thought beyond help, but on a new economic base that drew on the new wealth of incomers and tourists to the countryside. The elegiac tendency of writing about the crafts comforted many of these new consumers, providing an altruistic justification for their consumption. It also justified the higher price of crafted products which were pushed beyond the economic reach of their older markets.

Behind the image of rural industries we can discern explanations for the acquiescence of rural organisations to the recommendations of the Scott report. Alongside an analysis of the complex and intertwined relationships of new and old power in rural society it is important to understand the way that printed and broadcast media provided paradigms for the arguments of these groups. The negotiated settlement that governs the fate of rural industries between the wars can best be understood as the product of the interaction of these forces.

10 Agriculture in the wider perspective

John Sheail

BY the 1970s enough time had passed for the immediate post-war years to be the subject of historical enquiry – that emphasised the new beginnings for farming, forestry and that third force in the countryside, outdoor recreation and the protection of amenity and wildlife. Without doubting the novelty of what had been achieved, it was pertinent to show the extent to which those post-war advances had drawn heavily upon the advocacy and debate of the interwar years. It was an exciting time for such historical writing. The Cabinet and departmental files for the 1920s and 30s had just been released under the Public Records Act of 1969. A modest venture was *Rural Conservation in Inter-War Britain*. (Oxford University Press substituted the word 'conservation' for the author's choice of 'protection', so as to give the book greater reader-appeal.) Blaise Gillie, an official of the statutory planning division of the Ministry of Health in the 1930s, had kindly read the manuscript. He criticised it for giving a false sense of coherence to the extraordinary array of initiatives recounted, many of which he had first learnt of only by reading the book! The manuscript was adjusted to give a better sense of the piecemeal, uncoordinated endeavour of these years. A distinguished reviewer later admonished the author for failing to bring out sufficiently the evolving connectivity of all that was going on.[1]

A priority in the 1970s was to emphasise all the other interests and activities developing, alongside farming, in the interwar countryside. Some thirty years on, it may be timely to refocus upon agriculture and, more particularly, the challenges for that industry which continued to occupy more than three-quarters of the land space, but where an even higher proportion of people now lived and worked within towns and cities. Where once it had been the dominant industry, it had slipped to fourth, providing less than 20 per cent of breadstuffs and 40 per cent of livestock products consumed within Britain. The average landings of fish were roughly twice the value of beef sales. The paper explores both the consciousness and response of ministers and officials, and more particularly their expert advisers, as to the agricultural position, within the wider context of early endeavours to plan the countryside, as exemplified in the regional surveys of Patrick Abercrombie.

[1] J. Sheail, *Rural Conservation in Inter-War Britain* (Oxford, 1981).

A COMMONALITY OF EXPERIENCE

Histories are easier to write when focused on some particular sector or locality, but personal experience is rarely so tightly drawn. Tom Williams was Parliamentary Private Secretary to the Minister of Agriculture in the 1924 Labour Government, becoming Labour's expert on agriculture in the 1930s, the Parliamentary Secretary to the wartime ministry, and minister himself in the Labour Government which followed. Yet his working life had begun as a miner and trade-union official, before he entered parliament in 1922 to represent the Don Valley, part of the rapidly industrialising South Yorkshire 'concealed' coalfield. As a poor-law guardian, he knew well enough how conditions in the agricultural communities were worse than even in the pit villages.[2]

The connectivity of these seemingly disparate interests found physical expression in the impacts of large-scale surface subsidence and land drainage upon one another in the Don Valley. Where the engineer's solution to coal subsidence was generally to raise banks and install pumps so as to minimise the effect upon drainage, such large-scale disruption of the watercourses demanded something administratively more innovative. A Special Commission, representative of both the mining interests and local government, pressed for the appointment of a comprehensive drainage authority. A Doncaster Area Drainage Bill received the Royal Assent in May 1929, whereby the colliery owners were placed under a statutory obligation 'to obviate or remedy any loss of efficacy in the drainage system resulting from subsidence', with the royalty-owners contributing both to such costs and the fund created to meet outgoings after the mines had closed. Yet even before such local legislation was enacted, both the mining and farming interests perceived themselves to be threatened by the consequences of improvements to agricultural and urban drainage higher in the Don catchment. As Tom Williams expressed it, in Parliamentary Questions and debate, for every 8 gallons of water in the lower Don, only one originated in the Doncaster area. The Bentley colliery was almost flooded in September 1931. An even more disastrous flood occurred in May 1932, inundating colliery housing and some 11,000 acres of farmland. Although the newly raised ring-bank was sufficiently advanced to protect the Bentley pit, the efficacy of such remedial works to combat subsidence was clearly dependent upon large-scale improvements to the lower course of the river Don, undertaken by a drainage authority with the commensurate scale of resources. Without these, the expenditure of local interests would be wasted and many tons of valuable coal left unworked. A further hybrid Bill was enacted, whereby the Doncaster

---

[2] Lord Williams, *Digging for Britain* (1965); A. Taylor, 'Williams, Thomas', *Oxford Dictionary of National Biography* (2004), vol. 59, pp. 308–9.

Drainage Area was brought under the Land Drainage Act of 1930, but with 'the mining powers' and the representation of mining interests upon the catchment-wide drainage authorities preserved.[3]

Yet if there is, on the one hand, wide diversity of experience within any personal career and the history of a single place, those same interwar decades may be taken to illustrate common points of reference, most obviously of a financial kind. Only a week before the Doncaster flood of September 1931, the national economic crisis had caused the Ministry of Agriculture to withdraw all prospect of Exchequer support for land-drainage works. At that scale too, there was increasing propensity to use expert investigation. Lord Macmillan, a distinguished lawyer and chairman of many such enquiries, wrote of Britain's uniqueness in having so sophisticated a committee system as part of its constitutional procedure. Almost every topic capable of being legislated upon, or administered, was investigated at some time by a Royal Commission, Select Committee, Departmental Committee, or some other body of enquiry. The result was a vast accumulation of reports and proceedings of evidence. Macmillan was, for example, chairman of a Committee of Finance and Industry, which included such figures as Maynard Keynes and Ernest Bevin. Published in June 1931, its report took over eighteen months to prepare. The Stationery Office made a substantial profit from sales of the report as a textbook in political economy.[4]

Macmillan wrote in an introductory chapter of how such a period of economic depression was a testing time for institutions. Dogmas hitherto regarded as canonical were questioned, as 'our former easy-going ways' no longer ensured prosperity in 'a crowded and increasingly competitive world'. An institutional stage had been reached where conscious and deliberate management must succeed 'undirected national evolution'. As parliament was 'nagged' to intervene, the age-long conflict between liberty and government was renewed. Whilst truly promoting the liberty which came from 'securing better conditions of life', it was important that such changes in the concept of government should not impair initiative and independence. As never before, a definite national policy was called for. There had to be a 'peculiar delicacy' of balance, being innovative yet requiring such skills and experience as could only be entrusted to those whose business it was.[5]

---

3 J. Sheail, 'Yorkshire's "Sloughs of despond": an inter-war perspective on resource development in Britain', *Environment and History* 6 (2000): 379–98.

4 Lord Macmillan, *A Man of Law's Tale* (1952), pp. 183–4.

5 British Parliamentary Papers (BPP), 1930–1, XIII, Cmd 3897, Financial Secretary to the Treasury, *Committee on Finance and Industry*.

AGRICULTURAL POLICY

That more assertive approach to policy-making had been further stimulated by the Great War, or, more accurately, such preparation for post-war conditions as prompted the establishment of the new Ministries of Labour, Health and Transport, their purpose being 'to identify the needs of specific client groups and, within a range of potential practicalities, to fashion the appropriate response'.[6] Although not a new department, the Board of Agriculture and Fisheries was largely restructured for such executive purpose. A Bill, enacted in December 1919, subsumed its pre-war role as a monitoring and 'policing' agency (as in respect of disease control) within a more positive responsibility for stimulating and managing 'our oldest and greatest industry'. At the instigation of a private member's amendment, it had been elevated in name to the status of 'a real ministry'. As Sir Francis Floud, the Permanent Secretary, wrote later of the ministry, it was expected to act as the advocate of the farming and fishing industries in all their relations with the State, and to be 'the medium for all their difficulties and troubles'. The ministry 'must perforce trench on the preserves of other departments' in serving landowners, tenants and workers, and trawler owners and line fishers, as well as acting, say, as the voice of science in many branches.[7]

That was not to say the ministry could be a pliant servant. Independent judgement was called for. A sub-committee of the Cabinet's Agriculture Committee, in an investigation as to credit facility, remarked in a report of January 1923 of how, although commonly spoken of as a homogeneous industry, farming covered an immense field of diversified opinion and businesses, in which 'every degree of financial position, skill and condition of life are engaged'. Whilst an increase in the barley price benefited the grower, its higher cost as animal-feed hurt the livestock sector, which provided 70 per cent by value of English farm-output. The minister had both to abide by his collective responsibility for Cabinet decisions and be responsive to parliamentary pressures. As the same sub-committee report explained,

> the deep importance to the welfare of the nation of a prosperous agriculture warrants a peculiar interest being devoted by the State to the financial position of the food producer, an interest all the more necessary in a country whose population is predominantly engaged in urban pursuits and, consequently, slow to appreciate, except in times of grave

---

[6] R. Lowe, *Adjusting to Democracy: The Role of the Ministry of Labour in British Politics, 1916–1939* (Oxford, 1986), p. vi.

[7] Parliamentary Debates (PD), Commons, 121, 267–76; F. L. C. Floud, *The Ministry of Agriculture and Fisheries* (1927), preface.

national peril, the significance of agricultural prosperity to the well-being of the nation as a whole.[8]

That distinction between an industrial and a national policy was emphasised by Lord Ernle (the President of the Board of Agriculture in the latter part of the war) in a House of Lords' debate on the optimal arable area in July 1925. In terms of agriculture itself, there was no case for government intervention. Farming was more prosperous than most other industries because of its requirement over more than half a century to adjust to the kind of overseas competition as now pressed upon other industrial-sectors. If farmers could not cultivate profitably, they knew by experience that the remedy was to revert to grass. It was both sound and invited by fiscal policy. Production costs fell and the chances of a moderate financial return increased. Yet, from a national perspective, Ernle believed 'we were rather fiddling while Rome was burning'. Alongside memories of how grain stocks had fallen to as low as eight weeks in June 1915, greater domestic provision, whether home-grown or simply stockpiled, might enable greater concession to be made in naval-disarmament talks. The Cabinet's Committee for Imperial Defence, however, dismissed, in early 1925, any need to sustain the arable area above what was economically viable in peacetime.[9]

There persisted, however, a sense of agricultural policy being too important to leave entirely to the discretion of individual farmers. The report of the Agricultural Tribunal of Investigation, of three leading economists, observed how 'the prestige of farming' and 'amenity of the countryside' had traditionally been associated with 'the plough'. In correspondence of May 1925 with the Prime Minister, Lord Bledisloe, the Parliamentary Secretary, wrote of the difficulty for any civilised state to stand aside and allow 'the cultivated land of the country to revert to jungle through gross neglect'.[10] Through maximising the employment potential of arable (as opposed to livestock) farming, agriculture would also contribute to 'national stability' and the settlement of the Empire by those of British race. There was no better buttress to political and industrial unrest than the occupation of a large part of the countryside by those who owned what they cultivated. Yet the most immediate means of raising the

---

[8] BPP, 1923, IX, Cmd 1810, Minister of Agriculture, *Report of the Committee on Agricultural Credit*, 3–4

[9] PD, Lords, 61, 441–5; The National Archives (TNA), MAF 53, 66.

[10] BPP, 1924, VIII, Cmd 2145, Agricultural Tribunal of Investigation, *Final report*; Cambridge University Library, Baldwin MSS, 25; E. J. Russell, Obituary, *Journal of the Royal Agricultural Society* 119 (1958): 57–9. The owner of a 4,000 acre Gloucestershire estate, Charles Bathurst was ennobled in 1919. Chairman of the Lawes Agricultural Trust, he accepted office as Parliamentary Secretary, so he told Baldwin, out of regard to the minister, Edward Wood, a large Yorkshire landowner.

arable area were discounted. The electorate had rejected in December 1923 Baldwin's proposals for such tariffs as would protect domestic producers from overseas competition. Even if the nation could have afforded subsidies on a sufficient scale as to raise the arable area significantly, the farming bodies, recalling the wartime 'cultivation orders' and dispossessions, rejected them on the premise that regulation of their choice of crops and husbandry would inevitably follow. The disruption caused by the repeal of the Agriculture Act of December 1920, with its guarantees both of prices and wages, had, in any case, been an object lesson to both the Conservative and Labour governments as to the political and economic cost of such controversial policies as ran the risk of being scrapped by the next political party in government.[11]

Making a virtue of a necessity, the minister, Edward Wood, and Bledisloe contended that, rather than dragooning the agricultural community, the function of government was to encourage and materially assist the industry to organise itself more effectively. Such a policy should draw upon the unique qualities of agriculture. Although a primary industry, like mining, it was inexhaustible and indeed 'expanding' in nature, where the 'active organic material' was rightly developed.[12] Through encouragement of such confidence as caused farmers to undertake land drainage and tillage, scientific rotation and selective breeding, there would follow, albeit over time, increasing output and employment. In publicly abjuring any drastic, revolutionary or spectacular policy, Bledisloe characterised the agricultural White Paper, published in February 1926, as

> rather a genuine attempt of constructive character to lay the foundation of a more prosperous and contented countryside, yielding more food and timber, promoting much-needed confidence and security for the agricultural producer and a better outlook and opportunities of advancement for the industrious agricultural worker.[13]

RURAL POLICY

The White Paper was an obvious point of reference for Patrick Abercrombie, the author of a major essay, 'The preservation of rural England', published initially in the *Town Planning Review* in May 1926.[14] The Lever Professor of Civic Design at Liverpool university and President (that year) of the Town

---

[11] PD, Lords, 63, 215–16.

[12] BPP, Agricultural Tribunal of Investigation, 8–11.

[13] BPP, 1926, XXIII, Cmd 2581, *Agricultural Policy*; PD, Lords, 63, 223.

[14] P. Abercrombie, 'The preservation of rural England', *Town Planning Review* 22 (1926): 5–56, published separately in the same year by Hodder and Stoughton.

Planning Institute, Abercrombie had, through his consultancy work, become aware of the increasing potential for both the endogenous forces of rural development and exogenous pressures of urban decentralisation. Agriculture would be advanced, as the White Paper made clear, through improved credit facilities, better marketing, more smallholdings, land drainage, afforestation and rural industries, including the new sugar-beet factories. As Abercrombie speculated, fields would be enlarged and hedgerows removed. Rural housing, if pursued courageously and consistently, would in time alter entirely the character of villages. As to urban decentralisation, Abercrombie's recent 'civic survey' of Sheffield had shown the built area would have to expand by half again if room was to be found for the required industrial and commercial activity and housing at 'the modern rate of 12 per acre'.[15]

Rural planning had become as essential as town planning itself. As Abercrombie expressed it, 'Mr Baldwin's electricity scheme', multiplied by trade revival and legislative aid to farming and town clearance, would accelerate further a 'rural revolution'. The King's Speech of February 1926 envisaged a Bill to establish a national grid for the generation and transmission of electricity; to bring about better credit facilities for farming and to extend the provision of smallholdings, and to provide for slum clearance in the congested areas of numerous towns.[16] Ahead of the agricultural White Paper, the Cabinet had approved in August 1925 grant aid of £1 million over five years towards arterial drainage schemes undertaken by the requisite drainage authorities. There was no aspect of farming where negligence could cause greater injury, often over extensive areas of a catchment. Yet some £18 million a year were estimated to be lost in food value from this cause alone.[17]

The Scottish Secretary, Sir John Gilmour, had claimed, in a Supply Day debate of April 1925, the most important function of the Scottish Board of Agriculture to be the support of research and education. An earlier Departmental Committee report had described them as essential to the survival, let alone advance, of Scottish agriculture. The only effectual protection against competition was 'the adoption of improved and enlightened methods of husbandry based upon scientific investigation'.[18] Grant aid for university

---

[15] G. Dix, 'Little plans and noble diagrams', *Town Planning Review* 49 (1978); P. Abercrombie and R. H. Mattocks, *Sheffield: A Civic Survey* (Liverpool, 1924).

[16] Abercrombie, 'The preservation of rural England', pp. 21–3; PD, Commons, 191, 7–10.

[17] PD, Lords, 63, 368; TNA, MAF 53, 62; J. Sheail, 'Arterial drainage in inter-war England: the legislative perspective', *Agricultural History Review* 50 (2002): 253–70.

[18] PD, Commons, 182, 1867–75; Secretary for Scotland, *Report of the Departmental Committee* (Edinburgh, 1924), p. 42.

departments, agricultural colleges and independent research foundations, such as the Rothamsted Experimental Station, had been put on a more systematic footing since the appointment of the Development Commission. Each recipient was recognised as a leading centre in one of the eighteen major research-fields identified, Rothamsted's speciality was, for example, plant nutrition and soil problems. Where the House of Commons' Select Committee on Estimates criticised the industry for making so small a contribution to the costs of such important services, Bledisloe spoke for many in pressing for more effective communication of the results of such survey and experimentation, most obviously through demonstration farms and 'plots'.[19] The educational side had also received significant moneys as part of the 'compensation' awarded under the Corn Production Acts (Repeal) Act of 1921. Every county in England and Wales had used such grant aid to expand the role of the now-statutory agricultural committees.[20] Fifty-three had appointed agricultural organisers. Twelve had established farm institutes. The White Paper affirmed the need for sufficient funds both for research and education, including an advisory service in technical agriculture and in economics and farm costings. The efforts of the various colleges in the latter area were co-ordinated by C. S. Orwin of the Oxford Institute of Research in Agricultural Economics.[21]

The White Paper called for labour-saving machinery, new crop-species, and improved fertilisers and pest- and disease-control but, as an official commented of the King's Speech, there was an increasing realisation of how 'the economic side of Agriculture lagged behind the technical side'. Greater stimulus must be given to the more explicitly economic aspects. Further investigation by the ministry's Economics Division provided the basis for negotiations with the joint stock banks in establishing a system by which long-term agricultural credit could be given on the lines of the central land-banks of some European countries.[22] A Departmental Committee of Inquiry (the Linlithgow Committee), into the methods and costs of selling and distributing produce, was highly critical of the lack of readily available information on marketing opportunities. A survey by the ministry's economists of such markets and fairs, made as an extension of surveys already underway of the marketing of individual types of crop- and livestock-produce, found widely varying standards of provision

19 A. Rogers, *The Most Revolutionary Measure: A History of the Rural Development Commission, 1909–1999* (Salisbury, 1999); National Archives of Scotland (NAS), AF 43, 188; PP, 1924–5, VII, Select Committee on Estimates, *Second Report (Ministry of Agriculture)*, vii; PD, Lords, 61, 417.

20 The exception being the Soke of Peterborough; the Lancashire County Council met its full costs.

21 PP, 1924–5, VII Select Committee; PD, Lords, 61, 418–19.

22 Ministry of Agriculture, *Report on Agricultural Credit*, Economic Series 8 (1926).

and co-ordination. Northern markets were better organised than those in the South. There was an insufficiency of wholesale markets, but over-provision of livestock markets, in the English Midland counties.[23]

A 'somewhat exhaustive investigation' of the co-operative marketing of agricultural produce, the first in the ministry's orange-covered 'Economic Series' of booklets, found the picture rather 'gloomy', with 'some bright spots'. Arthur W. Street, the head of what had become the Markets and Co-operative Branch of the Economics Division, wrote of how the priority was not for further exhortation, or even 'the exemplification of its success' in countries like Denmark, but 'object lessons or demonstrations of how the methods of co-operation can be successfully applied'.[24] Bledisloe wrote later,

> The canker of individualism is the curse of our countryside and, however far-reaching and praiseworthy may be State guidance in the matter of improved marketing of produce, this canker can only be healed by the voluntary adoption of co-operative methods in every branch of agricultural trading and finance.[25]

TOWN AND COUNTRY PLANNING

The State was similarly implicated with other industries in their search for more systematic methods by which production costs might be minimised and marketing opportunities expanded. A Royal Commission on the Coal Industry (the Samuel Commission) reported in March 1926.[26] Its appointment prompted the Sociological Society to convene a conference in the rooms of the Royal Society of London, in October 1925, as an illustration of how sociology might inform 'the discussion and treatment of current ills with the quickening spirit of a synthetic science'. The opening speaker was the veteran biologist, planner and sociologist, Patrick Geddes, who perceived the Coal Crisis as a 'symptom of a deep-seated malady in the body politic' and, more positively, as evidence of 'a National Transition'. Britain had muddled along for so long, in some kind of 'Palaeotechnic mindset', not because of any lack of inventiveness but rather from a robust immunity of the 'Educated and Governing Classes' to science and its application. The papers given at the meeting

[23] PP 1924, VIII, Cmd 2008, Minister of Agriculture, Departmental Committee on Distribution and Prices of Agricultural Produce, *Final report*; Ministry of Agriculture, *Markets and fairs in England and Wales*, Economic Series 13 and 14 (1927); Anonymous, 'Arthur Street', *Public Administration* 29 (1951): 303–6.

[24] Ministry of Agriculture, *Co-operative Marketing of Agricultural Produce*, Economic Series 1 (1925).

[25] C. Turnor, *The Land: Agriculture and National Economy* (1929), pp. vii–xiii.

[26] BPP, 1926, LXIV, Cmd 2600, Royal Commission on the Coal Industry, *Report*.

otherwise dealt with more effective methods of converting coal to electricity, gas and coke, ways of maximising coal reserves, minimising transport and combustion costs, and mitigating pollution.[27] Abercrombie illustrated, in a final paper, how all the applied sciences might be brought together in planning the actual coalfields, as a further example of the wisdom of determining the use of land and natural resources on the basis of the 'systematic deployment of expertise', as opposed to 'the idiosyncracies of personal intuition'.[28]

Abercrombie, with the architect and surveyor of the Doncaster Borough Council, had broken new ground by not simply focusing on what was wrong with particular industrial and urban developments, but had drawn up a prescriptive regional analysis for that part of the Yorkshire 'concealed' coalfield, before the greater part of its development took place. Through determining by close and systematic study the optimal location, layout and design of development, they would create an opportunity to attain industrial prosperity without associated loss of amenity and health — so combining what Abercrombie described as 'a homely family life' with the level of amenities usually found only in a great city. Rather than a new city of the size and density of Leeds or Sheffield, the regional plan proposed ten or more communities around a central city, Doncaster, that was neither swollen nor tentacular but, in the truest meaning, metropolitan. Agricultural land, smallholdings, allotments and ample spaces for playing fields would form 'the natural matrix to these human and industrial aggregates, cementing them together and at the same time keeping them apart'.[29]

The statutory basis for such planning was the tightly drawn section of the Housing, Town Planning, &c. Acts of 1909 and 1919 as enabled local authorities to draw up such schemes as would ensure 'land in the vicinity of towns shall be developed in such a way as to secure proper sanitary conditions, amenity and convenience in connection with the laying out of the land itself and of any neighbouring land.' Adjacent property-owners would particularly benefit from preventing unsuitable development. A separate code for town planning was effected under the Town Planning Act of 1925. In as much as it was for the county borough or county district councils to prepare and submit town-planning schemes, and to give or refuse approval for development, everything hinged on the vigour and competence of the individual councils and their officials. Even where drawn up and enacted, such regulation was

27 V. V. Brandford (ed.), *The Coal Crisis and the Future: A Study of Social Disorders and their Treatment* (1926).

28 P. Abercrombie, 'The planning of a new coalfield in East Kent', in *The Coal Crisis and the Future*, ed. Brandford, pp. 35–40.

29 L. P. Abercrombie and T. H. Johnson, *The Doncaster Regional Planning Scheme, 1922* (Liverpool, 1922).

in no sense confiscatory. Property owners might claim compensation where denied scope to develop their land howsoever they wished.[30] Such a liability deterred such planning schemes from zoning areas exclusively for agricultural use. Abercrombie pressed nevertheless for an extensive tract west of the river Don to be so designated, as 'a valuable wedge of farm land approaching to within one and a half miles of Doncaster', its low-lying nature making it unsuitable for housing and its area far in excess of anything required for factory building.[31]

Abercrombie wrote of how planning schemes should encompass both the built-up areas undergoing redevelopment, and the more open countryside, a goal eventually realised under the Town and Country Planning Act of 1932. A powerful instance of the value of such comprehensive powers was his survey and report of 1925 for East Kent. In as much as coal and ironstone extraction had hardly begun, there was outstanding opportunity for preventative medicine, as opposed to remedial surgery.[32] Abercrombie cited the proposed East Kent coalfield in both his paper to the Sociological Society's meeting and in his extended essay 'The preservation of rural England'. Although 'at first blush one might say that a new coalfield was too exceptional', he warned of how what was occurring in Kent was 'a concentrated or speeded-up version' of what was happening or about to happen everywhere'. Although still a blank slate industrially, the greater part of East Kent was already 'a very complex palimpsest of civilised effort, past and present'. Abercrombie's purpose was to strike 'a just balance' between 'conservation and development', with certain parts preserved intact and inviolate, and others brought forward as something new but beautiful.[33] Of the eleven types of planning zone distinguished in his regional plan of September 1928, there were an 'agricultural zone proper' and another where farming would be pursued until and unless required as building land. As he emphasised, the retention of continuous areas of farmland would do more than anything else to preserve the tranquillity of rural life amidst the industrial changes of coal and ironstone working. Where the soils permitted, farming might become more intensive in meeting the greater demand for local food-supplies and, where particularly unsuited for 'petite culture', they might be afforested.[34]

In a country like Britain, which had 'not yet succumbed to dictatorship',

30 Sheail, *Rural Conservation*, pp. 65–75.

31 Abercrombie and Johnson, *The Doncaster Regional Planning Scheme*, p. 27.

32 Dix, 'Little plans and noble diagrams', pp. 337–8.

33 Abercrombie, 'The preservation of rural England', pp. 39–41.

34 P. Abercrombie and J. Archibald, *East Kent Regional Planning Scheme: Preliminary Survey* (Liverpool, 1925), and *East Kent Regional Planning Scheme: Final Report* (Canterbury, 1928).

Abercrombie emphasised how little would be achieved without what he called 'persuasive' planning. The pace and scope of any statutory regulation would be determined ultimately by public opinion. There had to be confidence in the 'expert' adviser. 'Business, Labour, and Local Administration' had to recognise the benefit of creating through co-operative endeavour 'a Plan', as opposed to either ignoring or competing with one another in producing 'a Chaos'. By doing so, planning guidance must ride as lightly as possible over free choice. The right course should emerge almost insensibly. It was a political process in which local organisations had an essential part.[35] The Minister of Agriculture, Walter Guinness, in moving the Small Holdings and Allotments Bill in July 1926, acknowledged the great changes taking place in rural life, but also the success of such movements as the rural community councils and the Women's Institute in demonstrating how a vigorous spirit of enterprise remained deeply rooted in the countryside.[36] The working relationship of such local bodies and their 'expert' advisers would be greatly enhanced, if combined and communicated through some central organ. Abercrombie's 'The preservation of rural England' led directly to the founding of what became the Council for the Preservation of Rural England later in 1926, followed two years later by a similar Council for Wales and the Association for the Preservation of Rural Scotland.

AN 'ELEVATED' VIEWPOINT

John Lewis Gaddis, in his lecture series *The Landscape of History*, wrote of how first-hand experience was not necessarily the best pathway towards recognising and understanding the significance of events. One was too often imprisoned by the immediate senses, and so distracted by the complications of everyday existence. Historians, writing from a more detached and elevated viewpoint, are much better placed to judge the significance and nature of what occurred.[37] Thus, Andrew Cooper, in tracing agricultural policy as a case-study of Conservative politics, perceived a modernising impulse in the 1920s. Stability might remain the watchword, but ministers, officials and their 'expert' advisers believed increasingly that it could be attained only through the expertise as had to be more systematically applied to the more efficient production and marketing of crops and livestock.[38] It was through such enterprise that a

---

35 Abercrombie, 'The preservation of rural England'.

36 PD, Commons, 198, 786.

37 J. L. Gaddis, *The Landscape of History: How Historians Map the Past* (Oxford, 2002), pp. 2–5.

38 A. F. Cooper, *British Agricultural Policy, 1912–36: A Study in Conservative Politics* (Manchester, 1989), pp. 64–93.

role could be perceived for government in helping to advance the infrastructure by which credit was given, research and education were expanded, and co-operative societies both cut costs and enhanced sales. The effect was integrative, in the sense that the same facility of encouragement and co-ordination was extended to urban and rural development generally, as through the expansion of road transport, suburbanisation and improvement in the health and housing of the industrial population.[39] As with the farmer's 'workshop' so with the countryside of which it formed so large a part, stability was to be attained not by resisting change, but through more systematic response, whereby rural planning, as with town-planning proper, sought 'a due balance between existing features, natural and historic, and new growth', as contributed as much to the well-being of the community and nation as a whole, as to the individual locality, producer and household.

Reference to the agricultural White Paper of 1926, the Ministry's 'Economic Series' of booklets and to Abercrombie's various writings complicates Gaddis's comparison of the contemporary and historical perspectives, in as much as the observer of current events may strive, as consciously as any historian for perspective and elevation in synthesising what was happening. Such curiosity and reportage may be motivated (as with the historian) by personal and institutional self-interest, but, as Lord Macmillan testified, ministers and parliament positively wanted such 'expert' synthesis. In that sense, Patrick Geddes exaggerated the lack of interest shown by the 'Governing Classes' in 'the scientific method'. Their difficulty was not so much in the approach as in the practicalities of its application.

Such intelligence offered the opportunity to reconcile what Lord Macmillan perceived to be the liberties, which went with a greater sense of well-being, with the full scope for personal initiative and enterprise. A basis was provided for reconciling Bledisloe's assurance, in the Lords' debate on the White Paper, of the Government's desire for the best possible use of agricultural land with equal recognition of how farming, of all industries, lent itself least to Government administration and control.[40] Historians have variously characterised as backward-looking attempts to accommodate proposals for the fullest food-production and employment with policies to secure the profitability of farming. They have, however, a resonance with attempts by such figures as Abercrombie to reconcile wider societal aspirations for town and countryside with the individual entitlements of those owning and occupying property. In drafting Abercrombie's terms of reference for his Sheffield Civic Survey of 1924, local councillors and officers wanted a plan for the whole city that would foster work and trade through improvement as the transport infrastructure, and renewal

---

[39] J. M. Lee, Editorial, *Public Administration* 61 (1983): 347–50.
[40] PD, Lords, 63, 322.

and expansion of the city's housing, with due regard to convenience, health and appearance.[41] For Abercrombie himself, such aspiration was encompassed within the fundamental triad – environment, function and organism – or, as translated by Patrick Geddes into the more immediate relationship, a triad of 'place, work and people'. The emphasis might vary. Abercrombie's focus was on 'place',[42] whereas that of the agricultural interest-groups was on 'work'. Each of the three elements was the subject of much study and succour, but, as Patrick Geddes again emphasised at the meeting of the Sociological Society, they were the integral parts of 'a living unity'.[43] Politically, the attainment of such a unity of economic and social factors gave government, both central and local, a unique and essential purpose.

But, as Richard Vinen wrote in his twentieth-century history of Europe, *A history in fragments*, everything had become more complicated. The speeches and literature of the interwar years give the impression of an unprecedented interest in technological change or, for the purposes of this chapter, 'the scientific method'. Yet conditions in those same years were economically and socially worse than anything which came before or after.[44] 'The complications of everyday life', as Gaddis called them, both limited perspective and impaired its attainment. A paper published in the *Transactions of the Highland and Agricultural Society of Scotland*, written by the advisory economist for the South-Eastern Agricultural College, illustrated how modest was the progress being made in disseminating a more business-like approach to farm management.[45] A colleague in Abercrombie's own department attacked the excessive sentimentality shown toward the preservation of single buildings, streets and settlements. There had been so little grasp of the urgency of a more systematic management of compete 'landscapes', with ever-expanding borders.[46] With renewed economic recession in the late 1920s, the consultant's reports remained, for a large part, heuristic tools. Rather than there being a single history, Vinen speculated as to how there being multiple histories, overlapping and intertwining. Such a view may most closely reconcile contemporary and historical perceptions of the 1920s, in the sense of discerning the inkling of some central purpose from the muddle which there undoubtedly was.

[41] Abercrombie and Mattocks, *Sheffield*, p. iv; G. Dix, 'Patrick Abercrombie', in *Pioneers in British Planning*, ed. G. E. Cherry (1981), p. 108.

[42] Dix, 'Little plans and noble diagrams', p. 342.

[43] Brandford, *The Coal Crisis*, pp. 10–11.

[44] R. Vinen, *A History in Fragments: Europe in the Twentieth Century* (2000), p. 7.

[45] J. Wyllie, 'Some problems in farm management', *Transactions of the Highland and Agricultural Society* 41 (1929): 21–46.

[46] W. A. Eden, 'Order in the countryside', *Town Planning Review* 14 (1930): 95–103.

11 Farming in the public interest: constructing and reconstructing agriculture on the political left

Clare Griffiths

INDIVIDUALISM VERSUS PUBLIC SERVICE

Farmers have often been closely associated with traditions of individualism. The enduring resonance of the notion of the 'yeoman' conjures up ideals of independence of character and independence of action. In some contexts this determination to do as one pleased could be a subject of admiration, even when it seemed to go against the interests of the community as a whole. In John Moore's novel *The Blue Field*, one man's obstinacy in the face of the dictates of the executive committees directing agricultural production during the Second World War becomes, perversely, a cause for celebration rather than condemnation. The farmer who refuses to plant the crops officially prescribed, only to grow a defiant blue field of linseed instead, is presented as a charming embodiment of old English spirit – with the ultimate pedigree that he is rumoured to be a descendant of Shakespeare.[1]

Such determined independence could make it difficult for farmers to find common cause with each other, yet alone to identify with the good of a wider community. The farmer and author A. G. Street commented on the reluctance of farmers even to participate in organisations to promote their own interests. The National Farmers' Union's chief problems, he observed, were its own members: 'Farmers are naturally individualists and do not take kindly to control or to co-operation.'[2] When Street was writing, in 1932, the NFU was in fact already well established and, far from simply living up to its motto of 'Defence not defiance', was actively lobbying for an interventionist approach in public policy: for the state to assume some responsibility for promoting farming prosperity. Nonetheless, the individualism of the farmer was readily linked with ideas connecting national characteristics with personal freedom and a wariness about the power of the state. On the left, such individualism was problematic. Farmers' inclinations and priorities appeared to be antithetical to

---

[1] J. Moore, *The Blue Field* (1948).
[2] A. G. Street, *Farmer's Glory* (1989 edn; first published 1932), p. 249.

the economic interventions and controls with which the political left became associated during the twentieth century. Farmers were singled out for criticism as asocial beings, whose selfishness overrode other considerations in their dealings with their employees, or with day-trippers walking through their fields, and which prevented them from rising to the challenge of putting the land in their custody to its best and fullest use.

During the 1920s, however, new ways of thinking about agriculture began to offer an alternative prospect, which ran contrary to this ready equation between farming and individualistic private enterprise. When Ramsay MacDonald outlined the Labour Party's first major agricultural programme in 1926, 'duty' and 'service' were prominent elements in his vision of a new and prosperous agriculture. He imagined that Labour might introduce 'a higher motive' into farming, hitherto shaped by narrow commercial and personal considerations. Individualism would be replaced by ideals of public service, where agriculturists exhibited 'pride of calling and public spirit'. MacDonald talked about the scope for a new psychology to take shape amongst the farming community, through 'evolutionary processes'.[3] Farmers would 'do their duty', and those who rendered 'a useful public service' would find the Labour Party to be a new, if rather surprising, political ally.[4]

This form of language was not peculiar to MacDonald, though it does seem to have held great appeal for him.[5] Dissenters from the 1926 programme, who wanted a more radical and socialist reconstruction of agriculture than the drafting committee was ready to concede, had their own ideas about transforming farming into a 'public service'. The Independent Labour Party took the theme as part of its own programme, and declared that agriculture should become 'a great social service',[6] and could not be left at the 'whims of individuals'.[7] Clearly the possibility of such a transfiguration was alarming to some of those confronted with this political rhetoric. In her 'political dialogues' from 1929 Winifred Holtby pictures a farmer who is shocked at the idea that Labour would reorganise farming as a 'social service'. A friend has to explain

---

3 Ramsay MacDonald to Jesse Hawkes, 6 Dec 1926, National Archives, MacDonald papers, PRO30/69/1171/652.

4 *A Prosperous Countryside* (Labour Party pamphlet, 1927).

5 On his ideas about 'public service' as a general aim for the new society, see J. R. MacDonald, *Socialism: Critical and Constructive* (1921), pp. 279, 282–3. He may have been influenced by an earlier formulation of the idea of the farmer as a 'public servant', in A. Hickmott, *Socialism and Agriculture* (1897), p. 15. MacDonald certainly owned a copy of Hickmott's book.

6 E.g. E. H. Hunter, of the ILP, speaking at the Labour Party conference, 1924: *Proceedings of the 24th Annual Labour Party Conference* (1924), p. 173.

7 F. S. Cocks, *Socialism and Agriculture* (ILP pamphlet, 1925).

to him what this means: 'I expect you think social services mean things like health visiting … But I believe that the Labour Party means by social service some industry organized for the good of the whole Community, rather than for a few individuals.'[8]

Like Holtby's puzzled farmer, we too need to ask what it meant for farming to be viewed as a 'public' or 'social' service. In essence, such formulations touched on the way in which agriculture should relate to the whole of society (both urban and rural) and contribute to the common good. They began to deny some of the special character of the rural nation which had been a mainstay of political and cultural attitudes towards agriculture. Rather than assuming that agriculture was inherently different, working according to its own rules, and ultimately justified outside practical, economic argument, political discussion on the left searched for ways to integrate agricultural policy into broader political programmes. Agriculture still commanded an awed respect from many urban politicians, as an area of policy unto itself, but increasingly it was considered important to draw connections between agriculture and other areas of policy. The agricultural sector came to find more explicit justification through ideas about the contribution which it could, and should, make to society. As agriculture was imaginatively reconfigured as a social industry serving national needs, it became easier for the left to adopt a more sympathetic attitude to the problems faced by farmers in a period marked by the decline of many areas of domestic production and widespread talk of agricultural depression. The notion of farming in the public interest, rather than under the influence of a narrow individualism, made it possible to acknowledge a significant place for agricultural policy within progressive visions of social and economic reconstruction, and to envisage practical supports to ensure the future prosperity of farming.

AGRICULTURE AND THE PUBLIC GOOD

Approaches to agricultural policy underwent significant change in the period between the two world wars. Several factors were important in shaping this development, one of the most prominent being the changes in the countryside itself in the aftermath of the First World War, particularly through the experience of de-control in 1921. Analyses from specialists in the developing fields of agricultural science and agricultural economics also added new elements to political debate about the nature of the problems faced by agriculturists, and the possibilities for tackling them. The emphasis in political debate more

---

[8] W. Holtby, *A New Voter's Guide to Party Programmes: Political Dialogues* (1929), p. 51.

broadly was shifting towards an interest in economics, and within the Labour Party this was amplified in the wake of the collapse of the Labour government in 1931: policy discussion in the 1930s became more engaged with questions of economic management and structure, and with looking at the working of industries, as much as the social consequences of industrialism. This had its influence on the way in which agriculture was viewed. Agriculture had tended in the past to be contrasted with 'industry' – which was, by implication, urban. During the 1930s, however, agriculture itself was increasingly described as an industry.

There was a further important aspect which influenced shifting attitudes towards agriculture on the left, and this was the campaign to win political support in rural Britain.[9] From the mid-1920s the Labour Party's policies towards agriculture and rural life were inseparable from efforts to wrest rural constituencies from their Conservative and Liberal allegiances. The countryside had been identified as a key electoral battleground: a lack of representation there was judged to be holding Labour back from its proper political destiny. The challenge of addressing the rural electorate provided Labour's major motivation for developing agricultural policies.[10] This need to produce a palatable, indeed attractive programme of proposals inevitably limited the scope of policy-making, encouraging reformist rather than radical measures.

It was in this context that the political left in Britain began to engage more seriously with agriculture. Before the 1920s, socialist and progressive policies on 'agriculture' tended to be concerned mainly with class interests within the countryside, and with the social conditions of those who were employed on the land. The Labour Party started to formulate a more comprehensive vision of agriculture during the First World War, and particularly from the mid-1920s. While politicians engaged in planning the reconstruction of agriculture, to rebuild its prosperity and encourage its economic development in particular directions, they were also 'constructing' agriculture, in the sense of articulating ideas about its nature and purpose.

In its agricultural programme from 1926 the Labour Party ruminated on how domestic agriculture might realise its proper destiny of prosperity, despite seemingly unpromising circumstances: 'how to ensure that rural Britain shall find its proper place in the national economy, make its due contribution to the

---

9 I discuss this in C. V. J. Griffiths, *Labour and the Countryside: The Politics of Rural Britain between the Wars* (forthcoming).

10 This was often explicit in discussions within the party: e. g. George Dallas, the main author of the party's 1926 agricultural programme, emphasised its importance in their efforts to 'win the countryside and secure a great Labour majority': *Report of the 26th Annual Labour Party Conference* (1926), p. 236.

national well-being, and in the doing of these things find its own salvation'.[11]
What was the 'due contribution to the national well-being' which agriculture
could make in the period after the First World War, and which might justify
the maintenance of the rural sector? The importance of agriculture within the
national economy, the fabric of society, and even national identity itself, had
often been assumed, rather than justified. Many on the left were also tempted
to regard rural Britain as making some vital, if essentially unexamined contribution to national life. But this viewpoint could not be without its critics. From
the perspective of the Labour movement, domestic agriculture had a case to
answer: it had an infamous reputation for perpetuating low wage levels and a
cowed work-force. In the face of arguments that British agriculture could not
sustain higher wages, Joseph Duncan pointed out that correlations between
well-run enterprises and good employment conditions should hold true on
the land as in other industries,[12] and many others were tempted to blame
farmers who were apparently too inefficient to be able to pay their employees a
proper wage. Christopher Addison believed that, whatever the financial position, the case for higher wages in agriculture must rest on 'humanitarian rather
than economic grounds'.[13]

When farmers claimed that market conditions did not allow for improved
standards of employment, some politicians were moved to suggest that the
current organisation of agriculture must be scrapped to make way for a system
which could pay a living wage. Forms of agriculture which were not profitable might reasonably be left to other countries, where they could be pursued
more efficiently.[14] Food imports had freed Britain from the need to maintain a
large farming population, and had also reduced prices for consumers: the case
for encouraging domestic agriculture was not straightforward. Indeed, self-
sufficiency had become politically tainted for some on the left, as an offence
against socialist principles and internationalism.[15] It was easy to pick up on
nationalistic anxieties about ensuring domestic production in the interests of

---

[11] *Labour's Policy on Agriculture* (Labour Party pamphlet, 1926).

[12] J. Duncan, *Memorandum on Immediate Steps in Agricultural Reconstruction* (issued
by Labour Party advisory committee on rural problems, 1918), p. 3.

[13] Christopher Addison to Ramsay MacDonald, 28 May 1931, National Archives,
MacDonald papers, PRO 30/69/244/276–7.

[14] See R. B. Walker, *Speed the Plough* (ILP pamphlet, 1924); *Labour's Aims* (Labour
Party pamphlet, Sep 1937).

[15] H. B. Pointing and Emile Burns, *Agriculture* (Labour Research Department, 1927),
p. 14, on the socialist policy of producing commodities where they could be grown
'easiest and cheapest'; comments on domestic sugar production in *Country Worker*,
Jan 1935.

national defence, though, unsurprisingly, by the late 1930s concerns about the security of the food supply were re-emerging across the political spectrum.

There were various other potential justifications for a domestic agriculture, including the centrality of farming in sustaining viable rural communities. In the later twentieth century, farmers' lobby groups had some success in promoting justifications for agricultural support based around arguments about stewardship of the countryside and maintaining the aesthetic and environmental qualities of the landscape. This argument was also given prominence through the insistence in the Scott Report of 1942 that farmers were 'custodians of the natural heritage of the countryside'.[16] In the interwar period such arguments appeared relatively rarely in political discussion on the left, though the 'untidiness' of an 'unkempt' and 'derelict' landscape was often cited as an indictment of bad farming practices.[17] More than anything else, though, agriculture's responsibilities towards the community at large were seen to lie in the production of food. Even when political pamphlets discoursed on the ugliness of a derelict, sometime arable landscape, the offence to aesthetics was linked directly to a scandal of economic neglect: fields of weeds, undrained acres. As a publication from 1934 noted, 'the listlessness of slow decay is everywhere apparent … Sadly lacking over vast stretches of land is any sign of active, energetic cultivation, that obvious eagerness to make the fullest use of every half-acre of soil – the visible proof of a prosperous husbandry.'[18] Productivity was the debt that agriculturists owed to society for their use of the land. If land was an asset, held in trust for the community, then the 'frivolous or neglectful holder' should not be tolerated.[19] To put the land to full use was the farmer's most direct form of public service. In the opinion of most left-wing politicians, that public service would only be heightened when – by some means as yet unclarified – that land belonged legally, as well as morally, to the community.

Land nationalisation was one of several key elements in Labour's agricultural programme which seemed unlikely to win the party much support amongst farmers. Since most farmers' ambitions through the 1920s and 1930s were to return to state support, yet avoid state control, the policies which were most likely to prove popular with them were not easily compatible with left-wing priorities. When Ramsay MacDonald, as Labour prime minister, summoned a conference of representatives from the agricultural industry to

---

[16] L. D. Stamp, 'The Scott Report: a new charter for the countryside', *Geographical Magazine* 15/9 (Jan 1943): 396.

[17] E.g. descriptions of landscape in *How Labour Will Save Agriculture* (Labour Party pamphlet, 1934).

[18] *How Labour Will Save Agriculture*.

[19] Noel Buxton, in *The Book of the Labour Party: Its History, Growth, Policy, and Leaders*, vol. 2, ed. H. Tracey (1925), p. 40.

discuss policy in 1930, protective tariffs and subsidies were specifically ruled out as topics for debate.[20] Unfortunately these were the farmers' main demand at the time, pushed back onto the public stage in strident fashion through a series of demonstrations on the plight of British farming. After the 'Great Betrayal' of 1921, when Lloyd George's government removed the guaranteed prices provided by the Corn Protection Acts, farmers concentrated much of their public energy on attempts to have them reinstated. They were, however, far less happy to see the return of that other component of agricultural policy from the First World War: the minimum wage. Wage regulation had been another casualty of decontrol in 1921, but its reinstatement was a priority for the first Labour government, in 1924. Here, Labour's agricultural policy was addressing the interests of its most obvious constituency in the countryside, and the return of the wages board, albeit in a weaker form than its 1917 predecessor, came to be cited as an illustration of Labour's commitment to rural issues. It was not an issue with which farmers could identify; indeed, they regarded wage regulation as directly contrary to their interests. Until the Second World War the NFU remained opposed to the minimum wage, and many farmers argued that high wage bills were bankrupting their businesses.

THE ROLE OF THE FARMER

It might have been expected that Labour would apply the same class distinctions within agriculture as it identified in other sectors of the economy, and define its potential constituency of support accordingly. Yet, although classifications were applied, which made it clear that farmers were not regarded as 'workers', there was no corresponding assumption that Labour should limit its campaigns to pursuing votes only amongst farm labourers. The farmers were also within the party's sights. The ambition of winning the farming vote was not as absurd as it might appear. Farmers as a group have tended to be anti-socialist, but in the 1930s and 1940s some of them seem to have been rather more receptive to what the Labour Party had to offer – partly as a consequence of the fact that the other parties appeared to have lost interest in their votes, and were demonstrating little inclination to make any promises to restore agricultural prosperity. In a party pamphlet from 1928, aimed specifically at a farming readership, G. T. Garratt (himself recently retired from a career in India, and now farming a hundred acres in Cambridgeshire) warned farmers that they faced a stark choice: between the Conservative Party's policy of doing nothing to address the problems of British agriculture, and Labour's proposals to reorganise agriculture as a public utility. He promised a future

---

[20] National Archives, MacDonald papers, PRO 30/69/244/219–22.

in which supplies and prices would be stabilised, farmers would enjoy greater security, and their position would be 'more dignified and independent'.[21]

This potential transformation in the position and status of farmers became the Labour Party's main focus in its campaigns to capture the farming vote. Rather than attempting to convert this unsympathetic audience to the mainstays of a socialist platform – improvements to the lives of farm workers, and the goal of national ownership of the land – Labour concentrated on how farmers' own fortunes might actually benefit within a reformed agriculture. Land nationalisation was rarely emphasised as a point of principle, but rather presented as the means to achieve a more favourable economic setting in which to farm. Once the state was the nation's landlord, it was promised, tenants would enjoy the benefits of investment in the land which modern capitalist landlords had ceased to provide.[22] Heavily mortgaged owner-occupiers, meanwhile, would have an opportunity to release their capital and transform their farms into going concerns. Only in these circumstances of social ownership of the land, Labour argued, could the state contemplate investment in what would remain essentially private enterprises. Farmers were given the prospect of a new role, farming on behalf of the community and with the active encouragement of public investment in developing efficient and scientific cultivation.

More immediately attractive than the potential for greater investment in agriculture were Labour's promises to boost farm incomes. At the 1929 general election one of the party's commitments was to 'make farming pay'. A decade or so earlier, that somewhat ambiguously phrased objective might have been construed as a threat to exact retribution from a culpable industry, but at the end of the 1920s it conveyed the intention to restore agricultural prosperity and offer farmers a better deal than they had under the Conservatives. In place of the tariffs and subsidies which farmers themselves were calling for, Labour offered the possibilities of 'stabilisation' of agricultural prices, and later of 'guaranteeing' prices as a route to allow farmers the security to plan ahead and develop their production for the longer term. These guarantees were based on expectations about the potential to control markets and supply, with safeguards to ensure that the customer was not disadvantaged as a result. The issue of agricultural protection was the most difficult aspect of policy within Labour's attempts to position itself as the party most committed to agricultural

[21] *The Farmer and the Labour Party: Fair Reward for All* (Labour Party pamphlet, 1928).

[22] See, for example, Tom Williams's comments (*Labour's Way to Use the Land* (1935), p. 6) that, despite the many criticisms which could be made of landlordism in the past, landlords in the eighteenth and nineteenth centuries had at least taken an interest in farming and helped to promote good husbandry.

reconstruction. The old fear of 'dear food', and the political damage which this might wreak amongst the urban electorate, was still the most powerful obstacle to granting state assistance to agricultural producers. But the first Labour government's action in protecting the nascent sugar beet industry showed that exceptions could be justified in the interests of developing new sectors, boosting home production of foodstuffs, and expanding employment.[23]

For many politicians on the left in the 1930s the practical problem about implementing subsidies and other forms of state support was that, whilst these seemed likely to increase the income of producers and market middlemen, they lacked effective controls to ensure positive social outcomes in the interests of the wider community. In the House of Commons debate on the Wheat Act of 1932, Clement Attlee (deputy leader of the Labour Party, and a former assistant to Christopher Addison at the Ministry of Agriculture) was prepared to acknowledge the argument for at least temporary support for the troubled grain-producers, equating this to the need for measures to help depressed industrial and mining communities. However, he insisted that protection could only prove acceptable where it was clear that an industry was being run to proper standards, and for public benefit. The ultimate expression of this would be control of the enterprise, 'by the community in the interests of the community'.[24]

There was a further significant argument against using subsidies to support agricultural production for the future, on grounds of economic development. As the second Labour government struggled to answer protests from arable farmers in 1930, and respond to demands for transitional support to keep land under cultivation during a time of extreme economic hardship, the Economic Advisory Council advised against any state assistance. The EAC argued that support for wheat-growing was contrary to agriculture's long-term interests, and that, like other depressed industries in Britain, the future of farming lay in rationalisation and the development of more efficient and profitable fields of production.[25] Though the National Government subsequently chose to introduce deficiency payments to support grain-producers, Labour could not see this as a sustainable route to achieving agricultural prosperity. A Labour pamphlet issued in response to the Wheat Act argued that English farmers could simply not compete with the prairie farming practised in other countries. Instead they should concentrate on areas of farming 'for which our country and our soil are admirably adapted and specially favourable, such as poultry

---

[23] On the implications of the sugar subsidy, see E. A. Attwood, 'The origins of state support for British agriculture', *Manchester School of Economic and Social Studies* 31 (1963): 145.

[24] *Hansard*, 5th series, Commons, 262, cols. 1134–9, 2 Mar 1932.

[25] CAB 24/213, C. P. 244 (30).

farming, stock breeding, meat production, pig rearing and so on.'[26] It is worth noting the fundamentally optimistic vision behind this analysis: that, by concentrating on the right commodities, British agriculture still had the potential to function as an economically viable industry.

The idea of using the land in the most appropriate manner was not just about the scope to restore agricultural productivity, but was one of the essential components of an agriculture defined around serving the public interest. Agriculture's contribution to the national diet was naturally one of the primary ways in which British farming could be justified. But in response to contemporary debates about nutritional standards, links between the practice of farming and the needs of the community became more specific. In the late 1930s Labour spokesmen sometimes explored the possibility of constructing the agricultural industry around promoting higher nutritional standards: subsidising food consumption, in Morgan Philips Price's words, 'to aid the health diet of the people'.[27] Philips Price's proposal would have defined farming output directly in accordance with the nutritional needs of the whole population, encouraging positive patterns of consumption through state subsidy for those 'health foods' whose price under the free market often acted as a deterrent to working-class consumers. A 1937 party pamphlet, *Labour's Policy of Food for All*, argued that agriculture should be organised around this as its 'primary purpose': to provide people with the healthy foods they needed, at prices which were within their reach.[28]

The chief 'health foods' which were at issue here were fresh fruit and vegetables and fresh liquid milk. Eggs and meat were also elements considered to be underrepresented in the diet of the population at large. It was therefore ironic that the major focus of the drive for agricultural protection in the early 1930s had been on the very commodity which was regarded as dominating the national diet to a harmful degree – wheat. To wean the working classes from their dependence on bread, margarine and sugar products, Labour policy argued that they should have better and cheaper access to healthy foodstuffs. Part of this would be achieved by reforms in marketing, a subject which was given a great deal of attention from the late 1920s, and identified by Christopher Addison as an approach which was capable of yielding positive social benefits, even whilst the essential organisation of capitalist agriculture remained intact. But another important element in Labour's agricultural programmes was the emphasis given to farmers' inability to satisfy this market for healthy food from their current production. Modern agriculture was criticised

[26] A. Salter, *The Bread Tax* (Labour Party pamphlet, 1932), p. 11.

[27] M. Philips Price, 'Scientific agriculture and the consumer', *Labour*, Dec 1936.

[28] *Labour's Policy of Food for All* (Labour Party pamphlet, 1937)

as wasteful: its produce reached the consumer at vastly inflated prices, which failed to stimulate demand and thus resulted in the scandals of milk being thrown away or used for non-food purposes, and foodstuffs rotting because they could not be sold. It was argued that farmers had scarcely begun to capitalise on the possibilities offered by the domestic market for healthy, fresh food. Diversification of production had become a commonplace, urged on farmers following the collapse of grain prices during 1930, and which some had been calling for from at least the 1870s. It was not seen simply as a way of moving out of unprofitable sectors into markets where British agriculture might be competitive. It also promised to address real needs within the community, for quantities of reasonably priced, nutritionally valuable foodstuffs, which were currently in short supply. Here the interests of the community, and especially of poorer families, might intersect with the interests of farmers: farmers would find their market 'in the stomachs of the poor'.[29]

By 1939 the issue of nutrition was recognised as a dominant theme in defining agricultural policy on the left, of greater influence than those questions of land ownership and social relations which had once informed rhetoric about the future of agriculture. In the final years before the Second World War the Labour Party seemed to have found a way to bridge the gap between rural producers and urban consumers, and unite them in a social enterprise to raise national standards of living. It advertised its programme under the reversible banner of 'Food and Farming / Farming and Food'.[30] The electoral efficacy of this approach could not be tested, as the expectation of a general election was deferred by the outbreak of war. However, it did suggest a means of defining responsibility and accountability on the part of agriculturists, whilst at the same time offering them a promising economic future. Here was an example of what the 1926 programme had been searching for: a way in which agriculture might 'make its due contribution to the national well-being, and in the doing of these things find its own salvation'.

THE FUTURE OF FARMING

On one level, the idea of agriculture operating for the public good offered a way of linking different electorates and suggesting that they had mutual concerns: that the urban electorate should take an interest in the fate of agriculture, and that, conversely, the farming community could not safely set itself apart from the rest of the nation. But the notion of farming in the public

---

[29] *Labour's Policy of Food for All.*

[30] E.g. in Labour Party leaflets from June 1938, and as the subject of one of the issues in Labour's four-part series *Your Britain.*

interest also provided new justifications for treating agriculture as a special case within the economy, and for responding to farmers' requests for support in a harsh market. It opened up the potential for a social covenant between farmers and the general public, and, more directly, between farmers and the government. If farmers were responsive to national needs, they would deserve help and respect for their enterprise. Such treatment would be dependent on their willingness to fulfil their social role and public duty.

In the 1930s the use of phrases like 'public duty' or 'social service' was not as common as it had been when MacDonald was leader of the Labour Party. However, across many groups on the political left, even including the Communist Party,[31] ideas which these phrases had begun to express were becoming more rounded, and were being developed into specific policy positions. These approaches opened out different understandings of the social role of the farmer, and of the relationship between agriculture and the national community. Through commitments to the principle of land nationalisation, and to the desirability of making agriculturists accountable to the community, socialists appeared to offer more stick than carrot to the farmers. But by establishing assumptions about mutual dependency and common interests between town and country, the left was in fact able to envisage a range of supports to encourage them to rise to the challenges of boosting productivity, modernising and diversifying. Definitions of how farming might make a contribution to the welfare of the community as a whole paved the way for interventionist measures to confirm its status and underwrite its future prosperity.

---

[31] As expressed, for example, in the rural magazine *The Country Standard.*

12 Farmworkers, local identity and conservatism, 1914–1930

Nicholas Mansfield

W HEN I was a child in the 1950s, my next-door neighbour was an old railwayman called Sam Fairweather – a Methodist and Labour voter – who in September 1914 had walked 27 miles in one day to enlist at Bury St Edmunds barracks. Twenty-odd years ago, when I was interviewing elderly Norfolk farmworkers about George Edwards and the early days of the National Union of Agricultural Workers (NUAW), the conversation invariably turned from labour movement activism to the trenches in which, almost without exception, they had volunteered to serve. Indeed they saw the union, politics, the Great War and their younger selves as inextricably mixed, in a way which confused those schooled in a left-wing historiography.

Another puzzle awaited me when working on the unions in the Welsh Marches -Shropshire and neighbouring counties. At first sight it seemed fertile and unresearched ground. In the periods before and after the Great War, for the farmworkers' union the county was second in importance only to its Norfolk heartland. The unions here did quite well until about 1920, when in parallel with those in other parts of the country they declined, ostensibly because of agricultural depression. Yet Marcher farming, unlike that of the south and east of England, was not entirely governed by the price of wheat, and could be comparatively prosperous. The failure of agricultural trades unionism in Shropshire is mirrored in politics, with debacles like the Ludlow bye-election of 1923, demonstrating that most of the rural poor not only declined to vote Labour, but also actively chose to vote Conservative.[1]

My book *English Farmworkers and Local Patriotism, 1900–1930* tries to grapple with some of these issues, and argues that underlying cultural factors and the political consequences of the Great War motivated the relatively understudied ununionised farmworkers. In particular, within the Marches a distinctive local identity, augmented and soon surpassed the potentially stronger class identity, a process which may be applicable to other parts of rural England during the interwar period.[2]

---

[1] See N. Mansfield, 'Agricultural Trades Unionism in Shropshire, 1900–1930' (unpublished PhD thesis University of Wolverhampton, 1997).

[2] N. Mansfield, *English Farmworkers and Local Patriotism, 1900–1930* (Aldershot, 2001).

RURAL LIFE IN THE MARCHES

The traditional toast 'All Friends Around the Wrekin' eloquently summarises that strong regional identity and apparent classlessness of rural life in the Marches. Shropshire and neighbouring counties were remote. Its identity was defined in opposition to Wales and the Welsh, a real case of ancient enmity surviving into modern times, which could be shared by all classes of rural society. The gentry families, often established for centuries, commanded loyalty and rewarded it with an active and paternalistic involvement in local government. Their typically small or medium-sized estates weathered comparatively well Lloyd George, wartime time death duties and even the post-war depression. The underlying pastoral nature of agriculture cushioned the blow of the recession, and the very localised farming systems of the Shropshire 'pays' could contribute to relative prosperity. Whilst the growth of the West Midlands conurbation in the nineteenth century seemed to threaten the Shropshire gentry with a potential enemy as bitter as the hated Welsh, in the twentieth century its bountiful markets, typified by the Cadbury Brothers, proved a godsend to local agriculture.[3]

The Marcher gentry usually lived locally, and their amusements were connected with agriculture. Fox-hunting was a more important activity here than in other parts of England. Shropshire had more packs of hounds than Norfolk, which had twice the acreage and population. Farmers were encouraged to hunt, decreasing tensions between them and the gentry. Parts of the agricultural economy were geared to its needs, and even the poor were given ancillary roles in an activity which typified the organic society at peace with itself, which was the Marcher ideal.[4]

Genuine pride in the craft of the farmworkers' job was evident in the Marches, and encouraged by gentry and farmers. Tied cottages had large gardens, and, especially in the hillier south and west of Shropshire, there was access to grazing on common land. Squatting had been encouraged by landowners keen to exploit the mineral rights in economically marginal areas. On the Stiperstones and Clee Hills workers combined shifts in mining or quarrying with small-scale lifestyle farming, in a peculiar hybrid of independence and paternalism.[5] Working-class institutions retained the air of patronage. Marcher friendly societies, whether the village-based clubs (like the Wem Cow Club, which prospered into the 1930s) or branches of the national

---

3 Mansfield, *English Farmworkers*, chapter 2.

4 Mansfield, *English Farmworkers*, pp. 43–6. See also N. Mansfield, 'Foxhunting and the yeomanry: county identity and military culture', in *Our Hunting Forefathers: Field Sports in England after 1850*, ed. R. W. Hoyle (forthcoming).

5 Mansfield, *English Farmworkers*, pp. 40–4, 128–9.

affiliated orders, invariably had farmers as officers and gentry as their patrons and displayed little of the independent action which others have argued paralleled the chapel or union branch. Nonconformity was weak in Shropshire and had very little influence on the unions, and could be hostile to them, even in the 1870s. Instead the early Marcher unions themselves received gentry patronage, a phenomenon which again continued in various ways as late as the 1930s. Indeed, given the working-class cultural background of the area, it is extraordinary that the unions achieved as much as they did, and is probably indicative of the strength of class conflict.[6]

Although farmworkers supplied a good proportion of pre-war recruits to the army, Victorian military service was generally regarded as degrading and de-skilling, especially amongst 'respectable' working-class families. There was also relatively little connection, whether we consider officers or rank and file, between the 'county' regiment and the locality from which it was supposed to recruit. Pre-1914 regulars were a professional caste, cut adrift from their home districts. The social structure of the Territorial Army, though still underresearched, indicates that in most counties, part-time soldiers were spread out in drill halls across large geographic areas, and only came together for annual camp, giving little time to instill regimental spirit. By contrast, the county yeomanry (farmers' sons officered by gentry) used the comradeship of the hunting field, tempered in the nineteenth century by an anti-working-class police role, to develop a strong sense of identity based on county. Although less spectacular than the urban working class embrace of Lord Kitchener's appeal in 1914, the response of farmworkers was, over time, equally complete. It is likely that a quarter of a million volunteered; schoolroom patriotism, peer pressure and poverty being the main reasons: 'They said Kaiser Bill was coming over with his men ... all the youngsters went' and 'We were all damn glad to have got off the farms.' However, the threat of conscription and intimidation were used before the first month of the war was out, accompanied by a recruiting rhetoric which used historical military exemplars; Nelson in Norfolk, Cromwell's Ironsides in Cambridgeshire and the Marcher Lords in Shropshire. Probably for the first time, the county, rather than the village or district became a focus of local loyalty for working-class people. Comparisons were made with the recruiting efforts of ancient rivals, so in Shropshire the efforts of the old Welsh enemy were derided. Local dignitaries, often assisted by leaders of the labour movement and aided by the local press, made locally raised regiments the centre of a county identity, a process particularly noticeable in counties like Cambridgeshire, which did not have a strong collective image.[7]

[6] Mansfield, *English Farmworkers*, pp. 47–9, 128–9.

[7] Mansfield, *English Farmworkers*, pp. 80–90.

This county identity was also emphasised in the training of rural Kitchener battalions, when gentry or upper-class officers, very rarely from the same locality, found it a useful tool in instilling unit pride: 'We were all Norfolk chaps in my platoon. There were one or two educated chaps but most on us were all sort of uneducated. But with our sort o'slang we all kept together and got on better … We clicked in, in one lot: we all kept together.' Alongside this local identity, a unity based on class was also created, for the several dozen rural Kitchener battalions consisted mainly of farmworkers, and there is evidence that they took labour traditions with them into the army.[8] By contrast, farmers and their sons did not volunteer, but stayed at home and made money. After the introduction of conscription in 1916 the overwhelming number of the Military Tribunal appeals in country districts were by farmers' sons, as farmers retired or sacked their workers and brought their sons into their places: 'there [was] no more unpopular class than the tenant farmers in England … wherever you go you hear nothing but bitter complaints against the … farmers … as to their want of patriotism in keeping their sons back and sending their labourers to get killed, [and] the enormous prices they are charging for foodstuffs.' The leaders of the fledging farmworkers' unions were not slow to contrast the patriotism of their members with the self-interestedness of farmers.[9]

But conscription still fell largely on the rural poor, as did a number of other burdens which increased class tensions in the countryside: inflation, the wholesale lowering of the school-leaving age and the attempt to bully women back into field work. This war-weariness, though, was often combined with a pride in the working-class blood sacrifice and a determination to tilt the balance in their favour. From 1916 the unions grew in strength, the NUAW in particular took strike action when farmers refused to raise wages. In Shropshire a planned series of haysel and harvest disputes, based on the strongest branches, succeeded in raising wages throughout the county. This process continued unabated after the introduction of Agricultural Wages Boards in 1917, and, with unions pushing for a share in post-war prosperity, they experienced an astronomic growth. This was paralleled by almost identical increases in the membership of rural branches of the railway unions and in the now largely forgotten radical ex-service organisation – the National Federation of Discharged and Demobilised Soldiers and Sailors. Together these formed Labour parties in the last few weeks of the war, contesting the 'Coupon' election of

---

[8] Mansfield, *English Farmworkers*, pp. 86–102.

[9] Mansfield, *English Farmworkers*, pp. 104–6, 112–14. For typical press reports of Tribunal hearings see *Shrewsbury Chronicle*, 2 Jun 1916, where a hunt servant was given exemption, and 3 Jun 1916, where the chairman of the Ellesmere Tribunal declared: 'Farmers are not doing their duty. If we allow these boys to stop at home we shall be become the laughing stock of the country.'

December 1918 and making inroads into local government. With the collapse of the Liberals in districts like Shropshire, Labour found itself, almost over-night, the main opposition to the Tories.[10]

However, the farmworkers' economic and political success in the Marches was fragile, and the tide began to turn in the early summer of 1919. Whilst a widespread haysel strike by the NUAW in north Shropshire was settled in the union's favour, in neighbouring counties the decision of the rival Workers' Union to carry on working caused defeat, victimisation and bitterness between the two unions. As national agricultural depression began to bite, wages and union membership in the Marches fell catastrophically. An attempt by the NUAW to organise a county-wide strike in the spring of 1923, in support of the larger Norfolk dispute, petered out, again undermined by the Workers' Union. Within weeks the Labour candidate at the Ludlow bye-election was humiliatingly beaten into third place, polling barely a thousand votes. In a process which continued through the interwar period, many Labour support-ers voted with their feet and migrated to the city, typically from the Marches to the suburbs of the Birmingham conurbation. Their defeat though was not just at the hands of the agricultural depression but was the result of a dynamic set of new culturally conservative village institutions, which combined with older paternalism, formed an unbeatable combination for post-war radicalism.[11]

POST-WAR VILLAGE INSTITUTIONS AND ORGANISATIONS

The National Farmers' Union (NFU) rapidly established itself as significant in the post-war world, moving from a pre-war preoccupation with particular problems of livestock husbandry to being the employers' negotiators for the wage level settlement in the county's premier industry. It coolly and successfully countered the threat from organised labour, during, for example, the wave of strikes in 1919. In the 1918 election the NFU ran candidates in Worcestershire and Leominster, with programmes focusing on the difficulties of tenant farm-ers. However, the NFU in Shropshire showed little conflict with landowners, ostracised those few farmers who expressed support for the emerging Labour Party, and specifically voted to support the Conservative Party. By 1922, in con-junction with the local press, it was sponsoring a 'Brighter Villages' campaign which helped maintain a loyalist consensus in the countryside.[12]

---

[10] Mansfield, *English Farmworkers*, chapter 5, and N. Mansfield, 'The National Federation of Discharged and Demobilised Soldiers and Sailors, 1917–1921: a view from the Marches', *Family and Community History* 7/1 (May 2004).

[11] Mansfield, *English Farmworkers*, chapter 6.

[12] Mansfield, *English Farmworkers*, pp. 171–2, and *Shrewsbury Chronicle*, 21 Jan 1920.

The NFU was only one of the new institutions which were significant in this campaign. Ploughing matches had been used by nineteenth-century agricultural societies as a way of strengthening the pride and interest of the workforce but had died out in the late Victorian period. Now they were revived, along with hedging competitions and sheepdog trials linked to the growth of local agricultural shows, and were rewarded with prizes and cups presented by the gentry and were publicised with features and photographs in the county press. This combination of recreation and education may also be linked to the appearance at the end of the 1920s of the first Young Farmers Clubs, fostered by the NFU, and seen as deliberately harmonising the interests of farmers and farmworkers.[13]

Women's Institutes (WIs), having originally developed in Canada, first appeared in Shropshire in 1917, sponsored by the government to aid the war effort. Some historians see WIs as feminist organisations which campaigned on important welfare issues. However, evidence from the Marches shows fairly mundane activities – fruit-bottling and folk dancing – with the wives of the gentry taking a lead. In the ballot for Shropshire representatives on the National Executive Committee in 1933, both candidates were titled. WI branches were particularly involved in the spread of Empire Day festivities in the villages, another new development which underpinned the rural consensus:

> This meant half a day off school after the celebrations, to which the vicar, squire and parents were invited. Children entertained by showing their school work and singing songs from the National Song Book, patriotic songs such as Jerusalem, Rule Britannia and, of course, the National Anthem.[14]

In reaction to the post-war challenge from radical ex-servicemen, Conservative Party activists set up their own ex-service organisation, incongruously named the Comrades of the Great War. Officially it was non-political: 'Party politics would have nothing to do with the movement.' Nonetheless, using the rhetoric of the trenches, it successfully destabilised the radical National Federation of Discharged and Demobilised Soldiers and Sailors, weakening its links with the Labour movement through anti-socialist propaganda emphasising the pacifist record of the Independent Labour Party (ILP).[15] In addition,

---

[13] Mansfield, *English Farmworkers*, p. 174.

[14] Mansfield, *English Farmworkers*, p. 76, and Shropshire Federation of Womens' Institutes, *Shropshire within Living Memory* (Newbury, 1992), p. 243. See M. Morgan, 'Jam, Jerusalem and feminism', *Oral History* 23/1 (1995): 85–8.

[15] *Shrewsbury Chronicle*, 26 Sep 1919, Mansfield, *English Farmworkers*, pp. 152–4, and

the Comrades' wealthier ex-officer members were able to organise sponsor-ship for its club premises, and would sometimes lay on lavish entertainments at the country houses of rich members, which the poorer Federation could not rival. Indeed, the workerist Federation had already cut itself off from this sort of support by excluding officers from membership unless they had been promoted from the ranks. By 1920 the government offered to put the profits of wartime canteens at the disposal of a united ex-service organisation, and both Federation and Comrades coalesced into the British Legion. Its county struc-ture consciously imitated that of the county regiment. Although non-political, village Legion branches almost always chose ex-officer members of the gen-try for their officials. In Leebotwood, Shropshire, typically, the 'squire' Major Trevor Corbett, was elected chairman, a post he held concurrently with that of chairmanship of the Shropshire Agricultural Wages Board. By the end of the 1930s it was claimed of the British Legion: 'They differ hardly in any respect from a collection of Conservative working men's clubs.' Their 'anti-Bolshevist' politics probably contributed to the membership of only 10 per cent of eligi-ble ex-servicemen, although there is evidence that this proportion was higher in rural areas. Here it is clear that the Legion's combination of comradeship, paternalism, loyalism and county pride played an important role in fostering working-class conservatism in the interwar period.[16]

Other quasi-military organisations were successful at disseminating the shared patriotic values of 1914–18 into the post-war period. The village war memorial movement was clearly a potent weapon in uniting all levels of rural society in a common bond of grief, although its form and ceremony often retained the class tensions which sacrifice was meant to transcend. Nonethe-less the dedication of the village war memorial was often the opportunity for a community to redefine itself patriotically linked to its county or nation.[17]

Village war memorials were later supplemented by grander county and county regimental memorials that were erected, usually in county towns or appropriate cathedrals, which became the focus – in a militaristic form – of the Armistice Day commemorations in each area. However, the connection between remembrance and military patriotism was initially not a foregone conclusion; indeed, there was a decided move to commemorate the dead with utilitarian schemes, particularly village memorial halls. This notion was often

Mansfield, 'The National Federation of Discharged and Demobilised Soldiers and Sailors'.

[16] Mansfield, *English Farmworkers*, pp. 169, 184–5.

[17] Mansfield, *English Farmworkers*, pp. 181–2. For a fuller discussion of the subject, see N. Mansfield, 'Class conflict and village war memorials, 1914–24', *Rural History* 6/1 (1995): 67–87.

opposed by an alliance of gentry, clergy and farmers, who favoured capital expenditure on a stone cross or brass tablet – preferably in the parish church – rather than the ongoing cost of maintaining a hall. Nevertheless, local public opinion – sometimes with Nonconformist backing – often ensured that village halls were erected, frequently using cheap army surplus huts. They became the focus of the mildly hedonistic interwar popular culture of whist drives, dances and amateur dramatics. Although village halls were usually run by committees on which elites were dominant, these activities which they housed often genuinely involved all classes of rural society.[18]

The formation of the British Legion coincided with the development of Armistice Day in a militaristic form. Moreover, in many rural areas, 11 November was supplemented by additional celebrations which commemorated the county regiment. In Shropshire this was on 6 June – Bligny Day, celebrating the unique award of the French Croix de Guerre to a county Territorial battalion. By 1921 Bligny Day was celebrated by all battalions of the King's Shropshire Light Infantry, and parades, involving all ex-servicemen were established throughout the county. In celebrating the particular identity of Shropshire and its military prowess, the phenomenon had the effect of welding ex-servicemen to an establishment and military perspective at a time when returning soldiers had the potential to be subversive. In addition, it was used by the local establishment to ensure that its own regiment survived the anti-militarism and the Geddes axe of central government, when the Territorial Army came to be re-established in the early 1920s. The county yeomanry's hunting connections ensured its own survival, together with a reversion to its traditional policing role in the strikes of the 1920s.[19]

The cult of the county regiment was strengthened in the interwar period with the establishment of regimental museums, with an emphasis on the Great War, almost as an extension of the war memorial movement. They became, by the early 1930s, the showcases for regimental reunions whose rhetoric embraced all ranks in a way which would have been impossible to countenance for the pre-1914 regulars. County towns with barracks also began to stage military tattoos to strengthen the links between the regiment and the locality, a movement probably linked with the interwar historic pageant phenomenon. Tattoos were meant to encourage local enlistment, and, although poverty more than patriotism encouraged village lads to join up, there is certainly evidence that interwar recruits were more inclined to serve in 'their' county regiments than their pre-1914 predecessors had been. As the interwar period progressed,

[18] Mansfield, *English Farmworkers*, pp. 177–81.

[19] Mansfield, *English Farmworkers*, pp. 182–4, and Mansfield, 'Foxhunting and the yeomanry', p. 9.

service in county territorial battalions became more popular as anti-war revulsion lessened.[20]

THE RURAL HEGEMONY OF THE CONSERVATIVE PARTY

Quasi-military movements joined the other new village institutions – ploughing matches, Women's Institutes, Young Farmers' Clubs, Empire Day and village halls – in supporting the loyalist consensus. This cultural conservatism was underpinned by the rural hegemony of the interwar Tory party. Historically, the Conservative Party did well in Shropshire, with strong support from the gentry and farmers, but with the gradual extension of the franchise there was a need to woo the rural poor. The Representation of the People Act of 1918 transformed the political landscape, trebling the size of the electorate and creating huge rural constituencies.

The extraordinary skill of the Conservatives was in maintaining political control of this new system whilst subsuming cultural conservatism into the mores of rural society. Thus party politics became a class-based foreign import practised by the 'townee' Labour Party. A surviving Conservative minutebook from Lydbury North, Shropshire, dating from 1886 to 1924, when read in conjunction with the parish records, indicates the enmeshed network of gentry and farmer involvement in the party. One gentry family, the Plowdens, father followed by son, provided the Association Chairmen, and R. H. Newill, the Earl of Powis's agent, was the secretary (with the earl as a member) and a member of the NFU county committee was the canvasser. (Newill also acted as returning officer!) The local association was well organised, with fetes, whist drives and the visits of a cinema van. A surviving set of canvass cards for the adjoining village of Edgton and from 1923, shows an almost total Tory domination, with only two socialist votes and one Liberal. If, as seems likely, Tory organisation was as good in other villages, the Labour Party could offer little in opposition.[21]

Tory political domination was reinforced by the local press. Labour activists found that the press 'did the Conservative's work for them in rural areas … the local Conservative party had very little contact with the general public but got unusual publicity for Conservative activities.' The *Shrewsbury Chronicle*,

[20] Mansfield, *English Farmworkers*, pp. 185–6. On the growth of regimental museums, see P. Thwaites, *Presenting Arms: Representation of British Military History, 1660–1930* (Leicester, 1996).

[21] Mansfield, *English Farmworkers*, pp. 193–7. For a fuller discussion of these issues see N. Mansfield, *Farmworkers and Local Conservatism in South-west Shropshire, 1916–23*, in *Mass Conservatism: The Conservatives and the Public since the 1880s*, ed. S. Ball and I. Holliday (2002).

the main weekly Shropshire journal, was owned by Sir Beville Stanier, Tory MP for Ludlow until 1923. It was specifically anti-socialist after the war, even to the point of suggesting that the Labour Party had no place in the political process: 'Shrewsbury was not troubled with a Labour candidate, although Oswestry was.' Curiously it moved further to the right, and between 1922 and 1929 it expressed support for the British Facists and continued to show sympathy for Mosley's British Union of Fascists in the 1930s.[22] In counties like Shropshire the sophisticated propaganda techniques developed by Conservative Central Office were still supplemented by old-fashioned paternalism on special occasions, but, on the other hand, there is evidence that intimidation was also used by the Tories as a political weapon. The Labour parliamentary candidate for Oswestry, in 1924, inevitably perhaps, blamed his defeat on 'several glaring cases where people were almost afraid of being seen speaking to him. One man had told him that after the election he had lost his job. It takes real men and women to take their stand for Labour.' The Labour Party also listed intimidation as a factor in the debacle of the Ludlow bye-election: 'tenants who dared not show the Labour colours, everywhere the chains of feudal oppression.'[23]

Based on isolated rural groups of workers – typically railwaymen, quarrymen and organised farmworkers, themselves the minority of that work-force – the Labour Party in Shropshire had practically no middle-class activists at all. It therefore could not build on the post-war potential for drastic change, and let the initiative pass to the Tories. The largest Labour event in Shropshire consisted of 100 people at a rally in Ludlow, and even this involved bussing in supporters from other constituencies. This was puny compared to the numbers mustered by the Conservatives: the Junior Imperial League welcomed 600 to its Empire Day Dinner in Shrewsbury in 1924, and in 1926 claimed nearly 1,500 members. (Thousands of schoolchildren were also officially mobilised on the day.) By its gentle handling of crises like the 1919 railway strike, the General Strike of 1926 – when the Chief Constable could state: 'I feel I must express to all strikers my appreciation of their good behaviour during the strike' – and occasional farmworkers' strikes, Shropshire Conservatism showed its political skill. Even though from 1918 most of the Shropshire rural poor had the opportunity to vote for Labour candidates – with the exception of the Wrekin in 1929 – most chose not to do so.[24]

---

[22] Mansfield, *English Farmworkers*, pp. 193–4.

[23] *English Farmworkers*, pp. 188–9. As late as the 1945 general election, sackings and evictions of estate cottagers who had displayed Labour posters were reported: *English Farmworkers*, p. 203. During a bye-election in the Isle of Ely in 1973, a tied cottage tenant of my acquaintance was told to take down a Labour poster.

[24] Mansfield, *English Farmworkers*, pp. 195–7.

In addition, many union activists, rather than undertake the thankless task of attempting to organise fellow farmworkers, migrated from the land either to work on the railways or into the cities. Once these had gone, the majority of farmworkers felt their interests were protected by choosing to vote Conservative, as they did in the Ludlow bye-election of 1923 and consistently thereafter. Even the victory of 1945, the high tide of rural socialism, had little impact in Shropshire. Given the passage of time, the voice of the rural poor is muted, but one informant from the Shropshire WI's oral history project demonstrates the extent to which farmworkers were hostile to agricultural trades unionism, which in reality was relatively powerless:

> When Bert had his 14th birthday, the farmer was informed by the labour union that he should pay Bert three shillings and sixpence per week and that this would be increased every year. The farmer told Bert that he could not afford to pay such high wages, and he must give him the sack! Such was life in those days.

Such cottage conservative values were reflected at the highest level in the interwar Conservative Party. Stanley Baldwin's family made their money as Midlands maunfacturers, yet Baldwins's public image was as a bluff Shropshire farmer. It is no accident that his favourite author, Mary Webb, made her reputation as a chronicler of localism in the Marches. Baldwin's Conservatism successfully united local identity, county pride and loyalty towards a national Englishness in which ruralness had a central place: 'England is the country and the country is England.'[25]

---

[25] Mansfield, *Farmworkers and Local Conservatism*, p. 54; Shropshire Federation of Womens' Institutes, *Shropshire within Living Memory*, p. 158; and Mansfield, *English Farmworkers*, p. 197

3 British farming between the wars

Paul Brassley

THE interwar years are remembered, in the agricultural community, as a
time of hardship and depression. When I first went to work on farms,
in the early 1960s, many of the farmers who employed me had been farming thirty years earlier, and they spoke of low prices and incomes, decreasing
arable and increasing pasture, fewer crops and more livestock: 'dog and stick
farming' was the phrase used, because those were the main tools required to
look after extensively grazed animals. Their stories were confirmed later when
I began to read the writers of the period. Adrian Bell's *Silver Ley* (1931) ended
with a description of a great farmers' protest meeting at Cambridge; the final
part of A. G. Street's classic *Farmer's Glory* (1932), referring to the 1920s, was
entitled 'The Waning of the Glory', and John Moore, in *Portrait of Elmbury*
(1945), described the impact of agricultural depression on Tewkesbury between
1924 and 1927.[1] Le Gros Clark and Titmuss, writing a polemical Penguin Special early in 1939, asked, 'Can our home farming stand the strain of a protracted
war? We might reply by asking how far our home farming can stand the strain
of peace.'[2] Harkness argued that the 1920s and 30s saw a continuation of the
laissez-faire policies of the years between 1870 and 1914.[3] By the beginning of
the Second World War a widely accepted narrative of the previous two decades was already established.

The post-war historians soon began to tell the same tale: 'the land was
unchanging, but its fortunes declining', in the words of C. L. Mowat, one of
the first of them, and 'agriculture was left to its fate' according to Alan Armstrong, one of the more recent.[4] Others largely agreed with them.[5] Yet, as Joan

---

[1] A. Bell, *Silver Ley* (1931); A. G. Street, *Farmer's Glory* (1932); J. Moore, *Portrait of Elmbury* (1945), pp. 72–3.

[2] F. Le G. Clark and R. Titmuss, *Our Food Problem: A Study of National Security* (1939), p. 49.

[3] D. A. E. Harkness, *War and British Agriculture* (1941), p. 28.

[4] C. L. Mowat, *Britain between the Wars, 1918–1940* (1955), p. 250; W. A. Armstrong, 'The countryside', in *The Cambridge Social History of Britain, 1750–1950*, vol. 1: *Regions and Communities*, ed. F. M. L. Thompson (1990), pp. 134–5.

[5] K. A. H. Murray, *Agriculture*, History of the Second World War, Civil Series (1955), chapter 2; E. H. Whetham, *The Agrarian History of England and Wales*, vol. 8: *1914–1939* (Cambridge, 1978); J. S. Creasey and S. B. Ward, *The Countryside*

Thirsk has pointed out, the fact that farming had to change did not mean that it was inevitably unprofitable, and there were several examples of farmers who found successful responses to new circumstances.[6] The interwar period was a time when agricultural science and education were expanding, albeit from small beginnings, and productivity was growing. The volume of output rose. Why, then, was the image of depression so powerful, and to what extent was it justified? Those are the questions with which this chapter is largely concerned, but in order to make sense of them it is first necessary to sketch in the international and policy context within which British agriculture operated.

THE WORLD MARKET AND UK AGRICULTURAL POLICY

Between the wars the United Kingdom was an import economy as far as food and agriculture were concerned. On average, between 1920 and 1939, food, beverages and tobacco formed 45 per cent of UK imports. In 1937–8 imports accounted for 76 per cent of the wheat supply, 60 per cent of the barley supply, 81 per cent of the sugar supply, and significant proportions of fruit and vegetable supplies. The pattern was the same in meat and animal products: 50 per cent of beef, 62 per cent of mutton, 53 per cent of pigmeat, 21 per cent of poultry meat, 91 per cent of butter, 76 per cent of cheese, 39 per cent of eggs and 88 per cent of wool supplies were imported. Food imports as a whole accounted for about one-third of all UK imports (compared with industrial raw materials, which accounted for 22 per cent).[7] Once government support was withdrawn, in 1921, developments on world markets had a direct effect on the prices received by UK farmers. Interestingly, the more recent examinations of this period have very little to say about the world market, and Michael Tracy's work, which gave it the prominence it deserved, seems to have been forgotten recently.[8] There is no space in this chapter to tell the whole story, and two illustrations will have to suffice. The first concerns the wheat trade: world wheat production, inflated by the demand increases of the First World

---

between the Wars, 1918–1940 (1984); J. Brown, *Agriculture in England: A Survey of Farming, 1870–1947* (Manchester, 1987); R. Perren, *Agriculture in depression, 1870–1940* (Cambridge, 1995); A. Howkins, *The Death of Rural England: A Social History of the Countryside since 1900* (2003).

[6] J. Thirsk, *Alternative Agriculture: A History from the Black Death to the Present Day* (Oxford, 1997).

[7] T. Leisner, *One Hundred Years of Economic Statistics* (1989), p. 46; D. Britton and H. F. Marks, *A Hundred Years of British Food and Farming: A Statistical Survey* (1989), pp. 166–242; A. F. Wilt, *Food for War: Agriculture and Rearmament in Britain before the Second World War* (Oxford, 2001), p. 86.

[8] M. Tracy, *Agriculture in Western Europe*, 2nd edn (1982).

War, was already declining by 1920. Nonetheless, although the net surplus of supplies only amounted to about 7 per cent of production, that was slightly more than the import requirement of the largest importer, the UK.[9] Here was a sign of structural surplus. The effects of that, and of the impact of more general depression, were seen in the USA ten years later. Maize and wheat prices in 1931 fell to half of their 1929 levels. One-quarter of the US population lived on farms, and their incomes fell with these price falls. By 1930 54 per cent of farm families – some 17 million people – earned less than $1,000 per annum. The poverty line at that time was set at $2,000 per annum.[10] Similar problems affected many other countries.[11] Agricultural depression was a world-wide phenomenon. In Britain average wheat prices fell from 17s 0d per hundredweight in 1919 to 9s 10d in 1929. Barley prices fell from 21s 2d to 9s 11d per hundredweight over the same period, and prices of oats similarly decreased. Fat cattle prices nearly halved, as did fat sheep prices, and fat pig prices more than halved between 1920 and 1929.[12] The overall agricultural price index (API) for the UK fell from a peak of 16.33 in 1920 to a minimum of 6.27 in 1933 (1986 = 100). It subsequently rose again, but had only reached 7.38 by 1939. Part of this was the result of inflation and disinflation – the deflated API only fell from 235 to 144 in the same period – but the trend was clear.[13]

Depression, or at least low prices, were by no means unpredicted. In 1916 Sir Daniel Hall had pointed out that increasing the arable area in the UK would require some form of protection, and by 1919 it was clear that government support would at least be controversial, if it continued at all.[14] The Royal Commission appointed to inquire into the economic prospects of the agricultural industry was evenly split, half recommending continued price support and the other half its cessation. The latter group identified the potential danger of reliance on support: agriculture would be 'obliged to conduct its operations on the uncertain basis provided by guaranteed prices. These guarantees can

9 C. Kains-Jackson, 'The corn trade in 1919', *Journal of the Royal Agricultural Society of England* [hereafter *JRASE*] 80 (1919): 212–24.

10 D. Reynolds, *Rich Relations: The American occupation of Britain, 1942–45* (1995), p. 28.

11 See, for example, the memories of farming in New Zealand and Argentina in this period in J. Cherrington, *On the Smell of an Oily Rag: My 50 Years in Farming* (1979), pp. 33, 44.

12 R. E. Stanley, 'Agricultural statistics 1929', *JRASE* 90 (1929): 219–21.

13 P. Brassley, 'Output and technical change in twentieth-century British agriculture', *Agricultural History Review* 48 (2000): 60–84.

14 A. D. Hall, *Agriculture after the War* (1916), p. 128.

only be given by Act of Parliament, and no Parliament can bind its successors. Political opposition to guaranteed prices is certain.'[15]

In 1921 support was discontinued, and by 1922 Charles Orwin, head of the Agricultural Economics Research Institute at Oxford, was predicting the impact of lower prices: '... there is plenty of room for a further fall in markets before farming of one kind or another ceases to be a remunerative investment, but the country should be perfectly clear as to what is involved. The remedy for low prices is the reduction of costs and of output.' The same thing had happened thirty years earlier, he argued. In one of the southern counties, in a hamlet which once sent forty-four children to the village school, a farmer, a shepherd and a dog, all living elsewhere, eventually farmed the land by themselves, 'and today there can be seen a deserted village [he provided photographs to prove it] ... all within seventy miles of London, the centre of a state which imports more food per head of population than any in the civilised world.'[16]

The political pressures to change the trend were resisted. Bonar Law, the Conservative Prime Minister, told a deputation of farmers and farm workers in March 1923 that 'agriculture must lie on an economic basis'.[17] Both governments and consumers retained fond memories of the years of stability, free trade, and peace before 1914. It was probably, in the retrospective view of a near-contemporary, one of the factors behind the decision to return to the Gold Standard in 1925.[18] A few months later the Baldwin government, with Walter Guinness as Minister of Agriculture, produced the 1926 White Paper on agricultural policy, which again rejected the idea of agricultural protection or subsidy.[19] It was widely agreed, declared the White Paper, that agricultural policy should aim to maximise food output and provide a reasonable livelihood for the greatest number of people, but there was no agreement on how to achieve these aims. They might be brought about by increasing the corn acreage, but that could not be done without import controls or subsidies, neither of which the government would contemplate. The British farmer would be better advised 'to aim at meeting the demands of the population for meat and

---

[15] Royal Commission on Agriculture, 1919, *The Interim Report of the Royal Commission Appointed to Inquire into the Economic Prospects of the Agricultural Industry in Great Britain*. Cmd. 473, 1919, BPP 1919, viii. 1.

[16] C. S. Orwin, 'Commodity prices and farming policy', *Journal of the Royal Agricultural Society of England* 83 (1922): 9–10.

[17] Howkins, *The Death of Rural England*, p. 50.

[18] Harkness, *War and British Agriculture*, pp. 31–2.

[19] *Agricultural Policy*, Cmd. 2581 (1926).

milk'.[20] The policy proposed, therefore, was one of education and encouragement rather than coercion, to stimulate private enterprise and to protect farmers from 'the dislocation of reversals of policy'.[21] Free trade, in other words. But there were to be several measures aimed at improving agricultural efficiency, such as the provision of credit, drainage schemes, co-operative schemes, money for agricultural research and advisory schemes, support for the expanding sugar beet industry, and improvement of unclassified roads. All these, the White Paper argued, would increase confidence in the agricultural industry, and be 'far more effective than any alternative policies of a drastic and revolutionary character ...'[22]

The drastic change in policy began in 1931. The Conservative-dominated National Government that took office in August of that year could see some advantages in protectionism, although since industrial workers might spend up to 40 per cent of their total expenditure on food, it was also aware of the importance of cheap food.[23] It established tariffs on manufactured goods, but not upon major foodstuffs and raw materials. The question of how imports from the Empire should be treated then arose. At the Ottawa Conference in 1932 the UK agreed a series of preferential arrangements with Dominion countries whereby Empire produce would be largely exempt from the duties that were to be imposed on wheat, butter, cheese and sugar.[24] Since Canada provided 39 per cent of food imports to Britain, and Australia 24 per cent, assistance afforded to UK farmers by the move to protectionism was not great.[25] More significant was a variety of domestic policy initiatives: the 1932 Wheat Act, the establishment of the various marketing boards from 1933 onwards, the beef cattle subsidy of 1934, and the continuation of the sugar beet subsidy.[26] The 1937 Agriculture Act, with half an eye to increasing food production in the event of an emergency, introduced price subsidies for oats and barley and subsidies to reduce the cost of lime and basic slag (a phosphatic fertiliser).[27] A little earlier, in November 1936, the Food (Defence Plans) Department of the Board of Trade had been established. It would form the nucleus of a Ministry

---

[20] *Agricultural Policy*, clause 5.

[21] *Agricultural Policy*, clause 8.

[22] *Agricultural Policy*, clause 20.

[23] Harkness, *War and British Agriculture*, p. 41.

[24] Tracy, *Agriculture in Western Europe*, pp. 161–2. A detailed account of the negotiations on and effects of the Ottawa conference is given in T. Rooth, 'Trade agreements and the evolution of British agricultural policy in the 1930s', *Agricultural History Review* 33 (1985): 173–90.

[25] Wilt, *Food for War*, p. 87.

[26] Tracy, *Agriculture in Western Europe*, pp. 162–4.

[27] Whetham, *The Agrarian History of England and Wales*, vol. 8, p. 261.

of Food in the event of war, and it was a further sign of one of the major influences on agricultural policy at the end of the 1930s.[28] Nevertheless, in March 1939 Le Gros Clark and Titmuss thought it worth while to publish their Penguin Special warning of the dangers of famine in wartime.[29]

THE RESPONSE TO MARKETS AND POLICY

The foregoing discussion reveals the differences between the two interwar decades: to put it crudely, farming was left to its own devices in the 1920s and increasingly assisted in the 1930s. The effects of this could be seen in the changing prices received by farmers, although it should be remembered that the general level of retail prices (i.e. those measured by the Retail Price Index – the RPI) varied at the same time. Having been fairly stable in the first decade of the twentieth century, general retail prices began to rise from about 1909 and then doubled in the First World War, reaching a peak in 1920 before decreasing steadily in the 1920s and early 1930s. They bottomed out in 1933/4, but the 1940 price level was still below that of 1918. Agricultural prices as a whole (i.e. those measured by the agricultural price index – the API) followed the same trajectory, with a peak in 1919–20, a rapid decrease from 1920–2, and a fairly steady decline to 1933, after which they began to rise.[30] Between 1918 and 1939, after taking account of variations in the value of money (i.e. deflating the API by the RPI), there were twice as many years in which agricultural prices fell as there were years in which they rose. (See table 1.)

TABLE 1 Real agricultural prices (API deflated by RPI, 1986 = 100)

Year	Deflated API	Year	Deflated API	Year	Deflated API
1918	237.1	1926	166.5	1934	145.4
1919	240.0	1927	162.4	1935	152.4
1920	235.3	1928	167.8	1936	152.5
1921	193.1	1929	164.4	1937	162.2
1922	173.3	1930	155.0	1938	158.4
1923	171.5	1931	149.9	1939	150.0
1924	176.8	1932	147.7	1940	187.2
1925	174.2	1933	144.5		

Source: see text

[28] Wilt, *Food for War*, p. 59.

[29] Clark and Titmuss, *Our Food Problem*.

[30] Brassley, 'Output and technical change in twentieth century British agriculture', pp. 80–4.

Price trends in Britain thus followed world agricultural price trends, as would be expected in what was, as we have already seen, an import-dominated agricultural economy.[31] British farmers sold their output for less, and so had to sell more to maintain their receipts. A basket of farm goods that would have been sold for £240 (in 1986 prices) in 1919 would have realised only £144.5 (also in 1986 prices) in 1933. Thus the *volume* of output *rose* between 1920 and 1939 according to these calculations, and even rose a little – 10 per cent or so – between 1920 and 1934. (See table 2.)

TABLE 2 Volume of agricultural output

Period	Agricultural output (£m, 1986 prices)
1920-2	3,256.01
1923-9	3,335.07
1930-4	3,681.48
1935-9	4,133.72

Source: Brassley, 'Output and technical change ...', p. 84.

While this conclusion may be at variance with the popular conception of the interwar years, it does not seem implausible. Although the total area of agricultural land (i.e. arable plus permanent grass) decreased by about 2.7 million acres,[32] or roughly 10 per cent, and the lower-priced arable products exhibited decreasing acreages and declining or at best static outputs, production of the higher-priced products increased, as table 3 demonstrates.

Sugar beet, with the advantage of government support, was the only arable crop to increase significantly, reaching a peak of over 400,000 acres and 4 million tones in 1934, before declining slightly to the levels shown in table 3. It is interesting to note that the wheat acreage and output increased in the later 1930s, after the crop had received government support, whereas the later introduction of support for barley was only just beginning to make itself felt by 1939. Oats, on the other hand, declined in importance, along with horses, their main consumers. Pig numbers increased fairly steadily, and poultry numbers also increased, peaking in the early 1930s.

Dairy cow numbers and milk sales were increasing even before the Milk Marketing Board was established, but some of the extra output went into the lower-priced manufacturing market. There were still over 1,300 farmhouse cheese-makers in 1934, although their numbers began to decline. The number of producer-retailers, in contrast, was rising, reaching more than

31 Tracy, *Agriculture in Western Europe*, p. 129.

32 Murray, *Agriculture*, p. 22.

TABLE 3 Changing acreages, numbers and outputs
in major UK agricultural products

Product	1920–2	1931	1938–9
Declining or static			
Wheat area (million acres)	2.0	1.25	1.7
Wheat output (million tons)	1.75	1.0	1.6
Barley area (million acres)	1.6	1.1	1.0
Barley output (million tons)	1.0	0.85	0.9
Oats area (million acres)	3.2	2.5	2.0
Oats output (million tons)	2.1	1.9	1.7
Potato area (million acres)	0.7	0.6	0.6
Potato output (million tons)	4.5	3.0	4.0
Horses (thousand)	950	784	650
Expanding			
Sugar beet area (thousand acres)	8	234	345
Sugar beet output (million tons)	0.07	1.7	3.5
Sheep (million)	20	25.6	26
Cattle and calves (million)	6.7	7.3	8.1
Cows and heifers in milk (million)	3.0	3.4	3.6
Pigs (million)	2.5	2.9	3.8
Pigmeat (thousand tons)	299		423
Fowls (million)	29	59.6	60
Eggs (million dozen)	189		545

Source: Ministry of Agriculture, Fisheries and Food, *A Century of Agricultural Statistics* (1966), pp. 98–129; D. Britton and H. F. Marks, *A Hundred Years of British Food and Farming: a statistical survey* (1989), pp. 218 and 238.

63,000 by 1938.[33] Arthur Court's family in Wiltshire was among those that found selling liquid milk to the Board more profitable than cheese-making. Thus ended a family tradition of many years: 'I am not sure whether mother was glad about that or not … at least she could go to the Women's Institute meetings and not have to rush to get her cheese finished first.'[34] Liquid milk sales also began to supplant butter-making in South Devon, and in North Devon, traditionally a stock-rearing area, '… the erection of milk factories at Lifton, Torrington, Lapford … and the establishment of the Milk Marketing Board, coupled with the fall in the price of store cattle, has led many farmers

33 Whetham, *The Agrarian History of England and Wales*, vol. 8, pp. 252–4.

34 A. Court, *Seedtime to Harvest: A Farmer's Life* (Bradford on Avon, 1987), p. 44.

to transfer their energies to milk production'.[35] A similar trend to dairying was seen in the East Midland areas and central Norfolk that formerly fed bullocks on a combination of grass and root crops: 'The root break released is devoted to cash crops such as potatoes, sugar beet, and carrots.'[36] The same pattern of decreased arable, more permanent pasture, and greater reliance on dairying was found in Wales.[37] On the Yorkshire Wolds, however, where farmers had formerly made a good living from malting barley and big, mutton-producing, root-fed sheep, there remained 'a baffling state of depression', since the traditional farming system was 'based almost entirely on markets for products which appear to be suffering a more or less permanent eclipse'.[38] Maxton's survey confirms that British agriculture retained enormous variations, and that some regions found it easier to adapt to market forces than others.

Similarly, some farmers embraced change more easily than others, and we know more about them as individuals than we know about those who failed. The *Journal of the Royal Agricultural Society of England*, for example, ran a series on 'notable farming enterprises' in the 1930s in an attempt to dispel 'the false impression of the intelligence and ability of the average farmer in this country 'as a result of the period of depression which has weighed heavily upon the agricultural industry during the last ten years' (i.e. the 1920s).[39] The farming enterprises featured in the series, however, were hardly average. Sir Frederick Hiam, who farmed about 9,000 acres in the Fens, and George Baylis, with more than 12,000 acres near Newbury, operated two of the biggest farms in the country.[40] Messrs Parker and Proctor, who featured in a later article in the series, farmed 14,000 acres near King's Lynn, and, although the dairy farms of Mr Clyde Higgs near Stratford-upon-Avon extended to only 700 acres, they fed 350 Ayrshire cows supplying milk for five milk rounds in Stratford, Warwick and Leamington.[41] In other words, the enterprises featured in the series were mostly large ones, with ready access to capital for the purchase of livestock, buildings and machinery. Nevertheless, the series overall made the valid point that blind adherence to traditional products or methods was not the way forward in terms of low prices. The Alley brothers, for example, reduced labour costs by adopting a simple rotation of two cereal crops followed by bare

---

35 J. P. Maxton (ed.), *Regional Types of British Agriculture* (1936), p. 182.

36 Maxton, *Regional Types*, pp. 101, 122.

37 R. Moore-Colyer, *Farming in Depression; Wales, 1919–1939*, Welsh Institute of Rural Studies, Working Paper 6 (Aberystwyth, 1996), pp. 11, 26.

38 Maxton, *Regional Types*, p. 83.

39 H. G. Robinson, 'Notable farming enterprises: 1', *JRASE* 91 (1930): 20.

40 Robinson, 'Notable farming enterprises: 1'.

41 F. Rayns, 'Two decades of light land farming', *JRASE* 95 (1934): 117–35; J. A. Scott Watson, 'Mr Clyde Higgs' dairy farms', *JRASE* 97 (1936): 112–23.

fallow on a heavily mechanised farm near Fakenham in Norfolk.[42] In contrast, Mr A. H. Brown, on a dairy and corn farm in Hampshire, increased the intensity of production by his heavy use of fertilisers and purchased feedingstuffs. Similarly, George Henderson, who had only about a hundred acres of light land on the Cotswolds from the 1920s, was convinced that 'the solution must be intensity of production'.[43] The most prominent interwar farmers, however, such as the Hosier bothers, pioneered extensive dairy farming on light land, using moveable milking sheds known as 'bails'. By the end of the 1930s there were about 200 farms using this system in Wiltshire and the neighbouring counties.[44]

Further evidence of technical change might be found in the papers read to the Farmers' Club, a long-established group of the more prominent and financially stable members of the industry. In 1921, for example, they heard about scientific pig-breeding, in 1922 about milk recording. In 1927 Mr Hosier told them about his open-air dairying system, and in 1932 they had papers on recent developments in the early potato industry, fruit and vegetables and their production for canning, and the organisation and expansion of the pig industry. In 1934 Sir William Ray MP spoke about the application of electricity to agriculture, and Mr Boutflour, a prominent advisor, educator, and advocate of the use of concentrate feeds for milk production, spoke about dairy cattle.[45] Some farmers, at least, were reacting logically, if not always rapidly, to market forces, and falling cereal outputs did not imply a decreasing total volume of agricultural output.

COST CHANGES

What also mattered to farmers was how much money they made. If costs rose by more than output their incomes would fall, and vice versa, and the next step therefore is to examine cost trends, the calculation of which is not without its complexities. Some costs are relatively simple to evaluate; spending on feeds, fertilisers, seeds, and so on. Others, such as labour, are simple at first sight – they obviously include the wages paid to employed workers – but potentially more complex, for farmers and their families also perform some of

---

42 H. G. Robinson, 'Messrs S. E. and J. F. Alley's mechanized farming', *JRASE* 93 (1932): 157–65.

43 H. G. Robinson, 'Mr A. H. Brown's farms', *JRASE* 92 (1931): 151–62; G. Henderson, *The Farming Ladder* (1944), p. 18.

44 D. Taylor, 'Hosier, Arthur Julius (1877–1963)', *Oxford Dictionary of National Biography* (2004).

45 K. Fitzgerald, *Ahead of their Time: A Short History of the Farmers' Club* (1968), pp. 247–54.

the manual work on the farm, although they may not always be paid. Other costs, such as depreciation, can also present problems. In practice, therefore, cost calculations rely on the use of conventions to produce comparisons of like with like. For comparisons over time in this period there are further problems, first because the removal of the new state of Eire from the UK figures in 1922 produces difficulties in making comparisons with earlier years, and second because the value of money changed over time. The costs shown in table 4 include input costs, such as feed, fertilisers, etc., depreciation, and factor costs, meaning those for labour, net rent, and interest.[46]

TABLE 4 Total costs in current prices in UK agriculture, 1904–39

Period	Cost (£ million)
1904–10	146.32
1911–13	157.20
1920–3	274.94
1924–9	247.24
1930–4	211.94
1935–9	233.07

Source: Brassley, 'Agricultural output, costs, incomes and productivity'

Subtracting these figures from the figures for output, also expressed in current prices, produces values for the net farm income in the period, but in order to make valid comparisons over time these need to be adjusted by the retail price index. This is done in table 5, with the resulting net farm income in constant price terms also being expressed as an index. The principal conclusion to be derived from table 5 is that, in money terms, costs did not fall as much as output when farm prices fell in the 1920s. Expenditure on inputs such as fertilisers, feeds and seeds varied little once changes in the value of money were taken into account, and, although wages rates increased up to the late 1920s, the number of workers employed was falling, so the overall wage bill varied little.[47] The overall result, therefore, was that farmers were residual earners: they did well when prices were high and badly in the years of world surpluses when they fell. Net farm income in real terms (i.e. constant

---

[46] These problems have been discussed elsewhere, and therefore only the outlines of the argument are presented here. See P. Brassley, 'Agricultural output, costs, incomes and productivity in the UK, 1919–1940', in *Production et productivité agricoles dans le monde occidental (xiv–xx siècles)*, ed. J.-M. Chevet and G. Beaur (forthcoming).

[47] Harkness, *War and British Agriculture*, p. 37.

TABLE 5 UK net farm income (NFI), 1904–39

	Output (col. A) (£ m)	Total costs (col. B) (£ m)	NFI (A – B) (£ m)	NFI (constant prices)*	Index of NFI in constant prices
1904–10	170.55	146.32	24.23	939.1	100.0
1911–13	188.05	157.20	30.85	1,151.1	122.6
1920–23	409.35	274.94	134.41	2,150.6	229.0
1924–29	283.67	247.24	36.43	727.1	77.4
1930–34	245.47	211.94	33.53	746.8	79.5
1935–39	293.00	233.07	59.93	1,312.9	139.8

*The RPI used to convert the NFI to constant prices in this table is based on 1986 = 100, so the NFI in constant price terms is expressed in 1986 prices.

Source: Brassley, 'Agricultural output, costs, incomes and productivity'.

price terms) between 1920 and 1923 was on average more than double what it had been before the war, but was then cut by a factor of three for ten years. It rose again, significantly, between 1935 and 1939, but over the whole period the lean years far outnumbered the fat.[48] This might explain why farmers had bad memories of the interwar years. Those with traditional ideas about mixed farming and employing labour looked back to their grandfathers' stories of the years up to 1870, and remembered, like A. G. Street, the pre-First World War years of their youth, when the worst of the depression was past. Nevertheless, many of them responded to market forces and increased livestock output at the expense of arable, while cutting back on labour and economising on building and machinery repairs. They produced as much as ever, or more in volume terms, but not in traditional combinations. As a result, despite the downturn in prices and the fall in incomes, the agricultural industry's use of the nation's land, labour and capital resources was not necessarily wasteful or inefficient. Whether those involved enjoyed this new kind of farming is another matter. Street, writing in July 1931, was clearly proud of having changed his farming system so that his business survived, but he gives the clear impression that, for him, there was more comfort and pleasure in the sort of farming to which he had been brought up before the war.[49]

The interwar years were, for the farming industry, a mixture of decline and regeneration. There was increased emphasis on agricultural science, although how much was translated into practice is perhaps another matter. There were

[48] It is also worth noting that there could be significant differences between farms specialising in different enterprises: see Moore-Colyer, *Farming in Depression*, p. 25.

[49] Street, *Farmer's Glory*, pp. 229–68.

successful farmers introducing new techniques such as mechanisation and bail milking, and output, and perhaps even overall productivity, rose. But some farmers went bankrupt, workers left the land, farm incomes fluctuated a lot, and there was a feeling that dog and stick farming was not quite proper farming. There were some well-written books on country life, and their lament for traditional farming perhaps became equated with a wider lament for a lost rural innocence. The result was that the problems of traditional farming were emphasised over the successes of new systems and methods. The popularity of this farming literature, coupled with the increasing political effectiveness of the National Farmers' Union in highlighting agricultural problems, meant that the difficulties of the industry perhaps achieved a greater prominence in the image of the interwar countryside than they deserved.[50] Farming was only one part of the rural economy, but in this period it began to be seen as the dominant part, so its difficulties consequently affected the rural image as a whole.

[50] For the growing effectiveness of the NFU, see A. F. Cooper, *British Agricultural Policy, 1912–36: A Study in Conservative Politics* (Manchester, 1989).

14 Leckford: a case-study of interwar development

Roy Brigden

I STUMBLED across the Leckford estate in the 1990s, when I was using the agricultural press to familiarise myself with the farming and countryside of the interwar period. In contrast to the conventional picture of a countryside subdued by depression, what struck me most when looking through articles of the period was the tremendous energy and activity that was being regularly reported upon and described. All kinds of things appeared to be happening: new technology and equipment, new scientific practices, new forms of marketing and enterprises to add value to agricultural produce, diversification into new products and services. A common journalistic practice, especially during the 1930s, was to have a series featuring individual farmers and all the enterprising things that they were apparently doing to buck the trend of doom and gloom. *Farmers Weekly*, for example, ran a 'Successful Farming' series between 1934 and 1937, featuring a total of 170 farms; and *The Farmer and Stockbreeder* developed 'Successful Women Farmers', with seventy-seven different subjects between 1935 and 1936.

In the same vein, over a twelve-year period from 1925, *Country Life* produced a sequence of detailed studies of individual farms with such titles as 'Dairy Farming Extraordinary', 'A Modern Super-Farm' and 'A Pioneer Mechanised Farm'.[1] Their author was Henry Robinson (1897–1960), who was on the staff of the Midland Agricultural College, rising to become its Principal, before moving on to be the first Professor of Agriculture at Nottingham University in 1944. He sought out, in order to praise, examples of what he saw as the new business approach to farming, because change and innovation, allied to sound commercial sense, were the way forward. Of the Leicestershire farmer G. Golden, who had turned from a business career to concentrate on making a success of dairying, he wrote: 'One is sometimes inclined to think that those who make the greatest headway in farming today are the ones who are not tied down to the dictates of what is known as farming tradition and who will

---

[1] 'Dairy farming extraordinary', *Country Life*, 31 Oct 1935, pp. 658–60; 'A modern super-farm: the Crawley Court estate', *Country Life*, 7 Aug 1926, pp. 195–9; 'A pioneer mechanised farm', *Country Life*, 1 Feb 1933, pp. 156–8.

employ their own common sense.'[2] Such virtues were, in his view, to be found in company farms such as Culverthorpe Dairy Farm Ltd near Grantham, where the landowner was the chairman, the former farm manager was now the managing director, and the seventy-strong work-force was encouraged to buy preference shares in the business.[3]

It was obviously good copy to talk up novelty and innovation. These were clearly not ordinary farms or farmers, but men and women who, for one reason or another, stuck out from the crowd and seemed to have a success story to tell. So I started a programme of fieldwork to revisit some of these farms around the country out of curiosity to see whether they still harboured any links with that pre-war experience. A surprising number of them did. So began a fascinating journey of discovery into the past. To turn up, for example, at the farm near East Grinstead where Richard Borlase Matthews had conducted his crusade on behalf of electro-framing in the 1920s, and to find the family still there and the place littered with relics of his experiments, was quite extraordinary.[4] At Warnford in Hampshire, where R. P. Chester, a wealthy chemist, created the most extensive and scientifically developed of pig enterprises in the mid-1930s, the derelict hulks of Scandinavian-style pig-houses still littered the downland landscape.[5]

Elsewhere the new business farming of the interwar period, too, had left its mark, often in the concrete buildings that were a sign of the time. Ernest Debenham's (1865–1952) Bladen Farms in Dorset operated 6,000 acres through separate specialist enterprises in conjunction with ancillary companies that supplied feed and other inputs and marketed the produce.[6] Leonard Elmhirst's (1893–1974) Dartington estate, an experiment in running a local rural economy on a business model, continues to sport its magnificent concrete dairy farm of 1932.[7] Buildings from the former Ovaltine Egg Farms, for the mass-production of eggs along the most scientific lines, date from the same period, and today grace a Hertfordshire stretch of the M25 motorway.[8]

---

[2] H. G. Robinson, 'An all-round dairy herd', *Country Life*, 24 Dec 1927, p. 947.

[3] H. G. Robinson, 'Company farming and direct marketing', *Country Life*, 3 Dec 1927, pp. 851–3.

[4] See 'Business farming: R. Borlase Matthews', *Country Life*, 17 Apr 1926, pp. 617–21.

[5] 'Successful farming: R. P. Chester', *Farmers Weekly*, 27 May 1938, pp. 27–30.

[6] *Bladen Farms and Allied Businesses*, 1929 (Dorset County Record Office, D254; E2).

[7] See V. Bonham-Carter, *Dartington Hall: The Formative Years, 1925–57* (Dulverton, 1970).

[8] 'A model egg farm', *Country Life*, 11 Jun 1932, pp. 676–8.

THE LECKFORD ESTATE

I went to Leckford because it featured in another case-study series, entitled 'Notable Farming Enterprises', which was run by the *Journal of the Royal Agricultural Society of England*, and took in eighteen highly detailed reports over the decade from 1930 to 1940. The one on Leckford, written by L. G. Troup and published in 1937, was very extensive, and presented a glowing, largely uncritical account of the way the estate had been successfully turned round and refashioned along the most modern commercial lines:

> The outsider who has been privileged to make periodical tours of the Leckford estate cannot but be struck by the extraordinary high level of crop production achieved on a soil type which is not ordinarily given credit for much natural fertility. Moreover, the yields are increasing and the absence both of crop failures and dirty land is becoming more striking year by year.[9]

What I found at Leckford, almost hidden away, was a little world of its own and a researcher's gold-mine. Not only is the estate still intact, but by its peculiar nature it carries a strong sense of continuity which embodies a rich and unique record of past practice. As a result, Leckford subsequently became the centre-piece of my research into the quest for profitability in farming during the interwar period.[10]

The Leckford estate straddles a five-mile stretch of the River Test near Andover in Hampshire, and currently runs to 4,000 acres, of which 2,500 are in productive agriculture. Over 1,000 acres are down to cereals; there are two dairy herds, each of 200 head; 150 beef cattle; a 250-acre fruit farm of 60,000 trees; a free-range poultry unit; and a highly sophisticated mushroom-producing facility with an output of 20 tonnes a week. Leckford produce, such as milk, meat, mushrooms, flour, fruit juice, apples and eggs, can be found in Waitrose supermarkets because the Leckford estate is a constituent business of the John Lewis Partnership. This is one of the UK's top ten retail businesses and a producer co-operative of more than 63,000 employees, or Partners, operating twenty-six department stores and 166 supermarkets with a combined turnover approaching £3 billion a year. Leckford is both an agricultural enterprise and a rural haven for the Partnership. Thus it also incorporates two golf-courses

---

9 L. G. Troup, 'The Leckford Estate Limited', *Journal of the Royal Agricultural Society of England* 98 (1937): 140.

10 See R. Brigden, 'Farming in Partnership: The Leckford Estate and the Pursuit of Profit in Inter-War Agriculture' (unpublished PhD thesis, University of Reading, 2000).

and a wide range of facilities for organised sports; a holiday camp and guest houses; the unrivalled fishing of the River Test and excellent shooting across the chalk downland; and substantial areas of ornamental gardens and woodland. The estate today turns over £5.5 million a year and employs a little over 200 people.

The estate was purchased by John Spedan Lewis (1885–1963) in 1929. Having earlier taken over his father's Oxford Street department store, he was in the process of transforming the business into a major national force in high-street retailing. In the same year his ongoing experiments with profit-sharing schemes since the First World War also reached the point where ownership of the whole firm was vested in the work-force, and the John Lewis Partnership was formally established. As complex as its founder, the Partnership gave participation to the employees and a share in the results of their labour, whilst preserving a strictly hierarchical management structure and reserving almost exclusive power in the hands of Lewis himself. Thus, in his own words, on the one hand:

> No owner of Capital should charge for its use more than he might reasonably be willing to pay if he were a Manager. No Manager should charge for his services more than he might reasonably be willing to pay if he were a capitalist. All profits beyond these charges should go to the Workers, Managers and managed alike.

While on the other:

> No man proposes that in a time of plague the members of communities, whether they be regiments or factories or countries or what you will shall decide by mass-votes what medicine they will take. Things of that kind have to be left to experts.[11]

A paternalist, philanthropist and autocrat, Lewis was a tough businessman who used the highly successful empire he had created as a vehicle for his own idiosyncratic vision of social and commercial organisation.[12] At Leckford, he wanted to translate that philosophy into a rural context. Not caring at all for the social prestige that had often attracted businessmen of earlier periods into land ownership, Lewis intended to develop the estate as a rural retreat for his urban workers and as an example of regeneration in the countryside. Central

---

[11] These quotations are from J. S. Lewis writing in the Partnership in-house publication *The Gazette*. The first is from 1 Jun 1929, p. 295, and the second from 15 Oct 1932, p. 581.

[12] For a fuller exposition of his theory of industrial democracy see J. S. Lewis, *Partnership for All* (1948).

to this idea was the need to reorganise the estate's agriculture along business lines and show how it could operate at a profit.

With the agricultural depression entering its most severe phase, this was not perhaps the best of times to begin such an experiment. The two estate villages of Leckford and Longstock had suffered from years of neglect, and the land was run down to the point of exhaustion. A programme of cottage renovation was begun; community facilities such as a bath house and reading room installed; and social institutions and self-help committees mirroring those operating in the department stores inaugurated. The spirit of Partnership, with the objective of pulling its participants together for mutual benefit and the greater good of the enterprise, was everywhere laid down over the more traditional structures of village life. The latter, often operated or at least hosted by the established Church, had to back off or fall into line. No alternative was allowed. Though not a churchgoer himself, Lewis tolerated religion, but only in as far as his authority over his own rural dominion remained unchallenged.

Facilities for sports and games, both indoor and outdoor, were introduced and actively promoted. Leckford and Longstock teams, not only in football and cricket but in a range of sports, including tennis, bowls and golf, were soon competing against other local sides and other branches of the Partnership. Both the shooting – excellent on this chalk downland flanked by wooded belts for cover – and the fishing – on one of the best trout streams in England – were developed as separate enterprises in their own right, but reserved primarily for Partners. Lewis himself was a very keen sportsman and saw sporting activity, with its emphasis on individual performance within the framework of the team, as a powerful metaphor for the Partnership in which he played the part of both rule-maker and umpire. He was also an expert naturalist who insisted on ecological considerations and concern for habitats being taken fully into account when developments were planned. Lewis made his country home first at Leckford, and later Longstock. Some other properties on the estate were converted to provide weekend retreats for department-store middle and upper management. A small holiday camp was started in the 1930s to provide a cheap holiday for shop-floor workers and some extra labour at fruit-picking time. Before the war there was talk of establishing a private school on the estate that would do for education what the Partnership had done for retailing, but this came to nothing.

THE LECKFORD FARMS

The agriculture was treated in much the same way as the department stores and organised on the assumption that, with the application of sound business principles and the enlightened influence of the Partnership, progress would be made, and it would move into profit. Tenants were removed, the land taken in hand, and the several farming enterprises arranged into separate departments reporting to a managing director. He in turn was answerable to a board, over whose monthly meetings Lewis presided as chairman. The other members included leading lights in the Partnership, among them Bernard Miller, who was ultimately to succeed Lewis as chairman of the whole organisation, and outsiders who were invited on in recognition of their expertise in a particular field. One such was Samuel Levy Bensusan (1872–1958), journalist, farmer and commentator on rural affairs, who had recently completed an agricultural tour of the country, following in the pre-war steps of Rider Haggard and Daniel Hall, which was written up and published as *Latter-Day Rural England* in 1928.[13] The underlying theme was that farming could and should stand on its own feet as long as those involved freed themselves from the shackles of redundant thinking and adopted a more open-minded and business-orientated approach:

> Those who are interested may ask themselves what the real conditions of agriculture are just now, and they will find here at least an honest attempt to set them out with no prejudice in any direction, but with certain firm convictions. The first is that the urban population will never permit Protection to enter the realm of practical politics; the second that agriculture can thrive quite well without it, if only farmers will combine to help themselves instead of shouting at the top of their voices for State aid and for special advantages that are denied to the other industries that must struggle with them side by side.[14]

These were sentiments that chimed closely with Lewis's own views at the outset of his agricultural experiment, and resulted in Bensusan being invited onto the Leckford Board in 1930.

For Lewis, the most influential of these external advisers on the Leckford Board of the interwar years was his friend and neighbour Roland Dudley (1879–1964), pioneer of the new mechanised farming, whose Linkenholt estate was not far away.[15] An engineer by training, Dudley was, like Lewis, a multi-faceted individual and an intruder on the rural scene with urban business instincts that ruffled a few feathers amongst some of the more traditionally minded country gentry in the district. He was a genuine innovator with the

---

[13] H. R. Haggard, *Rural England: Being an Account of Social Researches Carried out in The years 1901 and 1902* (1902), and A. D. Hall, *Pilgrimage of British Farming, 1910–12* (1914).

[14] S. L. Bensusan, *Latter-Day Rural England, 1927* (1928), p. 10.

[15] See R. Dudley, *Modern Farm Machinery* (1935).

kind of uncompromising attitude which the confrontational Lewis could only admire. His *Times* obituary said that he:

> had a strength of character that belied his urban, industrial background. He was, outwardly, an explosive eighteenth century Improving squire with twentieth century ideas; and, inwardly, a most kindly and lovable man.[16]

Behind the board, with its responsibilities for running the Leckford estate, were the back-up services of a very large corporate operation. The accounting and estimating departments in London maintained running financial reports for the estate that compared actual results with those previously predicted, and turned these into forecasts for the following year. Each branch of the agricultural enterprise was accounted for separately, and the managers were required to make regular reports and submit estimates of all new requirements for sometimes intensive scrutiny and debate. All this information, including detailed minutes of board meetings and much else besides, was published internally. To make management accountable to the membership, it was a guiding principle of the organisation that everyone should have access to what was going on in the business. Initially, the Leckford material was published in the Partnership's central *Gazette*, but from 1935, as was normal with the branches, the estate started its own fortnightly version, which is still produced to this day.

What the *Gazette* reveals is a truer picture of the real struggle to make farming on the estate pay. For Lewis it was deeply frustrating to find that normal rules of business appeared not to apply, and that the problems of agriculture would not be spirited away by the application of sound management principles alone. The first few years in particular did not go well. A number of false starts were made; money was lost; and on several occasions Lewis threatened to give up on the whole enterprise. Initially, for example, it had been expected that the London Partnership would be able to absorb estate produce through the staff restaurants and shops for mutual benefit. This proved not to be the case because Leckford prices, based on the costs of production, could not compete with what was available nearer at hand in the London markets. A romanticised vision of the rural and urban sides of the Partnership working in harmony did not last long, and by 1931 the estate was being run as a separate business enterprise. A pig department was established in 1929, and the estate ran its own slaughterhouse for five years. It proved never to be profitable, in spite of the prizes won for the pedigree stock of Large Blacks and some measure of stability provided by the introduction of the Pigs Marketing Scheme

[16] R. Dudley, *The Times*, 31 Jul 1964.

in 1933. Costs were never fully under control, and only very substantial further investment in the most modern Danish-style methods and accommodation were likely to produce the levels of output and efficiency necessary. Even then, the volatility of the pig industry made nothing certain. To stem the tide of mounting losses, therefore, the department was closed in 1937, and the estate never returned to pigs.

The poultry enterprise at Leckford went much the same way. This was a branch of agriculture that was achieving a much higher profile by the early 1930s, and appeared to offer fair prospects for the efficient home producer. Official statistics showed a rise in birds kept in England from 22 million in 1921 to 57 million in 1934, and an average output per hen of 100 eggs per year compared to eighty before 1914.[17] Nevertheless, by 1924 egg imports were running at over 2,400 million a year, so there was much potential for an expanding domestic industry if due attention was paid to quality control, standardisation and marketing.[18]

The Leckford estate began with a laying flock of 1,275 birds and had plans to increase this rapidly to over 6,000. Problems soon emerged, however, and this goal was never achieved. A number of managers came and went in swift succession, the stock changed and the strategies changed, but no profits were forthcoming. Wafer-thin margins, in a sector where disease or similar catastrophe could always be just around the corner, remained the root cause. The price index of British eggs, for example, was 32 per cent lower in 1932 than it had been in 1929, and was to fall further over the following two years.[19] Cheap imports from places as far away as Egypt represented crippling competition, and, with full-scale protective marketing schemes for the industry not achieving lift-off, general-purpose medium-sized producers of the Leckford type were very exposed. Further investment in large-scale, low-cost specialised egg-production may have worked, and the Leckford Board certainly considered and came close to accepting this, but on a strictly commercial level it represented too much of a risk, and was ultimately rejected. Having tried but failed to make it work, the decision was made in 1936 to cut the losses and pull out. Only in the twenty-first century, with enough Waitrose customers prepared to pay a premium for a first-class product, has Leckford returned to egg-production.

Assessments of the whole estate operation in this pre-war period can take divergent views. On the one hand, here was a lumbering corporate bureaucracy

---

[17] Ministry of Agriculture and Fisheries, *Agricultural Statistics* (1921, 1934).

[18] Ministry of Agriculture and Fisheries, *Report on Egg Marketing in England and Wales*, Economic Series 10 (1927), p. 12.

[19] Ministry of Agriculture and Fisheries, *Agricultural Statistics* (1937), vol. 72 part 1, p. 104.

blundering around making mistakes in an environment that was quite alien to its accustomed line of business. On the other, here were some very astute commercial minds, hiring the best advisers and practitioners, making what they considered to be prudent investments on the evidence available, and still finding it impossible to achieve viable returns. More than six years were spent, at much cost in money and effort and visits from experts, in coming to the conclusion that Leckford was not suited to the production of soft fruit. It included a short period of attempting to add value with a small bottling and jam-making enterprise. The orchards, which were planted up soon after the acquisition of the estate, were given more of a chance because from the outset they were seen as a longer-term proposition. They could also absorb some of the labour that mechanisation of the crop lands was displacing. Even so, costs were much higher than expected, extending the expected start-up period, and the effects of bad seasons, such as the devastating late frost of May 1935, served only to increase the sense of frustration and disappointment. Nevertheless, Leckford's chalky slopes were particularly suited to apples and from 1936 the renowned fruit expert of the day, R. G. W. Bush was paying regular advisory visits.[20] By 1939 production from the maturing trees had reached the stage where the installation of cold storage on the fruit farm was justified, but it was only during the 1940s that the enterprise gradually moved into profit.

The two remaining farming enterprises at Leckford went against this tide by achieving some measure of success before the Second World War, but only because of the effects of market intervention. The dairy, comprising herds on both the Longstock and Leckford sides of the estate, did not fare well initially, and was completely revamped after 1930 with a new herd, new staff and the abandonment of unsatisfactory milking machinery in favour of a return to hand methods. Substantial losses were accumulated during these years, but then came the Milk Marketing scheme, which from 1933 brought stability to the trade and a reasonable return to the producer, with incentives for improvements in quality. Immediately dairying on the estate moved into profit, albeit small to begin with, and stayed there. The hitherto constant sense of crisis, wondering what next misfortune lay around the corner, was gone, and the enterprise could begin to think and plan ahead with some confidence for the future.

The experience of corn-growing on the estate was not dissimilar. Here, of all the agricultural operations, Lewis made the biggest commitment in modernisation and mechanisation, both in terms of policy and of investment. He had accepted the theory that technology held the key to the future of arable

---

[20] See R. Bush, *A Fruit Grower's Diary* (1950). This was a compendium of diary articles that Bush had been contributing to *The Countryman* magazine since 1935.

farming through its capacity to increase output and reduce costs, most notably of labour. It was a rather more ruthless vision of the countryside and some way from the creation of an idealised rural community which had been part of the objective, however woolly, at the beginning. For him, the future now lay between the owner-occupied smallholding and 'the really big farm, managed on the lines of large-scale business, that is to say, with costly machinery, far-sighted programmes and the scientific cutting-out of every sort of waste between the soil and the actual consumer of its produce'.[21] In this he was influenced by the example of his friend Roland Dudley and by correspondence with C. S. Orwin, Director of the Agricultural Economics Research Institute at Oxford University, where mechanised farming was subject to ongoing investigation. In his opinion the home farmer was at a severe disadvantage because he had to hire labour under conditions of employment and rates of wages imposed upon him by the standards of the towns. The only way round this was to take every step to increase the value of each man's output, and 'this must mean a reduction in the number of men employed and the increase of the machinery at their command'.[22]

Roland Dudley had been experimenting at Linkenholt since 1928 with a farming system that not simply replaced horses by tractors but rather involved the organised deployment of appropriate powered equipment across the whole corn-production process. Its advantages, as far as profitability was concerned, were in his view threefold. First, the soil was worked more efficiently and effectively by a new generation of heavy-duty implements designed for tractor-haulage. Second, working speed was enhanced, so that the preparatory operations could be completed at the optimum time for seed germination, whatever the weather. Finally, and most significantly, came the question of cost. Dudley produced detailed figures, recorded on his own estate, that at least appeared to show that mechanised farming, operation by operation, was cheaper than the horse equivalent.[23]

Integral to Dudley's system was the crawler tractor, which he favoured over the more conventional wheeled type, and the combine harvester. (See illus. 1 and 2.) In 1930 he was one of only four owner-operators of these machines in the country. By 1932 he was on the Leckford Board and persuading Lewis that the open corn lands and light soils of the estate made them ideal for a similar approach. In the autumn the first orders were being placed for a full

[21] J. S. Lewis writing in *The Gazette* [of the John Lewis Partnership], 23 Apr 1932, pp. 172–3.

[22] C. S. Orwin writing in *The Gazette* [of the John Lewis Partnership], 18 Jun 1932, pp. 310–11.

[23] Dudley, *Modern Farm Machinery*, pp. 11–20.

ILLUS. 1 & 2 Inter-War mechanised farming on the Leckford Estate, Hampshire, 1935: *(above)* crawler tractors; *(below)* combine harvester

complement of equipment, including crawlers, poly-disc ploughs, precision seed-drills, and a combine harvester. First one side of the estate and then the other were completely converted.

Leckford thus rapidly shot into prominence as a leader in this new kind of farming in the interwar period. Its effects were subject to the same kind of clinical examination that the Partnership's financial division gave to any innovation in one of the department stores. What the accounts show is a rather different story from the one confidently predicted by Dudley. They demonstrate that the only factor that made the mechanisation programme remotely sustainable was government intervention through the deficiency payments that came into effect with the Wheat Act of 1931. Without that support, and left to market forces alone, the price obtainable by the farmer for wheat, assuming the figures from Leckford were not wholly untypical, was quite unable to cover the true level of costs incurred. Even so, seasonal variations continued to exert a strong influence, and made the outcomes highly unpredictable. The exceptionally good year of 1934, for example, was followed in Hampshire by four wheat harvests that were all disappointing for different climatic reasons. Overall, the arable enterprise at Leckford from 1932 up to the war was more often in profit than not, but only because of the subsidy, and then only just.

CONCLUSIONS

The lesson learned overall was a hard one: the problems endemic to farming were a little more complex than they appeared at first sight from the world of high-street retailing. It was certainly a much more chastened Spedan Lewis that contemplated the prospects for the Leckford project on the eve of the Second World War. He would have liked to have demonstrated to a sceptical world that it was his Partnership philosophy, combined with its intrinsic qualities of sound business management, that was responsible for turning a run-down stretch of the English countryside into a thriving, and above all profitable, agricultural enterprise. It would have been the proof that he was looking for that his system, founded upon the principle of shared ownership, was indeed a model for successful business organisation on a scale to match any other. Finding that his magic formula did not work as expected, was not a pleasant experience. As a free-thinking, free market businessman, Lewis was loath to recognise that it was assistance from the state that made all the difference. But it was so, and remained so, during the war and after, as the estate began to enjoy real prosperity and thrive as a rural outpost of the Partnership.

15 The wheelwright, the carpenter, two ladies from Oxford, and the construction of socio-economic change in the countryside between the wars

Paul Brassley

DESPITE the title of this book, there is much to suggest that the common and traditional image of rural England between the wars is one of decline, of agriculture especially but also in rural crafts, trades, communities and culture. As one writer of the time put it, in a book almost inevitably titled *Gone Rustic*,

> ... I have wondered whether we have not lost something more valuable than a gold standard. For the blacksmith's race has gone forever from the earth ... there will be never again just this kind of tranquillity and honest worth. Generations, living simply, observing the seasons, self-reliant in work and pleasure, have bred the blacksmith's type. There will be a day when we shall try to revert to this type, but it will be in vain. The smithy will have changed to a garage on the village green, the lanes will all be straightened for motor-cars, the land cut up for speculative building, the old cottages renovated for week-enders. We cannot stay the hand of Time.[1]

Thus, through contemporary publications, the image begins to emerge. The process is carried on by subsequent authors, reinforced or contradicted by the contemporary reactions to events of national and local policy-makers, and overlain by both the perception and the reality of what actually happened.

The purpose of this chapter is to examine the construction of this image. In part, therefore, it considers the work of some of the authors of the time. It then refers briefly to the later work of rural sociologists and historians, before turning to the activities of the interwar rural policymakers. And finally it attempts to discover what was happening in one part of rural England – Devon – in the 1920s and 30s. And it does all of this with reference to rural crafts and

---

[1] C. Roberts, *Gone Rustic* (1934), p. 178.

trades other than agriculture, which have perhaps had less attention than they deserve in recent historiography.

THE LITERARY EVIDENCE

By the first decade of the twentieth century there were numerous books on the condition of rural England and the flight from the land, and this trend continued into the interwar years, with books such as *Farmer's Glory* and *Lark Rise*, which eventually achieved classic status.[2] The literary exploration of rural England was accompanied by a leisure exploration, by walkers, cyclists and, later, motorists, and the two were interrelated, in so far as the leisure activities helped to sell the books.[3] As Alun Howkins points out, many of these books were about farming and farm workers, but some of them were concerned with rural crafts or trades, and it is these that will be discussed here.[4]

One of the most influential of the genre was Sturt's *The Wheelwright's Shop*, first published in 1923.[5] It appears to be influential because it was picked out by Leavis and Thompson in their well-known *Culture and Environment: The Training of Critical Awareness*, first published in 1933, in which they bemoan the disappearance of the 'organic community' and glorify Sturt and the world he portrays as the antithesis of all they oppose – mass production, standardisation, and levelling down – and the embodiment of all they support.[6] It is easy to see why Sturt met with their approval. The whole book has a sepia-tinted elegiac quality, and he begins by explaining that in 1884, when he entered the business, it was a 'folk' industry with folk methods. His employees are described as friends of the family, custom, apprenticeship, and learning by tradition were important, and things were made to last. How different from the industrial world that Leavis and Thompson wished to attack. Towards the end of the book Sturt bemoans the importation of wheels from the USA and the introduction of a gas engine: it may have enabled the firm to survive, but it was 'the beginning of the end of the old style of business', and 'the men' became 'machine "hands"'. As such, their old relationship with their employer changed, and '... machinery has separated employers from employed and has robbed

---

[2] A. G. Street, *Farmer's Glory* (1932); F. Thompson, *Lark Rise* (Oxford, 1939).

[3] B. C. Batsford, *The Britain of Brian Cook* (1987); C. Brace, 'A pleasure ground for noisy herds? Incompatible encounters with the Cotswolds and England, 1900–1950', *Rural History* 11 (2000): 75–94.

[4] A. Howkins, 'The discovery of rural England', in *Englishness: Politics and Culture, 1880–1920*, ed. R. Colls and P. Dodd (1986).

[5] G. Sturt, *The Wheelwright's Shop* (Cambridge, 1923).

[6] F. R. Leavis and D. Thompson, *Culture and Environment: The Training of Critical Awareness* (1964), p. 87.

the latter of the sustaining delights which materials used to afford them'.[7] It was just the sort of thing that would not happen in Leavis and Thompson's organic community, of course. In fact, as Raymond Williams pointed out, the story of the recently disappeared organic community is a long-lasting and powerful myth that can be traced back to the Garden of Eden.[8] Moreover, Sturt saw himself as a writer first and a wheelwright second. Nevertheless, this is not to say that his book should be discounted. 'Myth' is a word with two meanings: it may be a fictionalised narrative, but it embodies a great truth, and the fact that *The Wheelwright's Shop* is still in print, by its original publisher, suggests that twentieth-century readers found something significant in it.

A year or so after the publication of *The Wheelwright's Shop*, the Institute of Agricultural Economics in Oxford produced a series of works on *Rural Industries in Britain*. The curious origins of this Oxford survey have been described in detail elsewhere.[9] It began with a pilot study of the Oxford district, the results of which were published in 1921.[10] The national survey, in four volumes, followed in 1926 and 1927. The first three of these were written by Helen Fitz-Randolph and M. Doriel Hay (the two ladies from Oxford), and the fourth, which dealt exclusively with Wales, was by Anna M. Jones, who was appointed in part at least for her ability to speak Welsh.[11] They had all carried out an extensive county-by-county survey of the whole country between 1921 and 1923, and described in great detail what they found. Its variety was enormous. In volume 1, which was mainly concerned with the wood-based industries, they mentioned coopers, turners, cloggers and tanners, makers of spelk baskets and trugs, fences, hurdles, besoms, hay rakes, barrel hoops and crate rods, as well as wheelwrights, blacksmiths, saddlers and makers of ropes, nets and halters. Volume 2 was almost entirely concerned with osiers and basket-making, and the rush, sedge, reed and straw industries. Volume 3 dealt mostly with the 'decorative' industries: spinning, weaving and dyeing, and lace-making, with additional material on rural potteries and an appendix on flint-knapping, an industry which sold its products to the flintlock trade, 'is already an anachronism', and produced 'consumption and other diseases of the throat and chest'

---

7 Sturt, *The Wheelwright's Shop*, pp. 200–2.

8 R. Williams, *Culture and Society, 1780–1950* (1962). E. P. Thompson quotes Williams in his introduction to the 1993 edition of Sturt.

9 P. Brassley, 'Industries in the early twentieth-century countryside: the Oxford Rural Industries Survey of 1926/7', in *People, Landscape and Alternative Agriculture: Essays for Joan Thirsk*, ed. R. W. Hoyle (2004), pp. 133–48.

10 K. S. Woods, *Rural Industries round Oxford* (Oxford, 1921).

11 H. FitzRandolph and M. D. Hay, *The Rural Industries of England and Wales*, vol. 1: *Timber and Underwood Industries and Some Village Workshops* (1926), vol. 2: *Osier Growing, Basketry, and Some Rural Factories* (1926), vol. 3: *Decorative Crafts and rural Potteries* (1927); A. M. Jones, *Rural Industries in Wales*.

among its workers. 'The supply of flint lock rifles to the natives of Africa ['who must be armed so that they can shoot game but whom it is politic to arm less efficiently than the representatives of the ruling race'] is hardly an end of sufficient importance to justify the continued employment of men in these unhealthy conditions.'[12] Volume 4 was concerned with the same range of industries as all the previous volumes, but dealt with Wales. In addition to describing the techniques of each craft or industry, they also examined earnings, costs, prices, marketing methods and foreign competition, and assessed the prospects of each. Rush-plaiters, for example, felt that the future of their trade was in doubt, whereas rush-cutters felt that their part of the trade was profitable and on the increase. This is perhaps why there is no overall conclusion to each volume, because what was important for one trade might be less so for another.

At this point, however, what is important is the difference in approach between Fitzrandolph and Hay and writers such as Sturt. Whereas Sturt looked back nostalgically to his youth and mourned the passage of the old craft techniques, FitzRandolph and Hay were concerned with what their survey had found, which they described in great detail, and how the observed trends could be explained – it was a matter of industrial scale economies and decreasing transport costs, according to C. S. Orwin's preface.[13] Sturt saw machinery as a threat, but for FitzRandolph and Hay it was an opportunity, and they wrote with approval of useful new machines such as the cross-cut, circular and band saws, lathes, and hand-morticing machines. They approved too of the diversification by wheelwrights into motor-body building; Sturt's shop moved in the same direction, and he saw it as a wise move 'from every point of view save the point of sentiment'.[14] Orwin, less sentimentally, reminded his readers of 'the danger of these small unorganized enterprises becoming sweated industries', so that the survival or revival of a traditional craft might not always be desirable.[15] Only at one point do the two approaches come near to touching: at the beginning of volume 1 of FitzRandolph and Hay is a 'Ballade of Rural Industries', which refers to industrialism as a 'cruel bereaver', and mentions 'Director of Survey, *and each believer / In revival* of village crafts like these' (my italics).[16] Unsigned as they are, perhaps these verses reveal more

---

[12] FitzRandolph and Hay, *Rural Industries*, vol. 3, pp. 161, 165.

[13] FitzRandolph and Hay, *Rural Industries*, vol. 3, p. vi.

[14] FitzRandolph and Hay, *Rural Industries*, vol. 1, pp. 176, 178; Sturt, *The Wheelwright's Shop*, pp. 201.

[15] FitzRandolph and Hay, *Rural Industries*, vol. 3, p. vi.

[16] FitzRandolph and Hay, *Rural Industries*, vol. 1. The ballade was based on Dante Gabriel Rossetti's translation of Francois Villon's *The Ballade of Dead Ladies*, in D. G. Rossetti, *The Works*, ed. W. M. Rossetti (1911), p. 541.

about the personal feelings of the surveyors than all the measured, level, third-person prose in the rest of the volumes.

These two contrasting works have been examined in detail because they exemplify the contrasting genres in the interwar rural industries literature. FitzRandolph and Hay produced the pioneering socio-economic study, and Sturt was the prototype for the elegies. Both had their followers (albeit the latter much more than the former), and it is interesting to examine both ways of seeing the changing position of rural trades and crafts in this period.

One of the first followers (whether conscious or not) of Sturt was Gertrude Jekyll, who is now better known as a garden designer. Batsford published her *Old English Household Life: Some Account of Cottage Objects and Country Folk* in 1925.[17] The cottage objects were arranged and described, with numerous photographs, chapter by chapter – fireplaces and hearths, candles, hearth implements, kitchen utensils, furniture – and then she branched out into cottage construction (in cruck, cob, wattle and daub, and stone), home industries (spinning and straw-plaiting), farm tools and implements, roadside gates and fences, bridges, and so on. 'The old five-barred gate, made of thoroughly sound oak by a country carpenter who knows and practises the good traditions' was described in minute detail, dimensions included, and produced a paragraph of praise for 'the comeliness of a thing that is well made and is exactly fitted to its purpose.'[18] She prefigured the Leavis and Thompson line in deprecating changes since the 1860s, referring to older, 'and, in many respects, better ways', and regretting the disappearance of 'the strong, simple and beautiful furniture, for the most part of oak'. The change she attributed to 'the increase in the use of steam machinery' and the subdivision of work, 'so that no one man has the satisfaction of seeing the labour of his hands completed and well done', and she compared the England of the 1920s with what could be found 'in the market place of a foreign town; ... crockery and simple clothing, wooden shoes and peasant tools, all coming straight from the producer'.[19]

More than a decade on from this, Walter Rose's book *The Village Carpenter*, which was published by the Cambridge University Press (also Sturt's publisher) in 1937, followed Sturt in describing the carpenter's work in detail, from the initial sawing of his timber to the making of gates, fences, pumps, mills, the various parts of new houses, and coffins. It was, Rose admitted in his preface, more an account of how things had been in the 1890s and earlier than of a carpenter's business in the 1930s, for after 1893 his family firm had

[17] G. Jekyll, *Old English Household Life: Some Account of Cottage Objects and Country Folk* (1925). The book was reissued in 1933, and there was a new edition in 1975.

[18] Jekyll, *Old English Household Life*, pp. 181–2.

[19] Jekyll, *Old English Household Life*, pp. 3–4.

become general builders. 'Outside influences were also at work, slowly but surely breaking down the age-long prestige of each craft; their separate exclusiveness was disappearing.' (pp. xvii–xviii). But while burying him, he was also there to praise '... the craftsman, a carpenter whose work is the expression of his life, to whom anything short of good workmanship is a degradation to which he will not sink.'[20] The power of the book, however, derives not from remarks such as these, but from its detailed portrait of the carpenter's trade. It was left to Frank Kendon, who helped Rose to write the book and contributed an introduction, to emphasise the innocence of a manual craft, implicitly contrasted with the muck and brass of urban industry:

> There is for half the world a deep-rooted association of domestic modesty, frugality and wholesomeness about a carpenter's shop ... clean-smelling work, the musical sound of his tools, his slow, kind, but masterly hands ... a child can watch a carpenter at work without risk of soiling; sawdust is cleaner than snow ...[21]

Rose himself might not have put it quite like that, but at the end of his book there is certainly the suggestion that the village remains the repository of important old skills which the town is in danger of losing.[22] The same theme was picked up by Dorothy Hartley in *Made in England*, in which she describes and illustrates the tools and techniques for making a wide range of products from wood, straw, reed, stone, metal, pottery, leather and horn, and wool and feathers:

> ... I want everyone to appreciate the work done by country people. Not for its commercial value, but because the work is done by independent people, and the character of these few independent people is as strong as the goods they make ... Our large towns are no longer representative of this old English stock. The big commercial enterprises are mainly concerned with making money ... Mass production and specialization in themselves need not destroy vitality ... But the whole trend of factory industrialization today is towards a few clever minds directing well-drilled obedient masses ...[23]

Again there is the distrust of money and commerce, and the disdain of the

---

[20] W. Rose, *The Village Carpenter* (Cambridge, 1937), pp. xvii–xviii, 74.

[21] Rose, *The Village Carpenter*, p. xi.

[22] Rose, *The Village Carpenter*, p. 139.

[23] D. Hartley, *Made in England*, 4th edn (1974), p. x.

urban masses; character and independence are valued, and they, apparently, are to be found in the countryside, making things to last.[24]

A similar rejection of industrialism and adoption of a craft as a 'spiritually fulfilling way of life' is found in Bernard Leach's *A Potter's Book*.[25] 'In a machine age', he wrote, 'artist-craftsmen, working primarily with their hands, represent a natural reaction valid as individual expression, and they should be the source of creative design for mass-production whether they work in conjunction with industry or not.'[26] Leach, however, represents a different category, the artist-craftsman. It is beyond the scope of this chapter to follow the emergence of this group, and in any case it is unnecessary, for the story has been told vividly and in detail by Tanya Harrod. But a brief discussion of the difference between the artist-craftsman and the artisan-craftsman is worth while at this point. Harrod cheerfully admits that she avoids defining crafts, but begins by looking at interwar 'artist craftsmen' (a term which at the time was also applied to women) and their activities in ceramics, weaving, textile printing, bookbinding, calligraphy and furniture-making among others.[27] In other words, these are not the crafts discussed and enumerated elsewhere in this chapter – the thatchers, blacksmiths, wheelwrights, carpenters, cobblers, hurdle and basket-makers and so on, for whose activities Harrod uses the term 'vernacular crafts'. The difference is partly in the markets they aimed at and the techniques they used, and much to do with the social class of the craftsmen, but the distinction is not absolute. Blacksmiths could produce decorative wrought-ironwork, wood-turners and others furniture, and a range of different kinds of people could describe themselves as potters. But the artist-craftsmen identified themselves by their rejection of new techniques and mechanisation – the paradox, as Harrod remarks, was that '… an important part of being modern was to be anti-modern' – by their desire to reform and elevate contemporary life, by their emphasis on truth to materials, and their desire to rediscover old tools and materials.[28] Romney Green, for example, dated the degeneration in furniture

---

[24] Although they are a little later than the period with which this paper is concerned, it is worth noting that others wrote in a similar vein: 'As common crafts grow scarce and die out, it occurs vividly to some people, that here is something precious …' (T. Hennell, *British Craftsmen* (1943), p. 7), and [it is a] 'disgrace to our social system that so fine a character as the country craftsman should have been allowed to disappear almost completely …' (N. Wymer, *English Country Crafts: A Survey of their Development from Early Times to the Present Day* (1946), p. 4). See also F. Derrick, *Country Craftsmen* (1945), and H. L. Edlin, *Woodland Crafts in Britain* (1949).

[25] T. Harrod, *The Crafts in Britain in the 20th Century* (1999), p. 38.

[26] B. Leach, *A Potter's Book* (1940), p. 258.

[27] Harrod, *The Crafts in Britain*, pp. 9–10

[28] Harrod, *The Crafts in Britain*, p. 145.

design back to the sixteenth century. The artist craftsmen often associated with marginal political groups such as Guild Socialism, Distributism, Social Credit (on the left), and other right-wing groups '... with novel, often anti-industrial, remedies for the seeming impasse of shrinking markets and rising unemployment'.[29] They were inspired by Eastern, African and South American art, and eastern philosophies, as well as local vernacular crafts. They often exploited the skills of artisans, but Harrod contends that 'skill as such was not valued in the interwar craft world', and that many of those who attained national reputations were not always personally skilful. They survived, she argues, partly because they made objects which looked like necessities but were marketed like luxuries, and partly because, like many of the better-known interwar artist craftsmen – Leach, Mairet, Peacock, Cardew – they 'were able to step outside the economic framework and resist the commoditisation of the goods they had made' because they had private means or patrons.[30] In many ways, therefore, the artist-craftsmen are irrelevant to the people and trades that form the main focus of this chapter; nevertheless, it is impossible to ignore them, if only because of the influence of the craft discourse on quangos such as the Rural Industries Bureau and on the construction of the craft image in the sort of books discussed earlier.

A reading of the interwar literature thus produces two different views of rural trades and crafts. In one, the traditional crafts are vanishing, save only for those which border on the arts, attract patronage, and appeal to the high-priced end of the market. In the other, the crafts are adapting, some faster and more successfully than others, to changing market conditions. Which is the more realistic picture?

HISTORIANS AND CONTEMPORARY COMMENTATORS

There are various ways of approaching the question posed at the end of the previous section. The most obvious is to examine the existing secondary literature, which, to generalise heroically, suggests that crafts were declining, although there were some efforts to prevent them from doing so.[31]

---

[29] Harrod, *The Crafts in Britain*, p. 145.

[30] Harrod, *The Crafts in Britain*, pp. 152, 168.

[31] C. Bailey, 'Making and meaning in the English countryside', in *Technologies of Landscape: From Reaping to Recycling*, ed. D. E. Nye (1999); J. Chartres, 'Rural industry and manufacturing', in *The Agrarian History of England and Wales*, vol. 7: *1850–1914*, ed. E. J. T. Collins (2000); J. Chartres and G. L. Turnbull, 'Country craftsmen', in *The Victorian Countryside*, ed. G. E. Mingay (1981); J. Saville, *Rural Depopulation in England and Wales, 1851–1951* (1957); W. M. Williams, *The Country Craftsman A Study of Some Rural Crafts and the Rural Industries Organisations in England* (Dartington, 1958).

Another source of information is the unpublished evidence of contemporary commentators. The first of these, in terms of chronology, was the Rural Industries Enquiry held by the Development Commission between December 1930 and February 1931.[32] Following only four years after the Oxford Institute survey, it approached the question from a different standpoint. Although the Oxford Institute survey was, as pointed out above, put in train because the Development Commission and the Ministry of Agriculture wanted to know more about the state of the rural industries that they were about to support, it attempted to produce this information by detailed survey of the tradesmen on the ground. The 1930 survey, in contrast, although also apparently concerned with whether or not government money was being wisely spent, chose to take evidence from those in charge of the spending, especially the Rural Community Councils (RCCs) and the Rural Industries Bureau. It produced some interesting data on trends in rural industries, although it concentrated, not surprisingly, on those trades to which the RCCs gave most attention: blacksmiths, wheelwrights and saddlers, and to a lesser extent, basket-makers. The Cambridgeshire RCC reported no observable fall in the number of craftsmen over the previous five to six years, except perhaps for thatchers, although saddlers were finding it hard to find new work (folio 2). In Cheshire, however, a survey of 420 villages showed that, since 1910, blacksmiths had diminished in number by 40 per cent, saddlers by 60 per cent, wheelwrights by 15 per cent, basket-makers by 75 per cent, and coopers by 50 per cent (fo. 69). Blacksmiths in Dorset were still finding a good deal of agricultural work, but saddlers, except in hunting districts, 'present great difficulty' (fo. 18), and similarly in Hampshire their work was 'practically gone' in villages (fo. 26). In Somerset there was still considerable demand for hurdles, but 'willows have been very depressed' (fo. 52). A survey of craftsmen in Leicestershire found 160 smiths, eighty to ninety wheelwrights, and thirty to forty saddlers (fo. 39), and in Lindsey (part of Lincolnshire) there were 288 smiths, 380 wheelwrights and fifty-eight saddlers (fo. 44). The problems of smiths, saddlers and wheelwrights were generally attributed to the depressed state of agriculture, the increasing tendency of farmers to buy in towns, and the decreasing number of farm horses. In Hampshire it was reported that a farm which had used to keep twenty-five horses had reduced the number to nine in two years, and on another the number had fallen from ten to three in the same time (fo. 26). In Leicestershire village saddlers were also facing competition from the large number of ex-servicemen who had been trained in light leather-work.

In the face of these developments, some craftsmen were diversifying: in Lindsey, wheelwrights had managed to survive by doing the carpentry in

32 National Archives, Development Commission archives, Rural Industries Enquiry, D4/421.

council housing schemes or by making furniture, and saddlers could produce motor upholstery (fo. 44); some smiths had become motor repairers (classes in acetylene welding and motor repair work were held in Derbyshire (fo. 15)), and others had turned to decorative wrought-ironwork. In Kent a survey of 207 blacksmiths compared their situation in 1930 with that in 1924. Of the seventy-five who had turned to ornamental ironwork, only 21 per cent reported a decrease in business, whereas of the 132 who were not doing ornamental work, 69 per cent reported a drop in business (fo. 34). There was a demand for garden fencing in Sussex, and the hurdle-making competition at the county show was well supported (fo. 55). And not all the new developments developed as planned: at Tarvin in Cheshire a Dr Morton had established a communal workshop in an old barn, and 'as a result a dramatic group had been started' (fo. 69). Equally, not all craftsmen were enthusiastic about diversification. They were reluctant to invest in electricity, or oxy-acetylene welding plant, or circular saws because they were old, or they felt that there was insufficient work to repay the investment. Generally, smiths in Sussex were not taking up the motor business (fo. 55). In Monmouth it was simply reported that 'the wheelwrights had not got to the point of making furniture' (fo. 46).

The enquiry also heard from a Mr Dixon, the manager of Country Industries Ltd, a co-operative which had been established in the early 1920s to sell country craft work.[33] He made the point that craftsmen needed agents because selling, especially to big firms, took time, and he also argued that British craftworkers sometimes priced themselves out of their markets, citing the example of a laundry hamper nearly 50 per cent more expensive than its foreign equivalent, and differing from it only in ways which involved useless labour. Not surprisingly, perhaps, foreign basketwork imports were estimated to be worth about £500,000 per year.

The conclusions of this 1930 enquiry, perhaps surprisingly in the light of the evidence, were quite positive:

> First, as to the present position and tendencies of the movement, looking back over nearly a decade of work. The original economist objection that to try and keep rural industries alive is like putting the hands of the clock back has been disproved; or if it has not been disproved, it has been shown that there is a large and lively group of people who do not believe it. Rural craftsmen have been unearthed, surveyed and catalogued: they have been agreeably surprised to find a sudden interest

---

33 A. Rogers, *The Most Revolutionary Measure: A History of the Rural Development Commission, 1909–1999* (Salisbury, 1999), p. 44. I am most grateful to Alan Rogers for the gift of his book; National Archives, D4/421.

taken in them and have generally responded: the village saddler alone
seems past repair ... (fo. 142)

However, they went on to admit that, for the trades ancillary to agriculture, the
main problem was that agricultural work was 'steadily diminishing' because of
the reduction in the arable area and the decreasing use of horses, which in turn
produced a decrease in demand for farriery and harness-making and decreasing expenditure on repairs. Rural craftsmen, smiths especially, were unwilling
to invest in electrification or oxy-acetylene welding plants because they were
perceived to be unprofitable, and there was now a shortage of young smiths
and wheelwrights because masters in financial difficulties were unwilling to
take on apprentices (fos. 147–61). Nevertheless, they argued, the introduction
of guilds and co-operatives, shows, propaganda, improvement of designs and
the introduction of sidelines 'have all helped to rekindle the embers of a slowly
dying fire' (fo. 142). In reality, the evidence produced by the enquiry might have
led it to rather different conclusions. It demonstrated that the most active
training demand was for 'classes connected with motors and welding', that
rural businesses were most successful when they turned to new products such
as fowl houses and garden fences, and that advice was most valued when it
helped to increase sales: 'As the end of the craft worker is usually not Art for
Art's sake, but the making of a living, the marketing of his goods is the end to
be kept in view' (fo. 143). But the purpose of the enquiry was not to determine
the commercial health of rural crafts and trades, but to decide whether or not
the Development Commission should continue to fund Rural Community
Councils when their existing funding from the Carnegie Trust ran out. Since
the promotion of rural industries was by this time the activity for which the
Commission was most widely known, even if most of its money still went to
fund agricultural research, it is hardly surprising that its report chose, in the
words of the popular song, to 'accentuate the positive and eliminate the negative'. And in this approach, it seems, it was probably supported by a powerful
assemblage of government departments and other agencies. The Ministries of
Pensions and Labour were interested in jobs for ex-servicemen at the end of
the war, and the Ministry of Agriculture and Fisheries had support for rural
industries written into its establishing Act in 1919.[34] Development Commission representatives had met civil servants and academics at the Welsh Office
in 1919 to discuss the establishment and development of rural industries.[35] In
the following decade the RIB (telegraphic address – indicatively? – 'Ruritania,

---

34 Rogers, *The Most Revolutionary Measure*, pp. 44–5; Brassley, 'Industries in the early
twentieth-century countryside'.

35 National Archives, D4/419: 'Note of a conference held at the Welsh Office, 29
December 1919'.

Westcent, London'), the RCCs and the Oxford AERI were all using the money resulting from this interest. It would be surprising to find that such a combination of policy-makers would be easily thwarted, and, indeed, Rural Community Councils did continue to receive government funding through the 1930s.

In order to support their claims for central funding the RCCs had to submit very full reports of their activities, down to the day-to-day activities of the Rural Industries Organiser, and these form another useful and previously unexploited source for the period from 1936 onwards. The Somerset RCC report for 1936/7, for example, lists the number of 'useful craftsmen' in the county – mostly blacksmiths, wheelwrights, thatchers and hurdle-makers, but also four basket-makers, four furniture-makers and woodworkers, three weavers, two potters and one rake- and tool-handle-maker – and describes current conditions in various trades.[36] Blacksmiths were said to be profiting from an increase in work as a result of better agricultural conditions, and finding that they could not do without oxy-acetylene welding plant. In contrast, only six or seven wheelwrights out of the sixty-one in the county were making new carts, not all were finding repair work, and 'many smaller village wheelwrights have taken to general carpentering and house decorating to augment their ordinary repair work'. Declining horse numbers also produced 'a real problem' for saddlers. Most basket-makers worked for big firms – meaning those employing up to about forty workers – and the industry was flourishing (although the following year it was said to be 'in crisis' as a result of an increase in willow prices from £19 to £32 per ton), but there was little demand for thatchers. In 1937 the Somerset RCC extended its work to the neighbouring county of Dorset, and the report of a survey made there in January 1938 provides some interesting contrasts with Somerset.[37] Thatchers, for example, were found to be enjoying good business conditions, although there were few younger ones. Blacksmiths, on the other hand, were less well off. Many shops had closed in recent years through the effects of the depression or the lack of a successor or the loss of implement agencies. Although there could be an overwhelming demand for repairs in the grass-cutting season, only a few had oxy-acetylene plant, and some smiths had taken to plumbing in outlying areas where mains water supplies had recently been installed. There were only five apprentice blacksmiths and six apprentice wheelwrights in a county with over 100 smiths and sixty-one wheelwrights, joiners and other woodworkers. Most wheelwrights now made most of their income from jobbing building and carpentry, and 'now regard their original business as a sideline ... [although] when

---

36 National Archives, D4/408, Somerset RCC report to the Treasury and Development Commission in support of claims for rural industries work.

37 National Archives, D4/408.

wheels go the farmer has to resort to the wheelwright, though sometimes the axle is removed and replaced by one from an old car complete with wheels.'

The report from the Lincolnshire (Lindsey) RCC for 1936/7 produced some discussion at the National Council of Social Service, which had a supervisory role for RCCs, as to whether the Lindsey RCC was doing what it was supposed to do.[38] The secretary, a Major North Coates, was said to be mostly interested in education, and, indeed, there was much on education and training in the Lindsey report. Farriery courses and tests for the RSS (Registered Shoeing Smith) qualification had been arranged, horse-shoeing and oxy-acetylene welding classes had been held at the county show in 1934 and 1935, and there was a fifteen-week course in motor and electrical engineering for rural boys who were bused into Lincoln Technical College. In the following year this course was repeated, and attended by seventy students from nineteen parishes, of which twenty-nine were farmers and farm workers, nineteen were drivers of farm tractors, threshing-machine engineers, mechanics or van drivers, while the rest were schoolteachers, rural craftsmen, shopkeepers, or unemployed.

Thus the pattern which emerges from these reports is one of considerable variation from one county to another, but an overall impression of decline in traditional trades, with little investment in new methods – rural electrification was a hesitant process – few apprentices, and an ageing work-force. The Lindsey report for 1938/9 contained a survey of the ages of 320 smiths, joiners and wheelwrights, and saddlers.[39] None was under thirty years old, and 42 per cent of the smiths, 32 per cent of the woodworkers and 61 per cent of the saddlers were over sixty. Where there was enthusiasm for new methods and training, it was not in the traditional crafts but in the new technologies. Motor vehicles and tractors, it would seem, produced the same interest among the rural youth of the 1920s and 30s that computers do among the rural youth of the present day, and with much the same impression on the older generation.

Despite the protests of the Development Commission, there was something in what the economists said: it was difficult to counteract market forces. Where a real demand existed, crafts and trades would survive or flourish. Otherwise they would be in difficulties. And circumstances could change fairly quickly. In 1939, for example, the Director of the Rural Industries Bureau tried to set up a training scheme for wattle hurdle-makers, on the grounds that there was now a new demand for hurdles as foundations for oil storage tanks, for freight packing in cargo boats, windbreaks on South African fruit farms, and shooting butts. Since the folding of sheep on downland, the traditional

---

[38] National Archives, D4/400, Lincolnshire (Lindsey) RCC report to the Treasury and Development Commission in support of claims for rural industries work.

[39] National Archives, D4/400.

market for hurdles, had declined, there were few skilled workers left, and there was now a need to train new workers.[40] Bill (later Sir William) Slater drew on the Dartington experience in evidence to the Scott Committee in 1942, and came to the same conclusion about the importance of economics.[41] He could speak with some authority, for the Dartington estate had been involved in promoting and thinking about a range of rural crafts and industries from the beginning of the Elmhirsts' involvement with it. The banners installed in the Great Hall to cut down reverberation had been made over ten years by Elizabeth Peacock (1880–1969) to symbolise the various departments of the estate. Dartington Hall products included indoor and outdoor furniture, turned ware, pottery, cider and fruit juice and textiles. In the 1930s the trustees had been financing their own rural industries survey in Devon.[42] 'There has been a very marked decline in the number of ancillary industries due to the mass production of the goods required for the farm', he said, so that smiths, wheelwrights and harness-makers were now mostly concerned with repairs, 'but with each advance in the mechanization of the farm their work becomes less'. Dartington's attempts to establish a variety of rural enterprises had convinced him that 'The rural craftsman must … seek his market amongst the more discriminate members of the higher incomed section of the population', but even then there was the danger that '… the craftsman products … will be copied by the factory and produced at a lower price. His markets are, therefore, continually being undermined.' The estate's 1937 catalogue shows eight wood turners working at the same bench, which suggests that it had already moved away from the idea of the individual craftsman producing his own or traditional designs.[43] This presumably reflected the importance that Slater attached to marketing. He cited Harris Tweed as a rural industry with an effective marketing organisation, and also emphasised the fact that 'the crofters weave only in their spare time': rural crafts were most likely to be successful as a supplementary industry to agriculture.

Therefore, interesting as it was, and influential as it may have been on the

[40] National Archives, D4/453, Rural Industries Bureau, Wattle Hurdle Making Scheme, 1939.

[41] Dartington Hall Archives, High Cross House, Dartington, Devon. Box Ag Econ 3 (1926–85), file D: evidence for the Scott committee, 1942, by W. K. Slater.

[42] This is confirmed in National Archives, D4/427, Correspondence between the Dartington Hall Trustees and the Development Commission on rural industries work in Devonshire, Jan and Feb 1940. For some time before February 1938 the trustees had been financing a rural industries survey in Devon by Mr Rex Gardner. It was to have been taken over by the newly formed Devon RCC, but the outbreak of war prevented this, and there were consequently misunderstandings over payments.

[43] Dartington Archives, 1937 catalogue of craft products.

up-market end of the craft industry, the Dartington experiment hardly provided a model which would keep the average blacksmith or wheelwright in the typical village. And to be fair to Slater, this is what he argued in his evidence to Scott, which contained far more about what constituted a suitable industry for a small rural town than about rural crafts *per se*. Thus the contemporary commentators produce the same conflicting impressions as the literary evidence discussed earlier: for some, it is the decline in traditional activities that dominates the picture; for others, it is the possibility of change and development that prevails. What counted, for the individual craftsman or tradesman in the village, was whether or not he was still in business and making a living. And the only way to see beneath the conflicts produced by the impressionistic evidence is to examine the trends in the numbers of rural craftsmen in this period.

THE QUANTITATIVE EVIDENCE

Unfortunately, it is easier to recognise the desirability of enumerating rural craftsmen than it is to count them. The best source for occupations is without doubt the Census Enumerator's book, which gives details of individuals, includes dual occupations such as 'blacksmith and publican', enables various age groups and genders to be separated, and allows precise location, all of which are desirable features in the statistics. But, given their hundred-year closure, these are useless for this period. They also require a lot of work to produce a national data sample. Consequently, previous investigators of rural employment have relied on the national summary data published from the census statistics. Chartres, especially, has made extensive use of these, with sophisticated data analysis to locate concentrations of specific trades.[44] For the purposes of this chapter, however, Chartres's methods are of little use, because they rely upon county figures, and each county contains both urban and rural areas. Wrigley tried to get round this problem by examining the difference between seventeen rural counties and the rest of England for ten trades over the years 1831–51.[45] It is possible to use his methodology for later years, up to 1911, but by 1931 definitions had changed to the point where it is not possible to produce comparative data. Moreover, although this method is more sophisticated than simply examining crude national totals, the rural counties still

---

44 Chartres, 'Rural industry and manufacturing'; Chartres and Turnbull, 'Country craftsmen'.

45 E. A. Wrigley, 'Men on the land and men in the countryside: employment in agriculture in early-nineteenth-century England', in *The World we have Gained: Histories of Population and Social Structure*, ed. L. Bonfield, R. M. Smith and K. Wrightson (Oxford, 1986).

contain significant urban areas. The only possible exception to this is the old county of Rutland, which contains one small market town – Oakham – but is otherwise reasonably rural. Saville used it in his work on rural depopulation, but only gives figures for 1911 and 1931.[46]

The alternative sources of occupational data for this period, the directories, are by no means perfect. They tend to underestimate the numbers involved, by comparison with the census, and they do not always reveal dual occupations.[47] Nevertheless, for want of anything better they have been used by several investigators for various purposes. Chalklin examined agriculture and transport, food processing and retailing, building and miscellaneous trades in twenty-five parishes in Lincolnshire between 1896 and 1933, finding that the blacksmiths, wheelwrights and saddlers survived fairly well into the interwar period, although the tailors and shoemakers were disappearing.[48] Saville, for his work on rural depopulation, also examined eighteen parishes in the South Hams, demonstrating that the total of shoemakers, carpenters and builders, blacksmiths, masons, tailors, wheelwrights and thatchers almost halved between 1910 and 1939.[49] However, he was using only a small sample: by 1939 the total was only sixty-one workers. Despite the problems of the directories, therefore, they have been used by several workers to produce occupational data, and in several parts of the country, although none involve very large sample sizes. Although the best reason for continuing to use them is the lack of anything better, it is interesting to note that when the Somerset Rural Community Council expanded its work to Dorset in 1938, it too used *Kelly's Directory* to identify the new county's craftsmen.[50] If it was good enough for the bureaucrats at the time, we might argue, it should be good enough for the historians studying them.

The procedure adopted in the following study, therefore, was to attempt to overcome the problems discussed above (small samples, geographical limitations, and the inclusion of urban settlements) by identifying a large number – seventy-six – of parishes in Devon. These parishes had a maximum population of no more than about 1,000 in 1931, and were selected more or less

[46] J. Saville, *Rural Depopulation in England and Wales, 1851–1951* (1957), p. 74.

[47] C. A. Crompton, 'Changes in rural service occupations during the nineteenth century: an evaluation of two sources for Hertfordshire, England', *Rural History* 6/1 (1995): 193–204; E. Higgs, 'Occupational censuses and the agricultural workforce in Victorian England and Wales', *Economic History Review* 48/4 (1995): 700–16.

[48] C. W. Chalklin, 'The decline of the country craftsmen and tradesmen', in *The Vanishing Countryman*, ed. G. E. Mingay (1989).

[49] Saville, *Rural Depopulation*, p. 212.

[50] National Archives, D4/408, Somerset RCC report to the Treasury and Development Commission.

randomly, by drawing a line on the map, selecting the parishes which it cut, and eliminating those that contained too many people. Their total population in 1931 was 28,789. There were 289,926 people in the smaller towns (those with populations of less than 8,000) and villages of Devon in 1931, so the data collected from the directories represent a 10 per cent sample of the rural county, distributed across it from east to west and north to south (see Map 1).[51] Directories for 1910, 1923 and 1939 were sampled, and the numbers of craftsmen and other occupations identified therein are shown in table 1.[52]

TABLE 1 Numbers in rural crafts and trades in 76 parishes in Devon, 1910–39

Occupation	1910	1923	1939
Thatchers	18	9	6
Masons	42	24	10
Builders	13	12	23
Carpenters	73	48	49
Wheelwrights	31	26	14
Blacksmiths	76	61	49
Shoemakers	50	30	22
Tailors	37	26	19
(subtotal)	(340)	(236)	(192)
Farmers	1,670	1,733	1,961
Shopkeepers	101	108	147
Pubs, hotels etc.	105	91	87
B&Bs, tearooms etc.	22	27	64
Food processing	117	93	65
Garages	1	9	40
Others	142	146	183
(subtotal)	(498)	(474)	(586)

Source: see text

These figures reveal the same trends as those identified by Saville (1957) in his case-study of eighteen parishes in the South Hams, albeit to a lesser extent.[53] They are not directly comparable, because three of Saville's parishes

[51] These figures are from the 1931 census, the results of which are reported in the 1939 directory.

[52] *Kelly's Directories of Devon*, 1910, 1923, 1939. Each of these was sampled from microfiche copies held in the Westcountry Studies Library, Exeter.

[53] Saville, *Rural Depopulation*, p. 212. Although Saville states in his table xxxiii that he has used eighteen parishes, he actually lists nineteen (see p. 178).

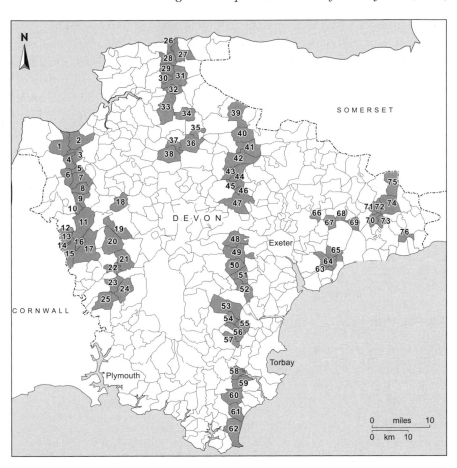

1 Woolfardisworthy	21 Bridestowe	41 Rackenford	61 Slapton
2 Parkham	22 Lewtrenchard	42 Witheridge	62 Stokenham
3 East Putford	23 Brentnor	43 Thelbridge	63 Bicton
4 West Putford	24 Mary Tavy	44 Washford Pyne	64 Colaton Raleigh
5 Abbots Bickingham	25 Lamerton	45 Woolfardisworthy	65 Newton Poppleford
6 Sutcombe	26 Trentishoe	46 Kennerleigh Bishop	& Harpford
7 Milton Demerel	27 Parracombe	47 Sandford	66 Clyst St Lawrence
8 Thornbury	28 Kentisbury	48 Tedburn St Mary	67 Talaton
9 Cookbury	29 Arlington	49 Dunsford	68 Feniton
10 Hollacombe	30 Loxhore	50 Bridford	69 Gittisham
11 Ashwater	31 Bratton Fleming	51 Christow	70 Offwell
12 Tetcott	32 Stoke Rivers	52 Hennock	71 Monkton
13 Luffincott	33 Swimbridge	53 Ilsington	72 Cotleigh
14 Northcott	34 Filleigh	54 Bickington	73 Widworthy
15 St Giles on the Heath	35 George Nympton	55 Ogwell	74 Stockland
16 Virginstowe	36 King's Nympton	56 Torbryan	75 Yarcombe
17 Broadwoodwidger	37 Chittlehamholt	57 Broadhempston	76 Musbury
18 Highampton	38 Burrington	58 Ashprington	
19 Beaworthy	39 Molland	59 Cornworthy	
20 Bratton Clovelly	40 Knowstone	60 Blackawton	

MAP 1 Parishes in the 10 per cent sample of rural Devon, 1910–39

– Totnes, Kingsbridge and Ivybridge – are small towns rather than villages, and so would have been eliminated from the sample discussed here. In Saville's sample the numbers engaged in the first eight trades in table 1 (thatchers to tailors) decreased by 48 per cent (118 to 61) between 1910 and 1939, with shoemakers and tailors being especially prone to disappear. In the all-Devon sample used here, the number of builders actually increases, although, given the similarities between the trades, it might be more realistic to add together figures for builders and masons and count them as a single trade. But the overall changes are not dissimilar to those found by Saville: a decrease of 43 per cent for the all-Devon sample, and of 42 per cent in fifteen parishes stretching north–south across south Devon from Tedburn St Mary to Stokenham. However, it is interesting to note that much of this change took place between 1910 and 1923: 104 tradesmen disappeared between 1910 and 1923, but only forty-four in the sixteen years between 1923 and 1939. So are the interwar years a period when rural crafts and trades had disappeared to such an extent that there were few left to lose, or are they a time in which the declining trend was bottoming out? Either explanation might have something to be said for it, but before deciding which is the most likely, it is interesting to examine the trends in the other part of table 1.

Saville provides no directory-derived evidence for other trades or occupations, but the information is available there, as can be seen from table 1. It is interesting to note that the number of farmers increases across the county, and this in a time of reputed agricultural depression. Although direct evidence is lacking, the most likely explanation is that this was a period of estate sales, so presumably not only did tenants take the opportunity to buy their farms, but also some of the bigger tenanted holdings, or perhaps home farms, were sold off to new entrants.

It is also interesting to see that numbers in the trades in the bottom half of the table, having declined slightly between 1910 and 1923, then increased in the next sixteen years. The trend was not uniform: the traditional forms of business in the hospitality industry – pubs and hotels – declined, as did the food-processing trades, which mean bakers, butchers and millers. In 1910 all but four parishes of the fourteen east Devon parishes sampled had food processors of some kind, but by 1939 eight parishes had none. Some of these businesses had probably been transformed into retailers rather than processors. Others clearly diversified their businesses. Even in 1910 a publican in Newton Poppleford acted as an agent for Gibbs' fertilizers, and in 1923 Albert Strawbridge of Colaton Raleigh was not only a shoeing and general smith but also an 'agent for the best kinds of agricultural implements, cycle repairs and accessories, and agent for leading makers'. At Gittisham in 1923 a carpenter also kept the post office. In other parts of the county there were similar examples of multiple occupations. The keeper of the Artichoke Inn at Christow in 1910 was a saddler, the miller at Filleigh in 1923 was also a coal- and reed-merchant, and at the same time the blacksmith at West Putford was also a grocer and the registrar of births, marriages and deaths. Blacksmiths seemed especially likely to branch out. At Sandford in 1910 John Westcott described himself as an agricultural engineer, thrashing machine proprietor, smith and wagon-builder; the blacksmith at Beaworthy in 1939 was also an agricultural engineer and oxy-acetylene welder, while his colleague at Bratton Clovelly was also the county instructor in farriery.

The impact of the motor car may also be detected in the directories. As table 1 shows, was there an increase in the number of garages, with forty in the seventy-six parishes surveyed by 1939. Garage proprietors often combined their trade with other occupations, as in the garage and grocery at Bratton Fleming, the garage and haulage contractor at Burrington, and the garage, ironmonger, hardware, cycle and wireless dealer at Ashwater, all in 1939. Other trades, too, developed to cater for the motor car and its passengers: road contractors, for example, and new types of business in the hospitality trades, such as bed-and-breakfast establishments, those providing apartments and farmhouse accommodation, and tea shops, such as the Little Sigford Tea Orchard near the developing tourist destination of Haytor on Dartmoor. William A. Beckley of Sutcombe presumably began as a wheelwright, but by 1923 he claimed to be also a general carpenter and motor car and carriage-body builder.

The final expanding category was the inevitable 'others'. The range of trades included therein was predictably vast. Some have an air of tradition, as with the higglers, hawkers, rabbit-catchers, corn- and seed-merchants, cattle-dealers, cider-merchants, tanners and gamekeepers. Some, like the jewellers, builders' merchants, insurance agents and fishmongers, one is perhaps surprised to find in small villages. Others illustrate the penetration of the professionals into the countryside: not only the medical practitioners and district nurses, but also the vets, surveyors, sanitary inspectors and architects. Others are just rarities: the teazleman, the herbalist, the convent and the architectural wood-carver. There are also the primary and manufacturing industries, such as the edge-tool makers at Dunsford and Ogwell and the mines at Bridford, Christow, Hennock and Ilsington. And finally there are the signs of what in hindsight appear to be diversification or development in the rural economy: the road contractor, the motor car proprietor, cycle dealer, haulage contractor, beekeeper, basket-maker, horse-trainer, and dressmaker. All of these are too few in number to provide, individually, any information on trends, but, taken together, they suggest that the rural economy was not incapable of change. The answer to the question posed earlier, about whether the decline in craft numbers had proceeded to the point where there were none left to lose, or whether the declining trend was bottoming out, might therefore be that the declining older crafts were to some extent replaced by more recently established trades; blacksmiths and garages are an obvious example. On the other hand, although it might be expected that numbers in the building crafts would decline more in the northern and western parishes, where population decreased more than in the southern and eastern parishes, there seems to be no evidence that this was indeed the case. Over the whole county, in fact, numbers in the building crafts (i.e. the first four of those listed in table 1) were remarkably stable in the interwar period. The most important discovery of this survey, however, is that the rate of decline in the sixteen years between 1923 and 1939 was slower than it had been in the thirteen years between 1910 and 1923. In fact, although the numbers of those in the traditional crafts declined, albeit at a slower rate in the interwar period, the numbers of those in the trades in the lower half of the table, having initially declined, rose between 1923 and 1939 to exceed their previous level. And taking all the non-agricultural occupations together, the increase in these trades was more than enough to offset the decline in the crafts between the wars.

EXPLANATIONS

How, then, if it is difficult to demonstrate quantitatively that the interwar period was one of rapid decline in rural crafts and trades, can the undoubted upsurge in elegiac literature be explained? One possibility is that it was simply a delayed reaction to the undoubted changes which occurred before the First World War and between 1914 and 1920. Another is that the Rural Industries branch of the Ministry of Agriculture, the Rural Industries Bureau and the AERI at Oxford were all intent on justifying their existence, although how this might provoke writers into action is difficult to see. A third possibility might be to see it as a reaction to change, threat and uncertainty. Writing in another context, Verrier argued that the First World War 'had left behind a vengeful Germany, a prostrate France, an isolationist America, and had produced a fascist Italy and a revolutionary Russia ...'[54] The old continental empires – the Russian, Austro-Hungarian, Hohenzollern German and Ottoman Turkish – which must have been remembered as political normality by the immediate post-war generation, had gone, to be replaced by new nations, democracies and totalitarian states. In the early 1920s King George V was said to be 'in a funk' about the 'danger of revolution', and in 1929 Beatrice Webb wrote of the 'senile hypertrophy' of the Empire.[55] In the decade of the General Strike and

---

54 A. Verrier, *The Bomber Offensive* (1974), p. 32.

55 P. Brendon, *The Dark Valley: A Panorama of the 1930s* (2000), pp. 43–4; see also M. Mazower, *Dark Continent: Europe's Twentieth Century* (1999).

the Great Crash the economy as a whole, not just the rural economy, was challenged. By the 1930s writers on both the left and right of the political spectrum were united in perceiving capitalism to be in crisis and decline. A global revolution leading to a socialist world state was an inevitability, according to H. G. Wells.[56] All over the world lower economic growth rates and higher inflation and unemployment led many to 'the belief that something was fundamentally wrong with the world they lived in'.[57] And in the countryside, this was a period in which more land changed hands than in any other short period since the dissolution of the monasteries.[58] Is it any wonder that some, such as the Elmhirsts and Rolf Gardiner, looked for radical solutions, while others looked for stability? In such a world the traditional crafts represented a haven of predictability, calm and comfort. Their continued survival meant that something remained of the old safe world; their disappearance implied the triumph of a newer and quite possibly less comfortable way of ordering society, especially in the eyes of the middle-class book-buying public.[59]

The willingness of the book consumer of the time to subscribe to the ideas and values implicit in the works of the wheelwright (Sturt) and carpenter (Rose) mentioned in the title of this chapter, and their contemporaries, is therefore part of the process of constructing the image of the period.[60] Subsequent investigations, especially those by Saville and Williams in the Dartington Hall Studies in Rural Sociology series, strengthened the picture so produced.[61] Miss FitzRandolph and Miss Hay, the two ladies from Oxford, and the sources of their funds, such as the Ministry of Agriculture, the Development Commission and the Rural Industries Bureau, were less elegiac in their approach, but their effect was much the same: they identified rural crafts and trades as a problem worthy of the policymaker's attention. It is immaterial that their solution to the problem differed from those who, by inference at least, simply wanted to maintain the world as it was for the sake of what they perceived as its traditional virtues. The existence of a policy implied that there was a problem to be solved. That there had indeed been a problem is suggested by the decline in numbers in rural crafts and trades in the years before and immediately after the First World War; whether the problem continued

56 Brendon, *The Dark Valley*, pp. 168–9.

57 E. Hobsbawm, *The Age of Extremes: The Short Twentieth Century, 1914–1991* (1994), p. 102.

58 P. Dewey, *War and Progress: Britain, 1914–1945* (1997), p. 160.

59 See Brace, 'A pleasure ground for noisy herds'; R. Moore-Colyer, 'Back to basics: Rolf Gardiner, H. J. Massingham and "A Kinship in Husbandry"', *Rural History* 12 (2002): 85–108.

60 Sturt, *The Wheelwright's Shop*; Rose, *The Village Carpenter*.

61 Saville, *Rural Depopulation*; Williams, *The Country Craftsman*.

to exist in the same form for most of the two interwar decades is much less clear. The Devon evidence suggests that, in some parts of the county at least, numbers were stabilising or perhaps even increasing. The fact that the composition of the rural crafts and trades sector in 1939 was not the same as in 1919 does not mean that rural craftsmen had vanished, although it may mean that they had adapted to changing economic circumstances. The two ladies from Oxford recognised this as early as 1926, and welcomed it; the wheelwright and the carpenter recognised it too, but certainly did not welcome it. And their sense of loss has been remarkably influential in constructing our view of socio-economic change between the wars.

❦ Conclusion

Paul Brassley, Jeremy Burchardt, and Lynne Thompson

WHETHER we consider it from a social, cultural, political or economic point of view, the English countryside between the wars is better char-acterised by growth and innovation than by stagnation or decline. In the long run perhaps the most important development was the changing size, com-position and nature of the rural population. Whilst the second half of the nineteenth century had witnessed declining population across most of rural England, the picture became more complex in the first half of the twenti-eth century. The change was especially marked in areas close to conurbations, such as the Home Counties, Warwickshire and Staffordshire (Birmingham), and Cheshire (Manchester). The population of the administratively rural dis-tricts of Berkshire, for example, increased by 54 per cent between 1901 and 1951, despite losing 11,844 acres to urban authorities.[1] The county's rural population increased by just over 6 per cent between 1921 and 1931, and by perhaps 20 per cent between 1931 and 1941.[2] Even the comparatively isolated and predomi-nantly agricultural western district of Hungerford recorded a rise in popula-tion of more than 13 per cent between 1921 and 1951.[3] Conversely, a sample of seventy-five rural parishes in Devon, chosen alphabetically from Abbots Bick-ington to Butterleigh, contained thirty-nine parishes in which the population fell from 1901 to 1931, and again to 1961, as compared to twenty-three in which it remained more or less constant and only thirteen in which it increased. In several of the expanding parishes the growth can probably be explained by their proximity to the larger towns, or, as at Bigbury, to the sea. Belstone, on Dartmoor, was close to neither sea nor town, but its population also expanded 'since', as Hoskins rather sourly noted, 'it was "discovered" fifty years ago'.[4]

As these figures suggest, the composition of rural society was also chang-ing radically. Howkins points out that by 1921 there were 297,968 coal miners living in rural areas – more than half as many as there were farm workers

---

[1] *Census 1901, Berks*, p. 11; *Census 1951*, p. 54.

[2] This figure is half the growth between 1931 and 1951, since there was, of course, no census in 1941. The assumption that growth rates were the same in the 1930s and 1940s is arbitrary but there is independent evidence of rapid growth in the county in the 1930s.

[3] *Census 1901, Berks*, p. 11; *Census 1951*, p. 54.

[4] W. G. Hoskins, *Devon*, new edn (Newton Abbot, 1972), pp.331, 523–5.

(see chapter 2). Besides workers in other extractive industries, there were also 177,521 transport and communication workers, mostly working in road transport, 168,798 metal workers and 135,218 building workers. Even more striking was the growth in rural white-collar workers. Commercial, public and professional occupations provided employment for 483,656 men and women resident in rural districts in 1921, little short of the number of farm workers. The rise of service-sector employment was especially marked in the Home Counties, accounting for 47 per cent of working residents in rural Berkshire, including the 12 per cent of total employment constituted by the rapidly growing census categories 'professional and technical, excluding clerical' and 'commerical, finance etc., excluding clerical'.[5] Gender patterns of employment were undergoing transformation too, with 36 per cent of the rural white-collar work-force female by 1921. A high proportion of these white-collar employees were commuters, a harbinger of the future. By 1951 as many as 52 per cent of employees resident in Abingdon Rural District worked outside it; 45 per cent did so in Cookham RD.[6]

Commuters were a diverse breed, ranging from the Morris Motors workers who cycled in to Oxford from the surrounding villages each day to the 'people who have amassed wealth out of ships, law, tea, pottery, ink, banking and "contracting"', who, according to F. E. Green, inhabited the 'high quality residential scatter' around Leith Hill, Surrey.[7] What they had in common, as Howkins puts it, is that they were 'in the country but not, at least in the traditional sense, of the country'. Yet whilst it is important to acknowledge the profound change that the influx of the 'new' countrymen and women brought, we should not exaggerate the decline of 'traditional' rural society. Certainly the number of agricultural workers fell but there was little reduction in the number of farmers. In some counties, in fact, the opposite occurred – in Brassley's sample of seventy-six Devon parishes (see chapter 16) the number of farmers rose from 1,733 in 1923 to 1,961 in 1939, an increase of 13 per cent, presumably a result of the breaking up and sale of estates.

If the composition of rural society was changing rapidly, so was social provision. Education was central to social improvement in the countryside at this time. Rural education felt the benefits of nationwide improvements in the school curriculum and leaving age, and in teachers' pay and conditions, albeit often belatedly. More distinctive, perhaps, was the nature of rural adult education. Following the Committee on Adult Education's *Final Report* of 1919,

5 *Census 1921, Berks*, pp. xxiv–xxxii, 26–7, 36–44; *Census 1951, Occupation Tables*, pp. 356–9.

6 *Census 1951 England and Wales: Report on Usual Residence and Workplace* (1956), pp. 44–6.

7 F. E. Green, *The Surrey Hills* (1915).

an impressive array of organisations attempted to provide classes for adults, including the Women's Institutes, Workers' Educational Association, Rural Community Councils and Local Education Authorities. By 1939 most counties had one or more full-time adult education tutors and several part-time tutors. Correspondingly the number of classes began to increase – in Oxfordshire there were twenty-two classes and courses of lectures in 1936, over and above those intended for the unemployed. Perhaps the most interesting development was, however, the village college movement (discussed by Adams in chapter 4), set in train by the socialist educationist Henry Morris. The first village college, combining meeting hall, library, adult education rooms and secondary school under one roof, was built in Sawston, Cambridgeshire, in 1930. It was followed by Bottisham and Linton (both 1937) and Impington (1939), all also in Cambridgeshire, and copied outside the county after the Second World War.

One of most frequent criticisms of rural education before the First World War was its lack of agricultural content. This began to change after the war. The Agriculture Act of 1920 required each county council to create a committee to supervise agricultural education. In the three years following the end of the war £3 million was set aside for agricultural education and research, whereby counties received up to two-thirds of their operating costs and four-fifths of the salary of agricultural organisers. Annual expenditure by LEAs on agricultural advisory and educational work rose from £213,602 in 1919/20 to £606,385 in 1938/9. Similarly, there were thiry-two county organisers in England and Wales with a staff of 166 in 1919, but fifty-five organisers with 468 support staff in 1938/9. The number of farm institutes administered by English and Welsh county councils increased from five in 1914 to seventeen in 1939; evening class provision and student numbers both more than doubled. In the West Riding fifty children aged between thirteen and sixteen attended continuation classes in 1933/4, whilst three years later 160 did. The energetic Colin Ross, county organiser for Devon, established mobile cheese and dairy schools, initiated field experiments in crop production and taught skills such as cider-making and oxy-acetylene welding. Students could go on to Seale Hayne College after completing a three-year part-time certificate course. The scale and range of agricultural education therefore increased substantially between the wars, foundations that were built on after 1945.

Education, especially adult education, was closely linked to leisure provision. An impressive array of new rural leisure organisations sprang into being during and after the First World War: the Women's Institutes, Village Clubs Association, Rural Community Councils, Village Drama Society and Young Farmers Clubs (YFCs) focused solely on the countryside, whilst the Scouts, Guides, British Legion and Workers Educational Association were also active in urban areas. Perhaps the most startlingly successful group were the Women's Institutes, which had more than 300,000 members by 1939. For the first time rural women were able to meet collectively and engage in social activities of their own making. The YFCs, whilst more narrowly framed, did aim to attract the children of farm workers as well as farmers. Nearly fifty clubs existed by 1928, although with fewer than 1,500 members. Grants from the Carnegie UK Trust, the Development Commission and, from 1935, a number of LEAs followed, and by 1939 there were 412 clubs with a membership of *c.*15,000. Adult men were perhaps less well catered for, although many belonged to the British Legion. In some counties, farming and horticultural discussion clubs were set up; there were twenty in Devon by 1939. Probably more popular than discussion was acting and by 1939, over 600 villages had affiliated to the Village Drama Section of the British Drama League (into which the Village Drama Society was absorbed in 1932). As in so many other aspects of rural social provision, the Carnegie UK Trust played a key role in promoting the development of village drama, channelling funds through the National Council of Social Service (NCSS) and National Federation of Women's Institutes to a Joint Committee for Music and Drama in the Villages. By 1939 nearly every county in England had a rural drama committee.

This proliferation of leisure provision was encouraged by the growing network of Rural Community Councils (RCCs) – independent county-level organisations that worked closely with local government and the rural department of the National Council of Social Service to co-ordinate voluntary social organisations in the countryside. Oxfordshire was the first county to establish a Rural Community Council (1922), and by 1942 there were twenty-four RCCs in 29 counties of England and Wales. One of their most urgent priorities was to encourage the building of village halls. It was widely recognised that, in the words of the annual report of the NCSS for 1931/2, 'Where there is no village hall there tend to be few village activities; the growth of active organisations is indeed almost impossible unless they can find an adequate meeting place.'[8] Village halls marked a quiet revolution in rural leisure. They were the first large indoor meeting places under public as opposed to private or sectional control. Before the First World War few village halls existed: in Oxfordshire only three are known to have been built before 1914, whereas there were at least seventy-five in existence by the end of 1939. The lack of large public meeting spaces in rural areas created particular difficulties for reformers and radicals in the nineteenth century: it was no accident the famous Wellesbourne meeting at which Joseph Arch founded the National Agricultural Labourers Union in 1872 took place under the doubtful shelter of a chestnut tree; and the red and

---

[8] National Council of Social Service, *Voluntary Service: Being the Annual Report of the National Council of Social Service (Incorporated) for the year 1931–2* (1932), p. 31.

yellow vans of late nineteenth-century land reformers had a practical purpose too. In terms of usage, however, it was the large public leisure activities such as whist drives, concerts, dances and plays that flourished most in village halls; indeed, many of the new leisure organisations established in the years after the First World War would have been unsustainable had halls not been built to accommodate them. For drama festivals 'the basic requirement was a hall with proscenium, scenery and blackout', and in 1932 and 1936 the Gloucestershire Drama Festivals had to be curtailed due to lack of suitable halls. Village halls 'stirred up no end of community activities and outings'; in Mansfield's words, they became the focus of 'the mildly hedonistic interwar popular culture of whist drives, dances and amateur dramatics'.[9]

Whilst the users of village halls may often have had hedonistic intentions, many of those promoting them had higher ends in view. This was nothing less than the creation of 'a new rural civilisation', a goal shared with the closely related village college and village drama movements. In the words of Henry Morris, 'without some such institution as the village college a rural community consisting largely of agricultural workers, small proprietors and small farmers will not be equal to the task of maintaining a worthy rural civilisation.' F. G. and Irene Thomas in Devon saw a similar role for village drama, providing a community focus, effort, mutual respect and, ultimately, rural regeneration. Revitalised community would provide the basis for a rural democracy, on the back of the introduction of virtual universal adult suffrage in 1918. At Liverton in Devon the Thomases established a drama committee to develop the villagers' skills in self-government and encourage 'group intelligence and collaboration'. In the words of the NCSS, 'the village has a special value as a school of democracy and whatever tends to draw out the capacity for self-government in village life is enhancing this value.'[10] For Henry Morris 'the village college will be the seat and guardian of humane public traditions in the countryside, the training ground of a rural democracy realising its social and political duties.'

Underlying the commitment to community and democracy was the assumption that rural people were different, possessing an ability 'to assess the quality of things that is easily blunted by the artificial environment of the streets' – an ability which could be 'easily corrupted by town influences that are permeating the countryside'.[11] There is a parallel here with the folk revival, primarily a pre-First World War phenomenon but still an active influence in

---

9 S. Stewart, *Lifting the Latch: A Life on the Land* (Oxford, 1987), p. 124. Mansfield: see chapter 12, above.

10 National Council of Social Service, *Constructive Citizenship: The Annual Report of the NCSS (Inc.) for the year 1930–31* ([1931]), p. 10.

11 NCSS, *Constructive Citizenship*, pp. 9–10.

shaping perceptions of rural culture in the 1920s and 1930s.[12] To this end it was important to discourage urban influences from adulterating rural community life, so the NCSS, for example, sometimes refused to give grants for village hall designs that failed to respect local vernacular architectural traditions, and efforts were made to prevent films being shown in some halls.

Whilst predicated on the maintenance of a sharp divide between urban and rural, the attempt to create a 'new rural civilization' carried the implication that rural regeneration could catalyse national regeneration, or, as W. R. Lethaby wrote in *Home and Country*, 'The country and country life are and must be the basis of national life.'[13] This equation emerged with a new strength and emphasis after the First World War, for reasons that have been extensively rehearsed elsewhere, in a crucial formative period for the identity of twentieth-century Britain. By 1926 Stanley Baldwin, seeking as ever to lay claim to an uncontroversial, even incontrovertible, centre ground, could pronounce 'England is the country and the country is England.'[14] Whatever the economic significance of the countryside between the wars, there can be no doubt that culturally the countryside had become absolutely central. The apogee was reached, perhaps, with the report of the Scott Committee on Land Utilisation in Rural Areas in 1942, which, as Christopher Bailey argues in chapter 10, 'cemented in place a literary, visual and popular discourse, so that anyone proposing economic development in rural areas would necessarily seem to be striking at the heart of the national heritage.'

Closely associated with this was the growth of a more broadly based preservationist movement than had existed before the First World War. Whilst pre-war organisations such as the Commons Preservation Society (1865), the Society for Checking the Abuses of Public Advertising (1893), the National Trust (1894) and the Society for the Promotion of Nature Reserves (1912) had small, overlapping, elite memberships, the Council for the Preservation of Rural England (1926) and the Ramblers Association (1935), perhaps the two most notable interwar environmental organisations, were more populist in their campaigning style, aiming to affect policy through influencing public opinion. Both represented predominantly urban interests and reflected the tremendous increase in popular leisure use of the countryside, enabled by the bicycle, omnibus and car, a shorter working week and more disposable income,

---

[12] G. Boyes, *The Imagined Village: Culture, Ideology, and the English Folk Revival* (1993).

[13] W. R. Lethaby, *Home and Country Arts* (1923), p. 16.

[14] The phrase was used by Baldwin in proposing the toast to England at the annual dinner of the Royal Society of St. George, held at the Hotel Cecil on 6 May 1924. The speech was subsequently printed in S. Baldwin, *On England, and Other Addresses* (1926).

and fostered by the new cultural centrality of the countryside and the publishing boom that gave expression to it.

Perhaps as significant as the popularity of rural preservationism was its self-consciously progressive character. As David Matless demonstrated in *Landscape and Englishness*, preservationism and the CPRE in particular was associated with an assertive modernism.[15] Patrick Abercrombie, whose 'The preservation of rural England' was the precursor to the formation of the CPRE, exemplifies the nexus between preservationism and planning in the 1920s and 1930s. Abercrombie sought, for example in his regional planning scheme for the new East Kent coalfield (1925 and 1928), to maintain what he saw as 'a very complex palimpsest of civilised effort, past and present' and to strike 'a just balance' between 'conservation and development'. Similarly, the CPRE's photographic essay *The Face of the Land* (1928) deplored the ruination of small country towns by untidy, out-of-scale advertising, but welcomed the clean modernist lines of the pylons of the new national grid. This embrace of *avant-garde* modernism and what was seen as the traditional character of rural England resonated with the apostles of rural regeneration. At Dartington Hall in Devon, for example, Leonard Elmhirst and his wife Dorothy attempted to provide a model of a progressive, modernised country estate by restoring the derelict medieval Great Hall whilst employing the architect William Lescaze to build the headmaster's residence, High Cross House, in the international modern style. In the same way Henry Morris chose the renowned Bauhaus architect Walter Gropius to design Impington Village College, intended to serve amongst other things as a centre for fostering distinctive rural traditions.

Preservationism, and its consequences for landscape and architecture, was one manifestation of the new centrality of the countryside in English culture. Another was the popularity of rural literature, both in the form of guidebooks, photographic essays and the like by publishers such as Batsford, and in the flourishing of the rural novel. As with preservationism, the interwar rural novel was more innovative than appearances might suggest. Although interwar rural novelists wrote principally for a middle-brow readership and eschewed the literary modernism of Joyce or Woolf, in their themes and subject matter many of them offered something more challenging than nostalgia. Women writers made a significant contribution to the genre, and social reform and feminism feature prominently in the works of novelists like Sylvia Townsend Warner and Winifred Holtby. *South Riding*, Holtby's last work, charts the social and economic downfall of the gentleman farmer Robert Carne with powerful empathy, yet ultimately sides unambivalently with the modernising influences of local government, welfare, education and the emancipation of women. Less

---

[15] D. Matless, *Landscape and Englishness* (1998).

obviously political were Constance Holme and Mary Webb, yet Holme's *The Lonely Plough* discreetly probes the ethical and technical adequacy of the estate system in what appeared to be its twilight whilst even Webb's novels refract contemporary social problems, such as the position of women, through their historical setting.

Webb's most successful novel, *Precious Bane*, contrasts its heroine's orientation towards wild nature with her avaricious brother's obsession with productive land. The distinction between 'earth' and 'land' can also be applied to interwar rural novelists. Most of the women writers mentioned in the previous paragraph were clearly 'land' novelists, whose interests were centred in the social worlds they describe. Webb, however, perhaps belongs with writers like T. F. Powys, Sheila Kaye-Smith or, on a larger scale, D. H. Lawrence as an 'earth' novelist, more interested in the spiritual power of nature than in social structure. At its most exaggerated and formulaic, the 'earth' novel deserved the withering satire of Stella Gibbons' *Cold Comfort Farm*. Yet writers like Lawrence and in a different way Williamson identified in nature and rural living a redemptive potential from which, in their view, humanity turned away at its peril. Williamson's enthusiasm for rural regeneration can hardly be separated from his admiration for Hitler; but profoundly as one may disagree with Williamson's political stance, his work is indicative of the energetic cultural response to rural change in the interwar period.[16] Williamson's belief in organic farming links him to contemporaries like Rolf Gardiner, H. J. Massingham, Sir Albert Howard and Lady Eve Balfour, whose ideas, as Philip Conford has shown, were a formative influence on the environmental movement of the second half of the twentieth century. Culturally as well as socially, then, the interwar countryside witnessed the emergence of influences that were to have a powerful effect after the Second World War.

Rural policy and politics follow a similar pattern. Interwar administrations did nothing on the scale of the Attlee government's rural legislation but the groundwork for almost all of it was laid between the wars. At an underlying level perhaps the most important development was the increasing consensus that government had a crucial role to play in organising agricultural and, indeed, rural land use more generally. There was widespread agreement that the right way to do this was by drawing on professional expertise. Abercrombie had argued in 'The preservation of rural England' that permissive

---

[16] This is surely worthy of further study – the chapters by Shaw and Rawlinson, and Moore-Colyer's work on Massingham in *Rural History* show how much the background of rural writers affected their work. R. J. Moore-Colyer, 'A voice clamouring in the wilderness: H. J. Massingham (1888–1952) and rural England', *Rural History* 13 (2002): 199–224.

planning legislation would achieve little; only statutory regulation, guided by the expertise of professional planners, could harmoniously reconcile the different pressures on land use. This emphasis was reflected in the county plans every county council was required to draw up under the 1932 Town and Country Planning Act. Agricultural policy evolved in a similar direction, with, as we have seen, substantial investment in education and research, and, from 1933 onwards, the creation of marketing boards to co-ordinate production, processing and distribution of agricultural products.[17] The predominantly Conservative governments of the 1920s and 1930s were not, as has sometimes been suggested, following a purely negative policy towards agriculture after 1921. On the contrary, as Cooper argued, they increasingly believed that only by the application of expertise could agricultural production and marketing become efficient.[18] The ensuing network of research, advisory and educational bodies and marketing boards pointed the way towards postwar developments such as the National Agricultural Advisory Service (NAAS; later ADAS). However, it is also important to acknowledge that the subsidies and protectionist measures of the 1930s marked a major departure from agricultural *laissez-faire*. The conventional periodisation that identifies the 1947 Agriculture Act as marking the reversal of a century-long era of peacetime free trade since the repeal of the Corn Laws in 1846 does not do justice to measures such as the sugar beet subsidy of 1925, tariffs on soft fruit and potatoes in 1931, the Wheat Act (1932), the beef cattle subsidy of 1933 or the Agriculture Act of 1937, with its subsidies for oat and barley production and for the use of lime and basic slag as fertilisers. Some of these measures had a major impact. The acreage of wheat fell from 2.0 million in 1920–2 to 1.25 million in 1931, but then rose to 1.7 million by 1938–9 in the wake of the Wheat Act. At Leckford the Wheat Act turned a loss-making arable operation into a profitable one. Since the Corn Production Acts (Repeal) Act provided for subsidies to be phased out only by 1923, in only two of the twenty-one interwar years was there not a major agricultural subsidy in place. It could be argued that rather than characterising policy between the wars as a reversion to *laissez-faire*, we should see it as

---

[17] Nora Ratcliff noted that 'we live in an age of centralization and control' and referred to the 'craze for organization' in the interwar years: N. Ratcliff, *Rude Mechanicals: A Short Review of Village Drama* (1938), pp. 14–15. John Spedan Lewis observed the same phenomenon more complacently, declaring that 'no man proposes that in a time of plague the members of communities, whether they be regiments or factories or countries or what you will, shall decide by mass votes what medicine they will take. Things of that kind have to be left to experts.' *The Gazette* [of the J. S. Lewis partnership], 15 Oct 1932, p. 581.

[18] A. F. Cooper, *British Agricultural Policy, 1912–36: A Study in Conservative Politics* (Manchester, 1989), 64–93.

a period in which government experimented with a variety of agricultural regimes, moving towards a combination of subsidies, advisory work and cheap food that pointed towards the post-war settlement.

It was, of course, the Labour Party that formed the first post-war government, and the evolution of Labour thinking on agriculture during the interwar period is, therefore, of perhaps as much importance as changes in government policy. As Griffiths demonstrates, Labour's attitude to farmers underwent a decisive change between 1918 and 1939. This was partly as a result of wider shifts in Labour's approach to economic policy. Whereas in 1918 Labour's primary concern was with the social consequences of industry, assumed to be urban, twenty years' later, with the experience of two periods in office behind it, the party's focus had shifted towards the economic management of industry, including agriculture. At the same time, Labour began to see farmers no longer as necessarily individualistic but potentially as public servants. The concept of 'farming in the public interest' made it possible to treat agriculture as a special case and to envisage subsidies for farmers. The *quid pro quo* was that farmers would be expected to put the land to its full productive use. Labour increasingly emphasised, for electoral reasons, that farmers could benefit from its policies: land nationalisation would go hand in hand with public investment in farm infrastructure, of the kind landowners were no longer able to provide. Advances in the understanding of nutrition in the 1930s, in the work of John Boyd Orr and others, also helped bridge the gap between Labour and agriculture – farmers could benefit the nation by producing high quality 'health foods' such as fruit, vegetables and milk, and deserved public support to enable them to do this. Once again, developments in the 1920s and 1930s pointed in the direction of, and provided the groundwork for, the wartime and postwar reconstruction of agriculture.

Policy was not, of course, the sole prerogative of politicians. The emergence of the National Farmers Union (NFU) as a powerful voice for farmers reflected the growing centrality of farmers to rural society, as many landowners disengaged from politics and farmworkers left the land in droves. By the 1930s the NFU's membership was over 125,000 (more than half of British farmers), and its leadership were enjoying increasingly close relations with government, exemplified by the appointment of Sir Reginald Dorman-Smith, president of the NFU from 1936 to 1938, as Minister of Agriculture in 1939. At a local level the picture is more complex. On the one hand, local authorities, especially county councils, took on an ever-widening range of responsibilities between the wars, especially in relation to welfare and infrastructure – schools, aspects of health care, drainage, road-building and so forth. This narrowed the scope for traditional landowner paternalism, as Winifred Holtby vividly describes in *South Riding*. The resources of local government were, however, limited, and the nexus between statutory and voluntary provision was pivotal feature of the interwar countryside. What voluntarism meant in practice varied greatly. Whilst the academics, educationists and university-educated professionals who led the NCSS, the RCCs and the WEA hoped that the halls, classes, societies, organisations and clubs they sponsored would supplant deference with democracy, their commitment to a separate rural culture could, as Adams has shown, undermine their liberating intentions. Furthermore, the brave new rural world envisaged by W. G. S. Adams, Grace Hadow and their co-workers in 1918–19 inevitably involved accommodation with the traditional elite when implemented on the ground: the Carnegie UK Trust notwithstanding, voluntarism remained dependent on those with land and capital to spare in the countryside, and even in the 1920s and 1930s that still meant mainly the larger landowners. But where the traditional elite did remain in the saddle, Mansfield's work suggests, they did so only by colonising the new social organisations and re-establishing the equilibrium of rural society on a new, more inclusive basis. In Shropshire, Mansfield describes the creation of a 'dynamic set of new culturally conservative village institutions', often with a military flavour, which contributed to the construction of a new 'loyalist' county identity. The chief rituals of this were the unveiling of war memorials, Armistice Day, Empire Day, the cult of county regiments and the associated military tattoos. Strengthened by this, the Conservative Party achieved complete electoral hegemony in the county between the wars. Whether a similar pattern obtained in counties less remote, agricultural and prosperously pastoral than Shropshire remains to be seen, but it seems safe to say that even where the traditional structures of rural social leadership remained intact, they did so as a result of a dynamic adaptation to a significantly altered social and political environment.

The economic fortunes of agriculture are central to the orthodox view of the interwar countryside as dominated by decline. However, Brassley points out that the volume of British agricultural output – surely the most important gauge of economic success – rose by 27 per cent between 1920–2 and 1935–9. Even when prices were at their lowest, between 1930 and 1934, the volume of output was higher than it had been in 1920–2. This is all the more impressive in view of the reduction of 2.7 million acres, or about 10 per cent, in the agricultural acreage. It was due at least in part to the flexibility and entrepreneurship of British farmers, who shifted production away from the arable sector into higher-value outputs such as liquid milk and meat. The number of cows in milk increased from 3 million in 1920–2 to 3.6 million on 1938–9, and of pigs from 2.5 million to 3.8 million over the same period. Collins and Brassley have argued elsewhere that agricultural productivity as well as output rose between the wars; especially in the context of a collapse in prices for some farm products and a glutted world market, the performance of the sector as a whole was very creditable.[19]

Agricultural depression was, in fact, a regional and subsectoral phenomenon. Strongly arable areas like East Anglia suffered most, but counties like Lancashire or Buckinghamshire, with good access to urban markets, or the traditionally pastoral counties of the north and west, made gains; low grain prices reduced costs for livestock farmers. Liquid milk and Thirsk's 'alternative husbandry' prospered; the Preston and District Farmers Trading Society were producing a third of England's eggs by 1931, for example, not a few of them ending up on the nearby breakfast tables of Blackpool landladies.[20] This was a typical example of the energetic, innovative response of many British farmers to the challenging price conditions of the interwar years. Brigden draws attention to the wide range of different approaches: A. H. Brown (intensive fertiliser and purchased feed use), the Hosiers (extensive dairying), R. P. Chester (Scandinavian-style pig-houses), the Alley brothers (reintroduction of bare fallows), Roland Dudley (mechanisation) and Spedan Lewis (modern business methods) were just a few who achieved prominence as radical innovators in the agricultural press.

What mattered most to farmers was not output or even productivity, but profits. But even here, it was only for a limited part of the period that decline is evident. Between 1924 and 1934 net farm income was indeed below pre-First World War levels, but between 1920 and 1923 it was far above them, and rose above them again in 1935–9.

The difficulties experienced by rural crafts in these years have also been exaggerated. Diversification was widespread and often successful: wheelwrights turned to carpentry or furniture-making, blacksmiths made decorative wrought iron, hurdle-makers could find a profitable alternative in garden fences or fowl houses. Above all, the motor trade provided opportunities: saddlers made upholstery, whilst wheelwrights and especially blacksmiths became motor repairers. In the long run the 'new' white collar and professional population of the countryside and the growth of rural tourism were to provide a vast new market for the rural crafts. Signs of this were already apparent before 1939. At Shinners Bridge on the Dartington estate, craft studios were constructed by the Elmhirsts, including a pottery for Bernard Leach. By 1935 Shinners Bridge had a car park and tea room, and sales of craft products were

---

[19] P. Brassley, 'Output and technical change in twentieth-century British agriculture', *Agricultural History Review* 48 (2000): 60–84; E. J. T. Collins, unpublished paper presented to the 2001 Economic History Society conference, Glasgow.

[20] A. Howkins, *The Death of Rural England: A Social History of the Countryside since 1900* (2003), pp. 72–3; J. Thirsk, *Alternative Agriculture: A History from the Black Death to the Present Day* (Oxford, 1997).

booming. As Jeremiah comments in chapter 9, 'it was evident that the culture of the craft experience in a beautiful landscape, enjoyed by the middle-classes in their new family motor cars, had been established.'

What, then, remains of the declinist case? The fortunes of landowners, not examined in detail in this book, might appear a clear-cut and major example of decline. The land sales cannot be gainsaid, although the often-cited figure that a quarter of the land in England changed hands between 1918 and 1921 has recently been challenged. Even here, however, closer examination suggests caution is called for. As Clemenson and Mandler have shown, most large landowners not only survived the first half of the twentieth century, but could be found prospering in the second half.[21] Those who owned land in urban or industrial areas did extraordinarily well; it is no accident that the Duke of Westminster remains, according to most rankings, the UK's wealthiest private citizen. As Michael Thompson suggests, it was probably the lesser gentry owning only agricultural land who suffered most. Even here, however, selling land was often a rational economic choice rather than a despairing necessity, switching assets from a low-yielding investment into typically much more profitable stocks and shares. This is a topic that remains worthy of further study, to determine whether estates were sold off because they were too small to be worth keeping, or in the wrong place, or badly managed, or the inheritance of a victim of the war, or any of the myriad alternative reasons.

Arable farming is another area where we might look to find evidence of decline. It is difficult to dispute that the acreage and profitability of most arable crops declined between the wars. Yet how significant was this? We should not equate the fortunes of arable with the fortunes of farmers in traditionally arable areas, since many successfully shifted to new enterprises. The stability of the number of farmers underlines the point. A stronger case for decline can be made out with regard to farm and craft workers. Howkins points out that the number of farmworkers declined by about 10 per cent between 1921 and 1930, and by a further 18 per cent by 1939. Yet incomes remained much higher than before the war. The number employed in the traditional rural crafts also fell sharply: from 340 to 192 in Brassley's Devon sample between 1910 and 1939. Most of this decline, however, appears to have occurred before the end of the war: already by 1923 numbers had fallen to 236. The rate of decline of traditional rural crafts actually fell during the interwar period. Furthermore, as with arable farming, the decline of a sector does not imply that the individuals involved in it necessarily lost out. The reduction of forty-four in the number of those employed in the traditional crafts in the Devon sample between 1923 and 1939 was more than counterbalanced by the increase of 112 in 'new' rural

[21] H. A. Clemenson, *English Country Houses and Landed Estates* (1982); P. Mandler, *The Fall and Rise of the Stately Home* (1999).

trades such as garages, shops and catering. It seems likely that many of the entrants into these 'new' trades had previously been involved in 'traditional' trades; a high proportion of rural garages, for example, were on premises that had once been blacksmiths' or wheelwrights' shops. This sample, however, is taken from one county only; it would be interesting to see if the same methodology applied elsewhere produced the same results.

This book does not purport to be a comprehensive history of the English countryside between the wars. Rather, it is a revisionist argument and a challenge to historians to undertake the detailed local studies that are needed if we are to flesh out the more nuanced view of the interwar countryside outlined here. What we do believe we have demonstrated is that, from whatever point of view one looks at the countryside in this period, there is abundant evidence of vitality and new growth, whilst the evidence for decline is less compelling than has usually been assumed.

Why, then, did contemporaries and the first generation of historians of the interwar countryside see this period as so strongly marked by decline? There were many reasons. One was that it in fact opened with a period of unusual prosperity for farmers (1914–21); the low prices and incomes of 1924–34 seemed all the more unbearable by contrast. Furthermore, some of those who suffered, notably large arable farmers and the lesser gentry, were influential, well connected and articulate. Another reason was that some prominent features of the 'traditional' countryside did badly in these years. Corn, especially wheat, had historically occupied a symbolic place at the heart of agriculture, whilst for much of the nineteenth century 'high farming', with its heavy capital and labour requirements, had been held up as the model. By contrast, the farming regimes that prospered between the wars were often less intensive. Drastically cutting expenditure on maintaining buildings and fences, cutting hedges and cleaning out drains, or allowing less productive land to 'tumble down' to waste probably contributed to the productivity gains achieved by interwar agriculture, but looked more like decline than regeneration. Similarly, some of the most successful branches of 'alternative agriculture', such as egg-production or dairying, had traditionally been associated with women, and were often seen as mere sidelines to the serious business of farming.

But, as many of the contributors to this volume have argued, literary representations of the countryside between the wars perhaps bear most responsibility for exaggerating the extent of decline. Often writing that was ostensibly about the countryside served to express other anxieties – about industrialisation, the subjugation of nature, the rise of democracy or the increasing economic and cultural domination of America. Such fears are unusually explicit in Mary Butt's novels and essays, but extended very widely: as Brassley notes, the 'lament for traditional farming became equated with a wider lament for lost rural innocence'. Henry Williamson's insistence that English grain yields were falling when in fact the opposite was occurring is indicative of the way in which perceptions of rural change were distorted by the political, social or moral imperatives they were made to serve (see chapter 6). Furthermore, the literary identification of the countryside with traditional agriculture and rural crafts – as opposed, for example, to the commuters, white-collar workers and non-agricultural manual workers who constituted such a large and growing proportion of the rural population – was shared and promoted by other increasingly powerful rural voices – preservationists, planners, the new rural social organisations, the organic movement and, of course, the NFU. The strength of these forces bears witness to the social, cultural, political and economic energy at work in the countryside between the wars. Ironically, then, it was the very breadth and vigour of regeneration in the countryside during the interwar years which contributed to popularising the belief that rural England was threatened with terminal decline.

Bibliography

Unless otherwise stated, all works are published in London, and relate to the date of publication referred to in endnotes.

Abbreviations:

AgHR = *Agricultural History Review*
JRASE = *Journal of the Royal Agricultural Society of England*
Rural Hist = *Rural History*

Abercrombie, P., 'The preservation of rural England', *Town Planning Review* 22 (1926).
—— and J. Archibald, *East Kent regional planning scheme: preliminary survey* (Liverpool, 1925).
—— and J. Archibald, *East Kent regional planning scheme: final report* (Canterbury, 1928).
—— and T. H. Johnson, *The Doncaster regional planning scheme, 1922* (Liverpool, 1922).
—— and R. H. Mattocks, *Sheffield: a civic survey* (Liverpool, 1924).
Adams, C., 'The idea of the village in interwar England' (unpublished PhD thesis, University of Michigan, 2001).
Addison, C., Viscount, *A policy for British agriculture* (1939).
Adult Education Committee, *The development of adult education in rural areas*, Adult Education Committee Paper 3 (1922).
—— *The drama in adult education*, Adult Education Committee Paper 6 (1926).
Andrews, M., *The acceptable face of feminism: the Women's Institute as a social movement* (1997).
Armstrong, W. A., 'The countryside', in *The Cambridge social history of Britain, 1750–1950*, vol. 1: *Regions and Communities*, ed. F. M. L. Thompson (Cambridge, 1990).
Ashby, A. W., and P. Byles, *Rural education* (Oxford, 1923).
Astor, W., Viscount, and B. S. Rowntree, *British agriculture: the principles of future policy* (1939).
Attwood, E. A., 'The origins of state support for British agriculture', *Manchester School of Economic and Social Studies* 31 (1963).
Bailey, C., 'Progress and preservation – the role of rural industries in the making of the modern image of the countryside', *Journal of Design History* 9 (1996).
—— 'Making and meaning in the English countryside', in *Technologies of landscape: from reaping to recycling*, ed. D. E. Nye (Amherst, 1999).
Baines, J. M., *Sussex pottery* (Brighton, 1980).
Baldwin, S., *On England, and other addresses* (1926).
Bamford, T. W., *The evolution of rural education: three studies of the East Riding of Yorkshire*, Research Monographs 1 (Hull, 1965).
Barrett, H., and J. Phillips, *Suburban style: the British home, 1840–1960* (1988).
Bates, H. E., *The fallow field* (1932).
Batsford, B. C., *The Britain of Brian Cook* (1987).

Beard, M., *English landed society in the twentieth century* (1989).

Bell, A., *Corduroy* (1930).

—— *Silver Ley* (1932).

—— *Cherry Tree* (1935).

Bensusan, S. L., *Latter-day rural England, 1927* (1928).

Best, R. H., and A. W. Rogers, *The urban countryside: the land-use structure of small towns and villages in England and Wales* (1973).

Betjeman, J., *Collected poems*, enlarged edn (1977).

Beynon, V. H., 'The changing structure of dairying in Devon since the 1930s', *Devon Historian* 11 (1975).

Blaxter, K., and N. Robertson, *From dearth to plenty* (Cambridge, 1995).

Bonham-Carter, V., *Dartington Hall: the formative years, 1925–1957*, 2nd edn (Dulverton, 1970).

Bowers, J., 'Inter-war land drainage policy in England and Wales', *AgHR* 46 (1998).

Boyes, G., *The imagined village: culture, ideology, and the English folk revival* (Manchester, 1993).

Brace, C., 'A pleasure ground for noisy herds? Incompatible encounters with the Cotswolds and England, 1900–1950', *Rural Hist.* 11 (2000).

Brandford, V. V. (ed.), *The coal crisis and the future: a study of social disorders and their treatment* (1926).

Brasnett, M., *Voluntary social action: a history of the National Council of Social Service, 1919–1969* (1969).

Brassley, P., 'Agricultural science and education', in *The agrarian history of England and Wales*, vol. 7: *1850–1914*, ed. E. J. T. Collins (Cambridge, 2000).

—— 'Output and technical change in twentieth century British agriculture', *AgHR* 48 (2000).

—— 'Industries in the early twentieth-century countryside: the Oxford Rural Industries Survey of 1926/7', in *People, landscape and alternative agriculture: essays for Joan Thirsk*, ed. R. W. Hoyle (Exeter, 2004).

—— 'Agricultural output, costs, incomes and productivity in the UK, 1919–1940', in *Production et productivité agricoles dans le monde occidental (XIV–XX siècles)*, ed. J.-M. Chevet and G. Beaur (forthcoming).

Brendon, P., *The dark valley: a panorama of the 1930s* (2000).

Brigden, R., 'Farming in partnership: the Leckford Estate and the pursuit of profit in interwar agriculture' (unpublished PhD thesis, University of Reading, 2000).

Brittain, V., *Women's work in modern England* (1928).

Britton, D., and H. F. Marks, *A hundred years of British food and farming: a statistical survey* (1989).

Bronstein, J. L., *Land reform and working-class experience in Britain and the United States, 1800–1862* (Stanford, 1999).

Brooke, J. R., 'Survival and revival', *Design for Today* (May 1933).

Brown, J., *Agriculture in England: a survey of farming, 1870–1947* (Manchester, 1987).

J. Burchardt, 'Reconstructing the rural community: village halls and the National Council of Social Service, 1919 to 1939', *Rural Hist.* 10 (1999).

—— *Paradise lost: rural idyll and social change since 1800* (2002).

—— 'Deference and democracy: village social organisations as rural institutions', in *Rural institutions in the North Sea area, 1850–1950*, ed. J. Bielemann, L. van der Molle and E. Thoen (forthcoming).

Burton, H. M., *The education of the countryman* (1944).

Bush, R., *A fruit grower's diary* (1950).

Butts, M., *A warning to hikers* (1932).

Cannadine, D., *The decline and fall of the British aristocracy* (1990).

Cavaliero, G., *The rural tradition in the English novel, 1900–1939* (1997).

Census of England and Wales 1921.

Census of England and Wales 1951: general report.

Chadwick, P. *Shifting alliances: church and state in English education* (1997).

Chalklin, C. W., 'The decline of the country craftsmen and tradesmen', in *The vanishing countryman*, ed. G. E. Mingay (1989).

Chartres, J., 'Rural industry and manufacturing', in *The agrarian history of England and Wales*, vol. 7: *1850–1914*, ed. E. J. T. Collins (Cambridge, 2000).

——, and G. L. Turnbull, 'Country craftsmen', in *The Victorian countryside*, ed. G. E. Mingay (1981).

Cheeseborough, A., 'A short history of agricultural education up to 1939', *Journal of Education Administration and History* 1 (1968).

Cherrington, J., *On the smell of an oily rag: my 50 years in farming* (1979).

Clark, F. Le G., and R. Titmuss, *Our food problem: a study of national security* (1939).

Clarke, P., *Hope and glory: Britain, 1900–1990* (1996).

Clemenson, H. A., *English country houses and landed estates* (1982).

Cocks, F. S., *Socialism and agriculture* (1925).

Comber, N. M., *Agricultural education in Great Britain* (1948).

—— 'Agricultural research and education in Yorkshire farming', *Journal of the Ministry of Agriculture* 22 (1948–9).

Committee on Post-War Agricultural Education in England and Wales, *Report*, Cmd. 6433 (1943).

Conford, P., 'A forum for organic husbandry: the *New English Weekly* and agricultural policy, 1939–49, *AgHR* 46 (1998).

—— *The origins of the organic movement* (Edinburgh, 2001).

Cook, W. R., *Braunton Young Farmers' Jubilee Book* (privately published, n.d.).

Cooper, A. F., *British agricultural policy, 1912–1936: a study in Conservative politics* (Manchester, 1989).

Cottenham Village College Local History Group, *Charity school to village college: Cottenham, Rampton, Willingham* (Loughborough, 1968).

Court, A., *Seedtime to harvest: a farmer's life* (Bradford on Avon, 1987).

Cox, G., P. Lowe and M. Winter, 'The origins and early development of the National Farmer's Union', *AgHR* 39 (1991).

Creasey, J. S., and S. B. Ward, *The countryside between the wars, 1918–1940* (1984).

Crittall, W. F., 'Peasant pottery', *Rural Industries* (Summer 1936).

Crompton, C. A., 'Changes in rural service occupations during the nineteenth century: an evaluation of two sources for Hertfordshire, England', *Rural History* 6 (1995).

Crosby, E. E. *A survey of the problem of education in rural areas* (1932).

Currie, J. R., and W. H. Long, *An agricultural survey in South Devon* (Newton Abbott, 1929).

Curry, W. B., 'The school', in V. Bonham-Carter, *Dartington Hall: the history of an experiment* (1958).

Curtis, S. J., *History of education in Great Britain*, 5th edn (1963).

Day Lewis, C., *The magnetic mountain* (1933).

Dearlove, P., 'Fen Drayton, Cambridgeshire: an estate of the Land Settlement Association', in *The English rural landscape*, ed. J. Thirsk (Oxford, 2000).

Deneke, H., *Grace Hadow* (1946).

Dennison, S. R., *Minority Report, Committee on Land Utilisation in Rural Areas* (1942).

Departmental Committee on Distribution and Prices of Agricultural Products, *Final Report*, Cmd. 2008 (1924).

Derrick, F., *Country craftsmen* (1945).

Design in Industry, Kitchens issue (Autumn 1932).

Devon County Agricultural Committee, *Scheme of agricultural education and training* (Exeter, 1926).

Dewey, J., 'The school and society', in *The school and society; and, The child and the curriculum* (1990).

Dewey, P., *War and progress: Britain, 1914–1945* (1997).

Dix, G., 'Little plans and noble diagrams', *Town Planning Review* 49 (1978).

—— 'Patrick Abercrombie', in *Pioneers in British planning*, ed. G. E. Cherry (1981).

Dott, A., 'The disabled officer in rural reconstruction', *The Nineteenth Century and After* (February 1919).

Douet, A., 'Norfolk agriculture, 1914–1972' (unpublished PhD thesis, University of East Anglia, 1989).

Dudgeon, P, *Village voices: a portrait of change in England's green and pleasant land, 1915–1990* (1989).

Dudley, R., *Modern farm machinery* (1935).

Duncan, J., *Memorandum on immediate steps in agricultural reconstruction* (1918).

Dybeck, M., *The village college way: the relevance of the Cambridgeshire village college philosophy to the present community education movement* (Coventry, 1981).

Eden, W. A., 'Order in the countryside', *Town Planning Review* 14 (1930).

Edlin, H. L., *Woodland crafts in Britain* (1949).

Edwards, B. *The Burston school strike* (1974).

Elmhirst, L. K., *Faith and works at Dartington* (Dartington, 1937).

Farnell, D. J., 'Henry Morris: an architect of education' (thesis for the Associateship Diploma in Secondary Education, Cambridge Institute of Education, 1967/8).

Ferguson, R. M., *A centenary of agricultural education and training* (Bicton, Devon, c.1973).

Fitzgerald, K., *Ahead of their time: a short history of the Farmers' Club, 1842–1967* (1968).

FitzRandolph, H., and M. D. Hay, *The rural industries of England and Wales*, vol. 1: *Timber and underwood industries and some village workshops*, vol. 2: *Osier growing, basketry and some rural factories*, vol. 3: *Decorative crafts and rural potteries* (Oxford, 1926, 1926, 1927).

Floud, F. L. C., *The Ministry of Agriculture and Fisheries* (1927).

Flynn, A., P. Lowe and M. Winter, 'The political power of farmers: an English perspective', *Rural Hist.* 7 (1996).

Fussell, P., *The Great War and Modern Memory* (1975).

Gaddis, J. L., *The landscape of history: how historians map the past* (Oxford, 2002).

Gardner, P. *The lost elementary schools of Victorian England: the peoples' education* (1984).

Garrity, J., *Step-daughters of England: British women modernists and the national imagery* (Manchester, 2003).

Gibbons, S., *Cold Comfort Farm* (Harmondsworth, 1939).

Gloag, J., *Industrial art explained* (1946).

Gloucester Rural Community Council, *Annual report for 1936*.

Glynn, S., and J. Oxbarrow, *Interwar Britain: a social and economic history* (1976).

Gold, J. R., and M. M. Gold, 'To be free and independent: crafting, popular protest and Lord Leverhulme's Hebridean development projects, 1917–25', *Rural Hist.* 7 (1996).

Graves, R., and A. Hodge, *The long week-end: a social history of Great Britain, 1918–1939* (1940).

Green, E., 'Members of the Rural Community Council I: The Workers' Educational Association', *Gloucestershire Countryside* 1 (Oct 1931).

Green, F. E., *The Surrey hills* (1915).

Grieves, K., 'Common meeting places and the brightening of rural life: local debates on village halls in Sussex after the First World War', *Rural Hist.* 10 (1999)

Griffin, R., *The nature of Fascism* (1991).

Griffiths, C., 'Red Tape Farm? The Labour Party and the farmers 1918–1939', in *Agriculture and politics in England, 1815–1939*, ed. J. R. Wordie (2000).

—— *Labour and the countryside: the politics of rural Britain between the wars* (forthcoming)

Haggard, H. R., *Rural England: being an account of social researches carried out in the years 1901 and 1902* (1902).

Hall, A. D., *Pilgrimage of British farming, 1910–12* (1914).

—— *Agriculture after the War* (1916).

Hardy, T., *Selected poems*, ed. D. Wright (Harmondsworth, 1938).

Harkness, D. A. E., *War and British agriculture* (1941).

Harrod, T., *The crafts in Britain in the 20th century* (1999).

Hartley, D., *Made in England*, 4th edn (1974).

Henderson, G., *The farming ladder* (1944).

Hennell, T., *British craftsmen* (1943).

Hepple, L., and A. Doggett, 'Stonor: a Chilterns landscape', in *The English rural landscape*, ed. J. Thirsk (Oxford, 2000).

Hickmott, A., *Socialism and agriculture* (1897).

Higgs, E., 'Occupational censuses and the agricultural workforce in Victorian England and Wales', *Economic History Review* 48 (1995).

Hirsch, G. P., *Young Farmers' Clubs: a report on a survey* (1952).

Hobsbawm, E., *The age of extremes: the short twentieth century, 1914–1991* (1995).

Holme, C., *The things which belong* (Oxford, 1949).

Holmes, C. J., 'Science and the farmer: the development of the Agricultural Advisory Service in England and Wales 1900–1939', *AgHR* 36 (1986).

Holtby, W., *A new voter's guide to party programmes: political dialogues* (1929).

—— *Anderby Wold* (1981).

—— *South Riding* (1988).

Horn, P., *Education in rural England, 1800–1914* (Dublin, 1978).

Hoskins, W. G., *Devon*, new edn (Newton Abbot, 1972).

Howkins, A., *Poor labouring men: rural radicalism in Norfolk, 1872–1923* (1985).

—— 'The discovery of rural England', in *Englishness: politics and culture, 1880–1950*, ed. R. Colls and P. Dodd (1986).

—— *Reshaping rural England: a social history, 1820–1925* (1991).

—— 'A country at war: Mass-Observation and rural England, 1939–45', *Rural Hist* 9 (1998).

—— *The death of rural England: a social history of the countryside since 1900* (2003).

Interdepartmental Committee of the Ministry of Agriculture and Fisheries and the Board of Education, *Report on the practical education of women for rural life* (1928).

Jackson, A. A., *The railway in Surrey* (Southend-on-Sea, 1999).

Jeffs, T., *Henry Morris: village colleges, community education and the ideal order* (Nottingham, 1998).

Jekyll, G., *Old English household life: some account of cottage objects and country folk* (1925).

Jenkins, I., *The history of the Women's Institute movement of England and Wales* (Oxford, 1953).

Jeremiah, D., 'Dartington – a modern adventure', in *Going modern and being British: art, architecture and design in Devon, c. 1910–1960*, ed. S. Smiles (Exeter, 1998).

Jones, A. M., *The rural industries of England and Wales*, vol. 4: *Rural industries in Wales* (Oxford, 1927).

Kains-Jackson, C., 'The corn trade in 1919', *JRASE* 80 (1919).

Kelly, M., *Village theatre* (1939).

Kelly, T., *A history of adult education in Great Britain*, 3rd edn (Liverpool, 1992).

Kennerley, A., 'Seale Hayne', in *The making of the University of Plymouth* (first draft) (Plymouth, 1999).

Kitteringham, J., 'Country work girls in nineteenth-century England', in *Village life and labour*, ed. R. Samuel (1975).

Labour Party, *Proceedings of the 24th annual Labour Party conference* (1924).

—— *Report of the 26th annual Labour Party conference* (1926).

—— *Labour's policy on agriculture* (1926).

—— *A prosperous countryside* (1927).

—— *The farmer and the Labour Party: fair reward for all* (1928)

—— *How Labour will save agriculture* (1934).

—— *Labour's aims* (1937).

—— *Labour's policy of food for all* (1937).

Larkin, P., *Collected poems*, ed. A. Thwaite (1988).

Lawson, J., *Primary education in East Yorkshire, 1560–1902* (York, 1959).

Leach, B., *A potter's book* (1940).

Leavis, F. R., and D. Thompson, *Culture and environment: the training of critical awareness* (1964).

Lee, J. M., *Social leaders and public persons: a study of county government in Cheshire since 1888* (Oxford, 1963).

—— Editorial, *Public Administration* 61 (1983).

Leisner, T., *One hundred years of economic statistics* (1989).

Lethaby, W. R., *Home and country arts* (1923).

Lewis, J. S., *Partnership for all* (1948).

Lockwood, C. A., 'The changing use of land in the Weald region of Kent, Surrey and Sussex, 1919–1939' (unpublished PhD thesis, University of Sussex, 1991).

Lowe, R., *Adjusting to democracy: the role of the Ministry of Labour in British politics, 1916–1939* (Oxford, 1986).

Lowenthal, D., *The past is a foreign country* (Cambridge, 1985).

Lymington, Viscount, *Famine in England* (1938).

McCulloch, G., *Educational reconstruction: the 1944 Education Act and the twenty-first century* (Ilford, 1994).

MacDonald, R., *Socialism: critical and constructive* (1921).

McLeish, M., 'A note on cottage industries in India', *Rural Industries* (Aug 1933).

Macmillan, H. P., Baron, *A man of law's tale: the reminiscences of the Rt. Hon. Lord Macmillan* (1952).

Mandler, P., 'Against Englishness: English culture and the limits to rural nostalgia, 1850–1940', *Transactions of the Historical Society* 6th ser. 7 (1997).

—— *The fall and rise of the stately home* (1999).

Mansbridge, A., *An adventure in working-class education: being the story of the Workers' Educational Association, 1903–1915* (1920).

Mansfield, N., 'Class conflict and village war memorials', *Rural Hist.* 6 (1995).

—— 'Agricultural trades unionism in Shropshire, 1900–1930' (unpublished PhD thesis, University of Wolverhampton, 1997).

—— *English farmworkers and local patriotism, 1900–1930* (Aldershot, 2001).

—— 'Farmworkers and local Conservatism in South-West Shropshire, 1916–23', in *Mass Conservatism: the Conservatives and the public since the 1880s*, ed. S. Ball and I. Holliday (2002).

—— 'The National Federation of Discharged and Demobilised Soldiers and Sailors, 1917–1921: a view from the Marches', *Family and Community History* 7 (2004).

—— 'Foxhunting and the yeomanry: county identity and military culture', in *Our Hunting Forefathers: Field Sports in England after 1850*, ed. R. W. Hoyle (forthcoming)

Martin, J., *The development of modern agriculture: British farming since 1931* (2000).

Matless, D., *Landscape and Englishness* (1998).

Maxton, J. P. (ed.), *Regional types of British agriculture* (1936).

Mazower, M., *Dark continent: Europe's twentieth century* (1999).

Meacham, S., *Regaining paradise: Englishness and the early Garden City movement* (1999).

Medhurst, A., 'Negotiating the Gnome Zone', in *Visions of suburbia*, ed. R. Silverstone (1997).

Miller, S., 'Urban dreams and rural reality: land and landscape in English culture, 1920–45,' *Rural Hist.* 6 (1995).

Mingay, G. E., *A social history of the English countryside* (1990).

Ministry of Agriculture and Fisheries, *Co-operative marketing of agricultural produce*, Economic Series 1 (1925).

—— *Report on agricultural credit*, Economic Series 8 (1926).

—— *Report on egg marketing in England and Wales*, Economic Series 10 (1927).

—— *Markets and fairs in England and Wales*, Economic Series 13 and 14 (1927).

—— 'Junior agricultural courses in Salop', *Journal of the Ministry of Agriculture* (1929).

Ministry of Reconstruction Adult Education Committee, *Final Report*, Cmd. 321 (1919).

Moore, J., *Portrait of Elmbury* (1945).

—— *The Blue Field* (1948).

Moore-Colyer, R. J., *Farming in depression: Wales, 1919–1939*, Welsh Institute of Rural Studies, Working Paper 6 (Aberystwyth, 1996).

—— ' Farming in depression: Wales between the wars, 1919–39', *AgHR* 46 (1998).

—— 'From Great Wen to Toad Hall: aspects of the urban-rural divide in inter-war Britain', *Rural Hist.* 10 (1999).

—— 'Back to basics: Rolf Gardiner, H. J. Massingham and "A Kinship in Husbandry"', *Rural Hist.* 12 (2001).

—— 'A voice clamouring in the wilderness: H. J. Massingham (1888–1952) and rural England', *Rural Hist.* 13 (2002).

Morgan, M., 'Jam, Jerusalem and feminism', *Oral History* 23 (1995).

—— 'Jam making, Cuthbert Rabbit and cakes: redefining domestic labour in the Women's Institute, 1915–60', *Rural Hist.* 7 (1996).

Morris, H., *The Village College: being a memorandum on the provision of educational and social facilities for the countryside with special reference to Cambridgeshire* (Cambridge, 1924).

Morris, R. J., 'Clubs, societies and associations', in *The Cambridge Social History of Britain, 1750–1950*, vol. 3: *Social Agencies and Institutions*, ed. F. M. L. Thompson (1990)

Mowat, C. L., *Britain between the wars, 1918–1940* (1955).

Muggeridge, M., *The thirties: 1930–1940 in Great Britain* (1940).

Mulford, W., *This narrow place: Sylvia Townsend Warner and Valentine Ackland: life, letters and politics, 1930–1951* (1988).

Murray, K. A. H., *Agriculture*, History of the Second World War, Civil Series (1955).

National Council of Social Service, *Third annual report of the National Council of Social Service for the year 1922* (1923).

—— *Cooperation in social service: being the annual report of the National Council of Social Service for the Years 1928–9* (1929).

—— *Constructive citizenship: the annual report of the NCSS (Inc.) for the year 1930–31* (1931).

—— *Voluntary service: being the annual report of the National Council of Social Service (Incorporated) for the year 1931–2* (1932).

—— *The Music and Drama Fund for Villages* (1935).

National Federation of Women's Institutes, *Annual Report of the National Federation of Women's Institutes, 1938–9*.

—— *Annual Report of the National Federation of Women's Institutes, 1949–50*.

'The new rural England', *The Architect and Building News*, 30 June, 7, 14, 21 July, 1933.

Newby, H., *Country life: a social history of rural England* (1987).

—— *Green and pleasant land: social change in rural England* (1993).

'Notes and news', *Gloucestershire Countryside* 1 (1931).

O'Grada, C., 'British agriculture, 1860–1914', in *The economic history of Britain since 1700*, ed. R. Floud and D. McCloskey, 2nd edn (Cambridge, 1994).

Orwin, C. S., 'Commodity prices and farming policy', *JRASE* 83 (1922).

Orwell, G., *Coming up for air* (1980).

Oxford Dictionary of National Biography, ed. H. C. G. Matthew and B. Harrison (Oxford, 2004).

Parker, D., '"Just a stepping stone": the growth of vocational education in the elementary school curriculum, 1914–1939', *Journal of Education Administration and History* 35 (2003).

Parker, R. A. C., *Coke of Norfolk: a financial and agricultural study* (Oxford, 1975).

Pedley, W. H., *Labour on the land: a study of the developments between the two world wars* (1942).

Penning-Rowsell, E., 'Who "betrayed" whom? Power and politics in the 1920/21 agricultural crisis', *AgHR* 45 (1997).

Perkin, H. J., *The rise of professional society: England since 1880* (1989).

Perren, R., *Agriculture in depression, 1870–1940* (Cambridge, 1995).

Pevsner, N. (ed.), *Cambridgeshire*, The Buildings of England Series (1970).

Philips Price, M., 'Scientific agriculture and the consumer', *Labour* (Dec 1936).

Place, G. W. (ed.), *Neston, 1840–1940* (Chester, 1996).

Pointing, H. B., and E. Burns, *Agriculture* (1927).

Ratcliff, N., *Rude mechanicals: a short review of village drama* (1938).

Raybould, S. G., *The English universities and adult education* (1951).

Rayns, F., 'Two decades of light land farming', *JRASE* 95 (1934).

Rée, H., *Educator extraordinary: the life and achievements of Henry Morris, 1889–1961* (1985).

—— (ed.), *The Henry Morris collection* (Cambridge, 1984).

Reynolds, D., *Rich relations: the American occupation of Britain, 1942–45* (1995).

Robbins, K., *The eclipse of a great power: modern Britain, 1870–1975* (1983).

Roberts, C., *Gone rustic* (1934).

Robertson, W. *Welfare in trust: a history of the Carnegie United Kingdom Trust, 1913–1963* (Dunfermline, 1964).

Robinson, H. G., 'Company farming and direct marketing', *Country Life* (3 Dec 1927).

—— 'An all-round dairy herd', *Country Life* (24 Dec 1927).

—— 'Notable farming enterprises: 1', *JRASE* 91 (1930).

—— 'Mr. A. H. Brown's farms', *JRASE* 92 (1931).

—— 'Messrs S. E. and J. F. Alley's mechanized farming', *JRASE* 93 (1932).

Rogers, A., *The most revolutionary measure: a history of the Rural Development Commission, 1909–1999* (Salisbury, 1999).

Rooth, T., 'Trade agreements and the evolution of British agricultural policy in the 1930s', *AgHR* 33 (1985).

Rørdham, T., *The Danish folk high schools*, trans. S. Mammen (Copenhagen, 1965).

Rose, J., *The intellectual life of the British working classes* (2001).

Rose, W., *The village carpenter* (Cambridge, 1937).

Rossetti, D. G., *The works*, ed. W. M. Rossetti (1911).

Rowlands, M. B., *The West Midlands from AD 1000* (Harlow, 1987).

Royal Commission on Agriculture, *The Interim Report of the Royal Commission appointed to inquire into the economic prospects of the agricultural industry in Great Britain*, Cmd. 473 (1919).

Royal Commission on the Coal Industry, *Report*, Cmd. 2600 (1926).

Royal Commission on the Distribution of the Industrial Population, *Report*, Cmd. 6153 (1940) [The Barlow Report].

'The rural boom', *Rural Industries* 6 (1927).

Rural Industries Bureau, *A memorandum on rural industries containing a suggested programme of work for a Rural Community Council* (1928).

Salter, A., *The Bread Tax* (1932)

Saville, J., *Rural depopulation in England and Wales, 1851–1951* (1957).

Scott, J. W. R., *The story of the Women's Institute movement* (Idbury, 1925).

Scott, L., *Report of the Committee on Land Utilisation in Rural Areas*, Cmnd 6378 (1942).

Scott Watson, J. A., 'Mr. Clyde Higgs' dairy farms', *JRASE* 97 (1936).

Secretary for Scotland, *Report of the Departmental Committee* (1924).

Selleck, R. J. W., *English primary education and the progressives, 1914–1939* (1972).

Sharp, T., *Town and countryside: some aspects of urban and rural development* (1932).

Shaw, M., *The Clear Stream: A Life of Winifred Holtby* (1999).

Sheail, J., *Rural conservation in interwar Britain* (Oxford, 1981).

—— 'Elements of sustainable agriculture: the UK experience, 1840–1940', *AgHR* 43 (1995).

—— 'Yorkshire's "sloughs of despond": an interwar perspective on resource development in Britain', *Environment and History* 6 (2000).

—— 'Arterial drainage in inter-war England: the legislative perspective', *AgHR* 50 (2002).

Shields, F. E. (ed.), *Fifty years not out! A history of the Young Farmer's Clubs in England and Wales* (1970).

Shoard, M., *This land is our land: the struggle for Britain's countryside* (1997).

—— *A right to roam* (Oxford, 1999).

Shropshire Federation of Women's Institutes, *Shropshire within living memory* (Newbury, 1992).

Simpson, A. W. B., *In the highest degree odious: detention without trial in wartime Britain* (Oxford, 1992).

Skidelsky, R., *Oswald Mosley*, 3rd edn (1990).

Snowden, H., *Born to farm in Devon: by horse and hand tool at Thurlestone, 1918–1939* (Totnes, 1998).

Stamp, L. D., 'The Scott Report: a new charter for the countryside', *Geographical Magazine* 15/9 (1943).

Stanley, R. E., ' Agricultural statistics, 1929', *JRASE* 90 (1929).

Steedman, C., *Childhood, culture and class in Britain: Margaret McMillan, 1860–1931* (1990).

Stevenson, J., *British society, 1914–45* (1984).

—— and C. Cook, *The Slump: society and politics during the depression* (1977); 2nd edn, *The Slump: society and politics, 1929–1939* (1994).

Stewart, S., *Lifting the latch: a life on the land* (Oxford, 1987).

Stewart, W. A. C., *The educational innovators*, vol. 2: *Progressive schools, 1881–1967* (1968).

Street, A. G., *Farmer's glory* (1959).

Sturt, G., *The wheelwright's shop* (Cambridge, 1923).

—— [as G. Bourne] *Change in the village* (1984).

Styler, W. E., *A bibliographical guide to adult education in rural areas, 1918–1972* (1972).

Taylor, A. J. P., *English history, 1914–1945* (Oxford, 1965).

Taylor, D, 'Growth and structural change in the British dairy industry, c.1860–1930,' *AgHR* 35 (1987).

Taylor, G., *History of the amateur theatre* (Melksham, 1976).

Tebbutt, H., 'Industry and anti-industry: the Rural Industries Bureau, its objects and work' (unpublished MA dissertation, V&A/RCA, 1990).

Thirsk, J., *Alternative agriculture: a history from the Black Death to the present day* (Oxford, 1997).

Thomas, F. G., *The new learning: an experiment with educational films in the county of Devon* (1932).

—— and D. I. Thomas, 'Fresh woods and pastures new: adult education in rural Devon', *Journal of Adult Education* 5 (1931).

Thompson, F., *Lark Rise* (Oxford, 1939).

Thompson, F. M. L., 'Town and city', in *The Cambridge social history of England, 1750–1950*, ed. F. M. L. Thompson, vol. 1: *Regions and communities* (Cambridge, 1990).

Thompson, L., 'The promotion of agricultural education for adults: the Lancashire Federation of Women's Institutes 1919–45', *Rural Hist.* 10 (1999).

Thorpe, A., *Britain in the 1930s: the deceptive decade* (Oxford, 1992).

Thurlow, R., *Fascism in Britain: a history, 1918–1985* (Oxford, 1987).

Thwaites, P., *Presenting arms: representations of British military history, 1600–1930* (Leicester, 1996).

Tichelar, M., 'The Labour Party and land reform in the interwar period', *Rural Hist.* 13 (2002).

Tracey, H. (ed.), *The book of the Labour Party: its history, growth, policy and leaders*, vol. 2 (1925).

Tracy, M., *Agriculture in Western Europe*, 2nd edn (1982).

Troup, L. G., 'The Leckford Estate Limited', *JRASE* 98 (1937).

Turnor, C., *The land: agriculture and the national economy* (1929).

Twinch, C., *Tithe war, 1918–1939: the countryside in revolt* (Norwich, 2001).

Verrier, A., *The bomber offensive* (1974).

Vinen, R. *A history in fragments: Europe in the twentieth century* (2000).

Walker, R. B., *Speed the Plough* (1924).

Waller, R. D., '1919–1956: the years between', in *A design for democracy* (1956).

Wallis, M., 'Unlocking the secret soul: Mary Kelly, pioneer of village theatre', *New Theatre Quarterly* 64 (2000).

—— 'Drama and the new learning for villages: F. G. and D. Irene Thomas, Dartington and rural adult education, 1927–33' (forthcoming).

Ward, C., *The child in the country* (1988).

Warner, S. T., *Lolly Willowes, or The loving huntsman* (1979).

Weaver, L., *Village clubs and halls* (1920)

Webb, M., *Gone to earth* (1954).

—— *Precious bane* (1956).

Whetham, E. H., *British farming, 1939–1949* (1952).

—— *The agrarian history of England and Wales*, vol. 8: *1914–1939* (Cambridge, 1978).

Wiener, M. J., *English culture and the decline of the industrial spirit* (Cambridge, 1981).

Williams, R., *Culture and society, 1780–1950* (1962).

Williams, T., *Labour's way to use the land* (1935).

—— *Digging for Britain* (1965).

Williams, W. E., *The auxiliaries of adult education*, Life and Leisure Pamphlets 1 (1934).

Williams, W. M., *The country craftsman: a study of some rural crafts and the rural industries organisations in England* (Dartington, 1958).

Williams-Ellis, C., *England and the Octopus* (1928).

—— (ed.), *Britain and the Beast* (1937).

Williamson, A., *Henry Williamson: Tarka and the last romantic* (Stroud, 1995).

Williamson, H., *Goodbye West Country* (Boston, Mass., 1938).

—— *The story of a Norfolk farm* (1940).

—— *The Phasian bird* (1948).

—— *A test to destruction* (*A chronicle of ancient sunlight*, vol. 8) (1964).

—— *The innocent moon* (*A chronicle of ancient sunlight*, vol. 9) (1961).

—— *The phoenix generation* (*A chronicle of ancient sunlight*, vol. 12) (1965).

—— *A solitary war* (*A chronicle of ancient sunlight*, vol. 13) (1966).

—— *Lucifer before sunrise* (*A chronicle of ancient sunlight*, vol. 14) (1967).

—— *The gale of the world* (*A chronicle of ancient sunlight*, vol. 15) (1969).

Wilson, W. R., *Devon Federation of Young Farmers' Clubs: 50 years, 1932–1982* (Exeter, 1982).

Wilt, A. F., *Food for war: agriculture and rearmament in Britain before the Second World War* (Oxford, 2001).

Wise, M., *English village schools* (1931).

Wiskemann, E., *Europe of the dictators, 1919–1945* (1966).

Woods, K. S., *Rural industries round Oxford* (Oxford, 1921).

Wright, P., *The village that died for England: the strange story of Tyneham* (1995).

Wrigley, E. A., 'Men on the land and men in the countryside: employment in agriculture in early nineteenth-century England', in *The world we have gained: histories of population and social structure*, ed. L. Bonfield, R. M. Smith and K. Wrightson (Oxford, 1986).

Wyllie, J., 'Some problems in farm management', *Transactions of the Highland and Agricultural Society* 41 (1929).

Wymer, N., *English country crafts: a survey of their development from early times to the present day* (1946).

Young, M., *The Elmhirsts of Dartington: the creation of a Utopian community*, 2nd edn (Dartington, 1996).

Index